Refiguring Women, Colonialism,
and Modernity in Burma

Southeast Asia

POLITICS, MEANING, AND MEMORY

David Chandler and Rita Smith Kipp

SERIES EDITORS

Refiguring Women, Colonialism, and Modernity in Burma

CHIE IKEYA

University of Hawai'i Press
Honolulu

© 2011 University of Hawai'i Press

All rights reserved

Paperback edition 2017

Printed in the United States of America

22 21 20 19 18 17   6 5 4 3 2 1

Library of Congress Cataloging-in-Publication Data
Ikeya, Chie.
    Refiguring women, colonialism, and modernity in Burma / Chie Ikeya.
      p. cm.
    Includes bibliographical references and index.
    ISBN 978-0-8248-3461-6 (hardcover : alk. paper)
    1. Women—Burma—Social conditions—20th century. 2. Women—
Burma—History—20th century. 3. Sex role—Burma. I. Title. II. Series:
Southeast Asia—politics, meaning, and memory.
    HQ1735.7 .I54 2011

                             2010040206

ISBN 978-0-8248-7281-6 (pbk.)

Designed by Janette Thompson (Jansom)

For Otōsan, Okāsan, and Christian

CONTENTS

Preface   *ix*

Abbreviations   *xiii*

Introduction   *1*

CHAPTER 1   The Colonial Setting   *14*

CHAPTER 2   Women on the Rise: Education and the Popular Press   *46*

CHAPTER 3   Between Patriotism and Feminism: Politicized and
Organized Women   *75*

CHAPTER 4   Modern Woman as Consumer: Fashion, Domesticity,
and the Marketplace   *96*

CHAPTER 5   Mixing Religion and Race: Intermarriage,
Miscegenation, and the Wives and Mistresses
of Foreign Men   *120*

CHAPTER 6   The Self-Indulgent *Khit hsan thu:* Culture, Nation,
and Masculinity on Trial   *143*

Conclusion   *163*

Notes   *171*

Glossary   *201*

Bibliography   *205*

Index   *229*

PREFACE

When I started my research in 2002, I had intended to focus on the Japanese occupation of Burma during the Second World War and the varied ways in which it was understood locally and within a broader context of Japan's rise as a non-European, modern, and imperial power. As is often the case with researchers, I left for the field with one topic and returned with another.

While waiting for government permission to access the Defense Services Museum and Historical Research Institute, which stores the majority of the Burmese material on the occupation, I thumbed through the Burmese- and English-language newspapers and periodicals published in Burma between 1910 and 1948, held at the Universities Central Library of Yangon University (UCL). There I was struck by images of "the modern Burmese woman" and the animated discussions about her. They raised numerous questions, but I wondered, in particular, why one of the most prevalent subjects of debate in British Burma had escaped the notice of historians of the colonial period. This and other questions led me to reflect on the relationships among gender, colonialism, and modernity and to examine how early twentieth-century transformations in colonial society, education, literary culture, politics, and the marketplace gave rise to new discourses about and practices related to women. I ended up spending the remainder of my time in the field investigating the press material at the UCL. It turned out to be one of the wisest decisions I have made as a scholar, not only because I never received access to the Defense Services Museum and Historical Research Institute but more importantly because it turned my attention to multiple Burmese-language sources that have been overlooked.

Previous studies of colonial Burma produced outside the country have tended to rely on English-language colonial-era documents, the majority of which are readily available in systematically organized public archives and libraries in Great Britain, chiefly the British Library. One reason why foreign scholars of Burma have relied on British colonial sources is that conducting research in Burma, where most holdings of Burmese-language as well as popular press material are located, poses taxing logistical challenges. The country's military regime has made it exceptionally difficult to carry out research in Burma. The Burma Socialist Programme Party, which assumed power after staging a military coup in March 1962, and the current military regime, the State Peace and Development Council, have both closely monitored the activities of local and foreign researchers and scholars, particularly those who work on post–World War II Burma. Applicants who apply for access to historical archives, many of which fall under the authority of one of the various government ministries, invariably encounter seemingly endless red tape and bureaucratic hurdles; the government rarely grants permission, and in many cases the applicant receives no reply at all. A successful applicant, upon finally arriving at the archives, finds that artifacts of popular culture such as newspapers, magazines, cartoons, and advertisements from the colonial period have not been microfilmed or preserved under appropriate conditions such as air-conditioning, despite the good intentions of the librarians. Material that has been acquired and catalogued may be missing, irretrievably damaged, or fast decaying. Navigating through the archives in Burma forces one to work with a diverse but patchy assortment of pieces and fragments of history. A great number of sources, such as many used in this study, may be found only outside traditional archival locations—for instance, from booksellers and in private collections. As a consequence of these difficulties, most scholars of colonial Burma continue to place undue emphasis on English-language, missionary, and British official documentation located in archives outside the country. Not surprisingly, their histories often reflect the typically distanced perspectives on genres of events that preoccupied the European and American authors of their source material—insurrection, religious reformations, and anticolonial resistance.

The following study integrates a wide range of primary sources from the 1900s to the 1940s, many of which have remained largely untapped until now. That I have been able to do so is a tribute to my parents, Osamu Ikeya and Daw Mya Kay Thee, whose support enabled me to gain timely access to public and private archives in the country and to carry out my research with relative ease. Their deep understanding of Burma, developed through a lifetime of living and working in the country, helped me comprehend, endure, and appreciate the ups and downs of conducting fieldwork in Burma. They have enriched my knowledge of Burma and its history, culture, and people immeasurably, and for that, I am forever indebted to them.

I am deeply grateful to other members of my family, especially Hitoshi Ikeya, Suzy and David Lyon, Auntie Daw Hnin Yee, Ma Mona, Ma Htay, Ko Maung, Ko Timmy, and the late Dr. Mohan. I owe an immeasurable debt of gratitude to my husband, Christian Lammerts, who read countless versions of this book. Without his constant warmth, patience, guidance, and brilliance, this book would not have come to fruition. He continues to serve as a model for the kind of scholar I should be.

Many others made the research for this project possible. I wish to thank Dr. Myo Myint, U Thaw Kaung, Kyaw Yin Hlaing, Dr. Khin Maung Win, Daw Kyan, Daw Mar Lay, U Tun Tin, Ino Kenji, Nemoto Kei, Takahashi Akio, Dobashi Yasuko, Dorothy Guyot, Ikeya Sadao, Ikeya Takeshi, Ikeya Hideko, Thak Chaloemtiarana, Gustaaf Houtman, and Vicky Bowman. I would also like to thank the staff of the India Office Records and Private Papers, the Universities Historical Research Centre Library at Yangon University, the UCL, the National Archives of Myanmar, and the Department of History at Yangon University. I extend special thanks to Daw Khin Khin Mya, Major Aung Myo, Daw San San May, Daw Mya Sein, and Dr. Kyaw Win.

The research for this project was also made possible by the generous financial support of the Institute of Historical Research at the University of London, AAUW (formerly known as the American Association of University Women), and Cornell University. I received several research travel grants from the Mario Einaudi Center for International Studies, the Department of History, the Southeast Asia Program, and the Feminist, Gender, and Sexuality Studies Program at Cornell University, for which I am very grateful.

In the process of writing this book, I have benefited from the assistance of many individuals, too numerous to name. I would like to thank the administrative staff and faculty associated with the Departments of History and Asian Studies, the Southeast Asia Program, and the International Students and Scholars Office at Cornell; the Simpson Center for the Humanities at the University of Washington; the Department of History at the College of the Holy Cross; and the Southeast Asian Studies Programme at the National University of Singapore. I extend special thanks to James Lees, Miriam Bartha, and Yolanda Youtsey. I am indebted to U Saw Tun, Bo Bo Lanzin, Nance Cunningham, Julie Pham, Maung Zeya, and Ma Moe Moe San for their assistance with copyright inquiries.

Throughout this project, I have relied on my extraordinary teachers, colleagues, and friends for encouragement, advice, and direction. I want to thank San San Hnin Tun, Keith Hjortshoj, David Wyatt, Kyoko Selden, Mark Lincicome, Douglas Kammen, Maitrii Aung-Thwin, Michelle Tan,

Peter Veil, Gopika Solanki, Natasha Hamilton-Hart, Goh Beng Lan, Alex Denes, Worrasit Tantinipankul, Doreen Lee, Tyrell Haberkorn, B. James Soukam, Curtis Lambrecht, Tobias Mayr, Luke Herbert, Rupesh Bhayani, Wan Kiatkanid Pongpanich, Aleena Pitisant, Mauro Merolle, Wondy Bekele, Sharon Wong, Matt Wessler, Wai Sann Thi, and Masao Imamura. I extend my deepest gratitude to Tamara Loos, Anne Blackburn, and Eric Tagliacozzo for their early guidance, invaluable suggestions and criticisms, and unwavering support over the years. They have been an inspiration. Lilian Handlin read an early draft of the entire manuscript. Her enthusiasm and generous comments were sources of much needed fuel at the time. I offer my heartfelt appreciation to Rita Kipp, David Chandler, Craig Reynolds, and an anonymous reader for their helpful suggestions and astute criticisms, and Pamela Kelly and Rosemary Wetherold, my editor and copy editor, respectively, for the application of their fine critical skills in the process of editing my manuscript. It remains only to add that responsibility for any remaining imperfections is mine alone.

An earlier version of a portion of chapter 2 was previously published as "The 'Traditional' High Status of Women in Burma: A Historical Reconsideration," in *Journal of Burma Studies* 10 (2005–2006): 51–81. Earlier versions of portions of chapters 4 and 6 appeared as "The Modern Burmese Woman and the Politics of Fashion in Colonial Burma," in *Journal of Asian Studies* 67, no. 4 (November 2008): 1277–1308, and are reprinted with permission of the Association for Asian Studies.

ABBREVIATIONS

AFPFL	Anti-Fascist People's Freedom League
AMSH	Association for Moral and Social Hygiene
BWA	Burmese Women's Association
CD Acts	Contagious Diseases Acts
GCBA	General Council of Burmese Associations
GCSS	General Council of Sangha Sammeggi
IAW	International Alliance of Women for Suffrage and Equal Citizenship
ICW	International Council of Women
INC	Indian National Congress
NCE	National Council of Education (Burma)
NCW	National Council of Women
NCWB	National Council of Women in Burma
UCL	Universities Central Library of Yangon University
YMBA	Young Men's Buddhist Association
YWBA	Young Women's Buddhist Association

Introduction

The Burmese novel *Mon ywe mahu* (Not out of hate), written by Ma Ma Lay in 1955, tells of a tragic romance between Way Way, a young woman from an ordinary Burmese Buddhist family, and U Saw Han, an older and thoroughly Anglicized and impious Burmese man working for a British firm. Set in British Burma immediately prior to the Second World War, the book focuses on the confrontation between Burmese tradition and Western modernity. There is nothing recognizably Burmese about U Saw Han, who has become in taste and habit a replica of a British colonial official. By marrying him, Way Way too loses her connection to her own culture. Unlike her husband, however, Way Way is incapable of acculturating, and her body rejects all things Western. She cannot keep down milk, a quintessentially Western staple; she becomes frail on a Western diet and miscarries; ultimately, she succumbs, not to the disease with which she is afflicted, but to the painful Western medication that her husband compels her to take. In this popular story, reprinted in at least five editions since its original publication and translated into English, French, Russian, Uzbek, and Chinese, Burmese tradition is portrayed as fundamentally at odds with Western modernity. The novel argues that Burmese and Western cultures are essentially incompatible and that their coexistence, let alone their union, threatens death. The failed pregnancy and demise of Way Way epitomize the futility and peril of the marriage of Burma and the modern West.

This image of a society that rejects foreign influences is an enduring vision of Burma, the country otherwise known as Myanmar. It is an image that has become more familiar in recent years through the xenophobic behavior of its military government, in power since 1962; examples of such behavior include its demonization of Aung San Suu Kyi—the leader of the pro-democracy movement and the National League for Democracy—as a minion of Western capitalist and imperial powers, and its refusal to allow foreign aid and workers into the country in the aftermath of the devastating Cyclone Nargis in 2008. By many scholarly and popular accounts, the fear and mistrust of the foreign and the perceived irreconcilability of "Burmese" and "foreign" cultures can be traced back to the experience of British colonial rule (1824–1942, 1945–1948) and the Japanese occupation of Burma (1942–1945), which left men and women in Burma deeply suspicious of and hostile towards the outside world.

Refiguring Women, Colonialism, and Modernity in Burma presents a different and as yet untold story about colonialism in Burma: of men and women who actively engaged with new and foreign identities, ideas, practices, and institutions and whose thoughts and actions crossed religious, racial, and cultural boundaries; of a society shaped by its openness to and participation in a culture and a world above and beyond the local or the national; of a modernity that offered alternatives to the either-or choice between Westernization and ethnonationalism. This forgotten or suppressed history of colonial interaction, imagination, and cosmopolitanism is intertwined with another hidden past, that of the "modern" women who came into view in 1920s and 1930s Burma.

FORGOTTEN HISTORIES: WOMEN IN COLONIAL BURMA

The early decades of the twentieth century saw a proliferation of complex discourses in the popular press on the "new woman" or "modern woman" the world over, from Japan, China, Siam, and India to South Africa, Germany, England, and America. The topics of these often controversial debates included female education and employment, the role of women in the home and the public arena, the sexual and political emancipation of women, and the relationship between women and consumerism.[1] British Burma was no exception. In colonial Burma, the "modern woman" appeared in image and text as student, wife and mother, earner and consumer, patriot and defector, pious and infidel, and "Burmese" and "Westernized" on the pages and covers of novels, newspapers, and magazines, and as the face of new lifestyles and commodities in advertisements, posters, paintings, and films. She was referred to by several terms, all of which described women of the *khit kala,* "women of the times":[2] *khit hmi thu* (up-to-date woman), *ya khu khit amyothami* (present-day women), *khit hsan thu* (trendy woman), *khit thit amyothami* (woman of the new era), and *tet khit thami* (girl/daughter of the era of advancement).[3] The woman of the *khit kala* not only signified redefinitions of femininity but also served as the privileged idiom through which intellectuals, writers, journalists, politicians, monks, and students discussed the possibilities and the challenges of the *khit kala* and the vital importance of *toe tet yay* (progress).[4] For some, she symbolized the renaissance of Burmese culture, while for others she evoked cultural degeneration. She expressed not only hopes for a new and reinvigorated Burma but also doubts and anxieties about the *khit thit* (new era) or *tet khit* (era of advancement). She was ubiquitous but elusive, ever resisting hard and fast definitions.

This book examines what the shifting and competing figurations of the woman of the *khit kala* reveal about what it meant to be or to become modern in colonial Burma, and investigates the political, social, and cultural aspirations that motivated the pleas for women to advance. What were the goals and consequences of the varieties of public commentary, social reforms, and protests that took place on behalf of women of the "new era"? What do discourses concerning modern-day women reveal about the impact of colonialism on the emergence of modernity in Burma and in colonized regions generally? This book addresses these questions through a parallel analysis of both imaginary and historical modern women in colonial Burma. On the one hand, I analyze literary and journalistic representations of the distinctive discursive typologies of "women of the times" in a diverse range of official and popular Burmese- and English-language documents and media produced between 1920 and 1940: the educated young woman, the politicized woman, the consumerist woman, the wives and mistresses of foreign men, and the self-indulgent and often Westernized woman. On the other hand, I attend to the practices of actual women who—whether pursuing higher education or careers in the medical, legal, bureaucratic, and journalistic professions alongside men, participating in legislative and party politics, joining antigovernment rallies and labor strikes, marrying "foreigners," or adopting new hairstyles and clothes—unsettled existing cultural norms and practices and contributed to new social formations and asymmetries.

What follows is the first book-length study of women in Burma to use gender as a category of sustained historical analysis. In her study of nineteenth-century British imperialism, Anne McClintock points out that "male theorists of imperialism and postcolonialism have seldom felt moved to explore the gendered dynamics of the subject."[5] Historical studies of colonial Burma by both "local" and "foreign" scholars have suffered from this common problem. More scholarship in English has been written about the colonial era than about any other in Burmese history.[6] Yet, and despite the conspicuous irruption of representations and discourses about women of the *khit kala* during the period in question, the existing literature on colonial Burma has failed to look at accounts by women or about gender.

That historians have accorded little importance to issues of gender says more about the limitations of methodological approaches that have shaped existing academic scholarship on colonial Burma than it does about their salience during the period in question. One such limitation is what Barbara Andaya has described as the "hegemony of the national epic in Southeast Asian historiography," a phenomenon that has privileged the writing of historical metanarratives that are "anchored by the lives of individuals (usually men) to whom evolution or liberation from foreign control is attributed."[7] Women are uneasily inserted rather than integrated into national histories of Southeast Asia.[8] In Burma, too, the nationalist metanarrative is written by and about leading nationalists (all men) who became elite political figures in independent Burma, and has long represented the only type of historiography that the government espouses or tolerates.[9] While some of these accounts mention the participation of women in nationalist movements, they merely "insert" women into the national epic for the purpose of glorifying the anticolonial struggle led by the Burma Independence Army, the predecessor of the current military regime. What little exists by way of studies that consider the historical pasts of women thus amount to a footnote in the official nationalist Burmese history. Such narrow analyses offer little, if any, insight into how women themselves experienced, perceived, and shaped the political, cultural, and socioeconomic landscape of colonial Burma. Not only do the women of the *khit kala* in this study fill this gap in the historiography of colonial Burma, but they broaden the understanding of colonialism and modernity in Burma beyond the level of politics and enable a fundamental revision of the reigning nationalist and anticolonial master narratives of political culture and society in colonial Burma.

HIDDEN MEMORIES OF COSMOPOLITAN BURMA

The historiography of colonial Burma is characterized by a singular tragic narrative: colonialism was a deeply traumatic and emasculating experience that left colonized men and women with no choice but to regard foreign people, norms, and practices as oppressive and exploitative. The British abolished the monarchy in 1886 and unceremoniously deported the last Burmese monarch, King Thibaw, and his immediate family from Mandalay into permanent exile in India.[10] With the abolition of the monarchy, the Buddhist monastic order, or sangha, was stripped of its traditional state patronage and supervision.[11] British colonial rule led to a sudden flow of investment capital from overseas sources, as well as to an unprecedented influx of adult male immigrants from the colonial metropole and British India who displaced the indigenous population from key administrative, commercial, and industrial socioeconomic niches created by administrative centralization, industrialization, and the development of a capitalist market economy.[12] The traditional agriculture-based economy became irrevocably tied to the colonial economy and hence to the global economic system, the malign effects of which were made palpable during the Great Depression of the 1930s, when an unprecedented number of Burmese farmers and traders sank into crushing debt.[13] Colonial policies and practices thus pitted the minority of foreign immigrants, who monopolized the processes and benefits of modernization, against the majority of tradition- and village-bound indigenous women and men who were deterred from taking part in or influencing their country's political, socioeconomic, and cultural development. This historical narrative of a conceptually and institutionally monolithic colonial modernity that made inevitable the rise of a nation antagonistic towards foreigners and indigenous "collaborators" continued to serve as a powerful genealogy for the isolationist, xenophobic, and antimodern tendencies of the military regimes that have governed the country since 1962.

No scholar was more important in constructing this master narrative of colonialism in Burma than the Fabian Socialist colonial civil servant and scholar John S. Furnivall (1878–1960). A Cambridge-educated Indian Civil Service officer who spent more than forty years in Burma (1902–1931 and 1948–1960), Furnivall produced much of the definitive secondary scholarship on socioeconomic life in colonial Burma and profoundly shaped the historical analysis of the impact of British colonialism on Burma, in particular, through his theorization of colonial Burmese society as a "plural society."[14] His theory of the plural society had a twofold significance. First, by "plural society," Furnivall meant a society in which ethnically and socioeconomically distinct groups—namely, Europeans, Indians, Chinese, and Burmese—lived side by side but separately, to meet only in the marketplace. In his pyramid scheme of the plural society, "foreign" men—that is, people of non-Burmese descent or mixed ancestry and predominantly non-Buddhists—occupied the apex: foreign men resided in Rangoon and dominated urban, prestigious, skilled, and well-paying jobs. Further down the pyramid were agrarians, Buddhists, and Burmese. The ethnically stratified socioeconomic groups retained their respective basic institutions such as kinship, religion, education, property, and recreation and "had nothing in common but the economic motive, the desire for material advantage."[15]

Second, Furnivall assumed that the economy in precolonial Burma was essentially agricultural, with limited trade founded on barter, and argued that the British colonial state exposed this traditional village economy of subsistence agriculture to the commercialized and monetized capitalist world economy. In the "plural society," social atomization, coupled with economic liberalization, resulted in the disintegration of local customs that formerly instilled, regulated, and fostered communal responsibilities and social cohesion. With no will or institution to advance social welfare, colonial Burmese society was left defenseless against unbridled market forces driven purely by the pursuit of individual profit. As Furnivall explains, the Burmese bore the brunt of the economically driven plural society: "In all that was distinctively modern in the [colonial] life of Burma, [the Burmese] had no part. . . . Burma was thrown open to the world, but the world was not opened up to [the Burmese], and the faster that development proceeded the further [the Burmese] lagged behind, for which a younger generation devised the catchword *auk kya, nauk kya.*"[16] The catchphrase *auk kya, nauk kya,* meaning "fall below, fall behind," captures Furnivall's depiction of colonial Burmese society. Burmese people fell behind and below Europeans, Indians, and Chinese and found themselves shut out of the processes of modernization.

Post-Furnivall historians of Burma have by and large reinforced the plural society model of colonial Burma.[17] In the only study of the Eurasian population in Burma, John C. Koop underlines the ethnic and socioeconomic segregation of the Eurasian community in colonial Burma, a community that resided primarily in Rangoon. He explains that Eurasians increasingly felt superior to the indigenous people: "One result of this was to restrict to a minimum social contacts between the Eurasians and members of indigenous groups, excluding relatives. . . . Eurasians proved to be politically reliable, and the British rulers preferred to employ them rather than indigenes in minor government positions, particularly in technical departments like the railways, posts and telegraph."[18] Studies of urban development in colonial Burma similarly emphasize ethnic separation. Christopher Bayly argues that colonial Rangoon, the heart of cosmopolitan Burma, was in fact an Indian city.[19] Sarah Maxim indicates that the urban landscape of colonial Burma lacked the more symbiotic relationship between the rulers and the ruled and the resulting "mestizo culture"—in which "immigrant groups intermarried with each other and with local peoples and developed a new, syncretic identity which was quite specific to this urban environment"[20]—that was characteristic of treaty port cities that existed prior to colonialism. The culture of the plural society, unlike a "mestizo" culture with its shared values and meaningful social intercourse, was characterized by conflict: "Everywhere there is rivalry and some degree of conflict between Town and Country, Industry and Agriculture, Capital and Labor; but when rural interests are Burman, and urban interests mainly European, with Burman Agriculture and European Industry, Burman Labor and European Capital, the elements of conflict are so deep-seated and so explosive that even the best will on both sides can hardly avert disaster."[21] Even Michael Adas, who points out that "[outside] of the political sphere, no niches were the total monopoly of any one group, and control of positions at different levels was continually changing,"[22] ultimately perpetuates the Furnivallian claim that an insurmountable divide between the modern colonizer (and eventually the Westernized local elite) and the traditional colonized defined colonial Burmese society. While noting that such modern public institutions as Western education and law were shared by Burmese people and foreigners alike, he nonetheless insists that the majority of Burmese people "adhered to their traditional institutions and participated only marginally, if at all, in Western institutions beyond those in the economic sphere."[23]

I argue that this interpretation of Burmese colonial history is deceptive for a number of reasons. First, it elides the fact that colonized men and women in Burma actively participated in the articulation of *khit kala* and *khit thit* ways of being and belonging and that they contested, albeit not always successfully, stipulations of exclusion that defined modern institutions and practices established or elaborated by the British administration. Second, it neglects the ambivalence and reluctance with which the colonial state sought to modernize "traditional" societies in the colonies, and the central role that colonized men and women, and colonials who were not agents of the state, played in the modernization effort. As chapter 1 shows, institutions typically associated with modernization such as government-funded public education, mass print media, and the public discursive sphere developed despite the apathy of and even interference by the colonial administration, and thanks largely to the endeavors of American Baptist missionaries, Buddhist monks, university students, party politicians, and wealthy businessmen and -women. For example, though the colonial administration had made educational reforms—specifically, the introduction and expansion of vernacular education offered outside monasteries—a priority as early as the mid-nineteenth century, less than a third of rural Burma had received provisions for such education in 1920. In fact, of the approximately six thousand institutions providing education in the 1920s, only seventy-nine were government schools; the rest were run under either indigenous or missionary management. The narrative of how the colonial state excluded the Burmese from modernity thus not only distorts the important roles the latter played as agents of modernity but also obscures the associations and unlikely alliances formed across the putative colonized/ Burmese/traditional and colonizer/foreign/modern divide.

In recent years, a voluminous literature on modernity has developed, seeking to further refine ever more sophisticated definitions of modernity (or modernities) and historicize and pluralize understandings and experiences of the modern.[24] This scholarship has reinforced the desirability of studies that complicate theories and definitions of modernity that give explanatory power to an abstract, agentless, and homogeneous colonial process or experience. There are no better embodiments of the intricate realities of colonialism and modernization in Burma than the women of the *khit kala* examined in this study.

REFIGURING WOMEN, COLONIALISM, AND MODERNITY

As the rich literature on the "new woman" or "modern woman" has demonstrated, she was a multivalent figure. The Japanese modern girl, or *moga,* "the vanguard of a changing age to battle old customs,"[25] symbolized at once the political, economic, and sexual emancipation of women as well as the potential of modernity to remove women from radical politics and enmesh them, instead, in frivolous consumerism.[26] If the modern girl in interwar England referred to a new generation of socially and financially independent working-class women, in interwar China she was viewed as a celebration of the superficial aspects of modern life, cultural loss, and existential alienation that modernity entailed.[27] In India and China, as Louise Edwards indicates, the modern woman "was part of a modernizing discourse that made possible the imagining of a new nation."[28] Images of the modern woman materialized cross-culturally as metaphorical shortcuts for varied expectations, projections, and anxieties that were brought about by processes of modernization.

In colonial Burma the woman of the *khit kala* served as a salient icon of modernity as well. She appeared in many guises and in her different forms she embodied modernities that were variously progressive, necessary, desirable, dangerous, and repulsive. The educated young woman, the patriot and feminist, and the consumerist housewife-and-mother and fashionista represented social equality, education, political organization and participation, science, and consumerism as hallmarks of modernity. At the same time, the fashionista, like the figure of the wife or the mistress of a foreign man, embodied a modernity defined by decadence, the loss of tradition, cultural dissolution, and continued European imperial expansion.

The woman of the *khit kala* was notable for her multivalence and her cosmopolitanism. She functioned as a cultural intermediary between the local and the global, occupying "the liminal space conjoining the indigenous and the imperial, the national and the international," and "continually [incorporating] elements drawn from elsewhere."[29] She brought into association old and new and familiar and foreign ideas, practices, and institutions. The fashionable woman wore high heels with the *longyi* (a saronglike ankle-length skirt). The patriot and feminist worked together with both local Buddhist organizations and international feminist associations. The housewife-and-mother raised her children on milk, biscuits, and Western medicine as well as Burmese dishes and herbal remedies. The educated young woman employed literary strategies and styles drawn from precolonial Buddhist commentarial texts to discuss progressive cultural politics in print media. The wife/mistress of a foreigner mingled with Indian, Chinese, European, and Christian and Muslim men and had mixed children. Discussions about women of the *khit kala* in colonial Burma were also informed to varying degrees by contemporary discourses about women that originated in specific locales but circulated beyond colonial and national boundaries—imperialist, nationalist, and feminist discourses about the "woman question," Christian missionary opinions about domestic science, Gandhi's *swadeshi* movement in British India,[30] and Marxist-Leninist literature from Britain. In other words, the discourses and representations of modern Burmese women "affiliated their users to a larger world rather than a smaller place."[31] They draw our attention to the cosmopolitanism that existed alongside and in tension with anticolonialism and nationalism.

Existing literature on cosmopolitanism in Southeast Asia has tended to emphasize, on the one hand, the role that the overseas Chinese people—due to their mobility, links to transnational networks, and positioning at the margins of the nation—have played as cosmopolitan cultural intermediaries and knowledge brokers.[32] On the other hand, recent studies of popular discourse on modernity in the British colonies in the region have emphasized the importance of English education, the English language, and English-language print media to the development of cosmopolitan and modern consciousness, with one study of colonial Penang characterizing the English language as the "de facto vehicle for local 'cosmopolitanism.'"[33] Even in her important study on the "indigenous interlocutor" Taw Sein Ko and his role as a cross-cultural broker between Burmese, Chinese, and European domains of knowledge, Penny Edwards discusses only English-language writings by the Sino-Burmese colonial official-scholar, supporting the notion that the English language was the de facto medium for cosmopolitan engagements with modernity.[34] These disparate developments in the scholarship on modernity and cosmopolitanism in Southeast Asia have had the combined effect of associating cosmopolitan thoughts and actions with diasporic and Anglophone communities and insinuating that indigenous people were unable to think and act locally *and* translocally, at least not in the local vernaculars.

This study shows that in colonial Burma the English language was not a privileged medium for debating modernity. Nor were Anglophone and diasporic communities the exclusive cosmopolitan cultural brokers. The development of the English language into a lingua franca did contribute to the rapid circulation of information and ideas in the region and facilitated cross-cultural discourse, but it did not monopolize cosmopolitan ideas and practices or the discourse on modernity. Just as those with affinities to Anglophone culture or an ethnically "Chinese" transnational community were able to participate in and contribute to local nationalist projects,[35] affinities to local communities did not preclude Burmese people from acting as cosmopolitan cultural brokers. Through feminine figurations of the *khit kala,* men and women in colonial Burma brought together signs and meanings of modernization refracted from multiple reference points to create plural visions of modernity that crossed religious, racial, and ethnic boundaries and operated beyond the social and political paradigms characteristic of nationalist and Furnivallian criticism. The modern Burmese woman disrupts the misleadingly discrete and stable binary categories such as "modern foreigners" and "traditional natives" common in many histories of colonialism and illuminates what Dipesh Chakrabarty has termed the "conjoined genealogy" of the modern.[36] Her forms force us to interrogate the multiple visions of modernity existing simultaneously under colonialism. She attests powerfully that "some people in the past have been able to be universal and particular, without making either their particularity ineluctable or their universalism compulsory."[37] This cosmopolitanism makes practices and discourses associated with women of the *khit kala* a field of inquiry that is perhaps unrivalled in its potential for rethinking historical narratives of colonialism and modernity in Burma.

THE PLAN OF THE BOOK

The first chapter of this book describes the colonial backdrop against which the modern woman emerged. It outlines the socioeconomic, political, and cultural transformations that made possible new discourses and practices concerning and involving women. I look at significant demographic changes triggered by the influx of single male colonists, immigrants and migrant laborers from England and British India, and the consequent increase in racially mixed unions. The rapid growth of an ethnically plural urban colonial society entailed the institutionalization of a plural legal system, as in British India, wherein cases related to family law were made subject to the "religion" of the persons involved in the dispute, and thus occasioned the codification of "Burmese-Buddhist" customary laws. Chapter 1 also examines the establishment of government-funded "secular" education, the formation of a popular commercial culture founded on mass print and visual media, and the related growth of the public discursive sphere, all of which shaped the urban landscape of colonial Burma. Subsequent chapters illustrate that these developments deeply influenced how local men and women imagined and made sense of who they were, articulated the boundaries of belonging and foreignness, and conceived of social and political power in gendered, religious, and ethnic terms.

Chapter 2 looks at the rise of educated women in the 1920s and the contemporaneous introduction of the first women's column "Yuwadi sekku" (Young ladies' eyes) in *Dagon Magazine.* The epistolary column, which featured letters ostensibly written by young women, was instrumental in the appearance of the iconic educated young modern woman who, together with the first generation of women journalists, intellectuals, lawmakers, and teachers, symbolized the aspirations of young women in Burma to become knowledge brokers, a vocation traditionally reserved for men. The column also served as a fertile site for addressing the contentious "woman question"—that is, whether and which conditions of women needed reform. The chapter shows that in Burma, as elsewhere at the time, the progress of women, especially through education, became the focal point of debates about modernization and nation building.

Chapter 3 examines the increasing politicization of women in the 1920s and 1930s. As a wife-and-mother of the nation, a Burmese woman was charged with the duty of safeguarding her home and family and raising her children to be devoted to their people and country. As a daughter of the nation, she was urged to participate in legislative and party politics, university boycotts, labor strikes, and anticolonial protests. The chapter demonstrates the dual obligations of women of the *khit kala* to the private and the public spheres of home and nation. The growing visibility of women in organized political agitation, however, was also a result of feminist efforts to mobilize women, as the activities of early women's associations in Burma reveal. The modern politicized woman was both a patriot and a feminist and intervened in the sufferings of others as patriotic feminists.

Two distinct images of the woman of the *khit kala* as consumer are analyzed in chapter 4: the fashionista and the housewife-and-mother. The former was associated with self-indulgent consumption while the latter was associated with wise and dutiful consumption. Yet both were closely linked to new bodily practices that placed emphasis on health, hygiene and beauty, self-improvement, and self-fulfillment and necessitated the use of scientific commodities. Both illustrate that what it meant to be modern was shaped by the rising culture of consumerism.

The remaining chapters examine censorious critiques of the sexual and sartorial practices of women of the *khit kala* in literary, political, and journalistic texts. Chapter 5 investigates negative representations of Burmese women who engaged in intimate relations with "foreign"—that is, non-Buddhist, non-Burmese—men. Chapter 6 returns to the fashionista and discusses critiques of her consumer practices and sartorial habits as frivolous, self-indulgent, and unpatriotic. These chapters illustrate that the intensifying nationalist appeal for women, as both signs and custodians of tradition, to protect and preserve the purity of Burmese-Buddhist culture led to the stigmatization of intermarriage and fashion as powerful symbols of disloyalty. They also argue, however, that neither the nationalist plea for traditionalism in the face of multiple modern and colonial temptations nor the changing tides of political movements sufficiently explain such criticisms. Attacks on the modern women were also symptoms of redefinitions of dominant femininity and masculinity.

The book ends, as it began, by turning to the writings of Ma Ma Lay. In the last chapter, I juxtapose two very different stories of colonialism in Burma that she told: *Mon ywe mahu* and *Thway* (Blood). The conflicting understandings of colonial encounters underlying these two novels bring us back to a consideration of the heterogeneous and uneven ways that Burmese men and women experienced and engaged with colonialism and modernity.

TERMS, NAMES, AND TRANSLATED QUOTATIONS

There was no single Burmese expression for the "modern woman" in colonial Burma. Several terms were used to describe her. Most of the various names for the modern woman were relatively generic and could be and were used interchangeably, though *khit hsan thu* and *tet khit thami* referred specifically to "fashionable" modern women and therefore had distinct connotations. To avoid confusion, I have used either *khit hmi thu* or "women of the *khit kala*," two terms that were widely used during the period under examination, to refer to modern Burmese women, unless a different descriptive term was used in the source material. When referring specifically to the "fashionable" modern woman, I use the term *khit hsan thu*.

My use of the term "Burma" also needs clarification. Whether to use "Burma" or "Myanmar" as the name of the country has become a controversial issue since the military regime officially renamed the country "Myanmar," a change rejected by the political opposition and by countries such as the United States that see the governing junta as illegitimate. Much ink has been spilled over this controversy, which I will not belabor here.[38] Suffice it to say that the usage of "Burma" over "Myanmar" or vice versa is often construed as a political statement. I use the terms "Burma" and its adjective "Burmese" not as a reflection of my political leanings but because they were the romanized terms most widely used to refer to Burma/Myanmar and its people during the period covered in this study.

There are no surnames in Burma, and therefore Burmese names appear in their full form at every occurrence in the book. In the bibliography, Burmese names have been alphabetized by the first letter of the first syllable of the name. Where appropriate, honorifics such as U,[39] Daw,[40] Ma,[41] and Maung[42] have been added to names, but these prefixes do not affect alphabetization nor appear in the bibliography.

Finally, a note on transliteration, transcription, and translation. In this book, I provide transliteration of Burmese words according to a slightly modified version of the Library of Congress Transliteration System.[43] For frequently used Burmese words, I provide the rough phonetic equivalent, followed by their transliteration in parentheses or in an endnote. Any unattributed translations are my own.

1

The Colonial Setting

The British colonization of Burma was piecemeal. It began in 1826 with the defeat of the Konbaung dynasty (1752–1885) in the First Anglo-Burmese War (1824–1826) and the loss of the provinces of Arakan and Tenasserim to the British government (see map 1.1). When the governor-general of the East India Company declared war on the Burmese in March 1824, the annexation of Arakan was not among the military and political goals. Arakan was a major source of tension between the British and the Burmese, however. The forty-year Burmese rule of Arakan (1785–1824) was marked by excessive levying of taxes and labor that led to exoduses of refugees into British territory and provoked Arakanese insurgency. That some Arakanese rebels had their bases in British territory and the British refused to surrender them to Burmese authorities aggravated cross-border relations. The continued expansionist policy of Konbaung monarchs, in Manipur and Assam in addition to Arakan, fueled border disputes and skirmishes, resulting in the longest and most expensive war in British Indian history.[1] By December 1825 the British had defeated the Burmese decisively, and in February 1826 the Treaty of Yadanabo was signed, including among its terms the cession of Arakan and Tenasserim and an indemnity of £1 million by the Konbaung government.[2]

Arakan grew into a major rice exporter, with its main port, Akyab, exporting more rice to Europe than any other port in the world until Rangoon surpassed it later in the nineteenth century.[3] Tenasserim proved to be a fiscal burden, however, failing to pay for its administration; there were even suggestions that the province be returned to the Burmese or sold to Siam.[4] Yet the appointment of Lord Dalhousie, known for his interventionist and annexationist policies, as governor-general of India ensured that British India would part with neither Arakan nor Tenasserim. Not only did he retain the

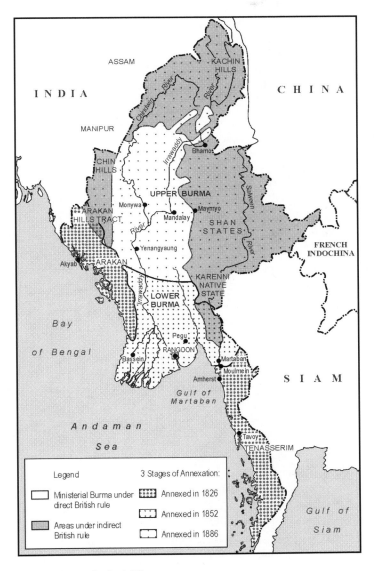

Map 1.1 Map of colonial Burma

provinces, but he also declared war on Burma in 1852, prompted by a complaint by captains of two British ships that they were unfairly fined by a governor in Rangoon for customs violations. Lord Dalhousie demanded that the Burmese rescind the fine and remove the governor in Rangoon. The Burmese accepted the terms, to which Lord Dalhousie responded with another ultimatum—pay the British one million rupees for the cost of having had to prepare for war—and proceeded to seize Rangoon, Bassein, and Martaban without waiting for a reply. Before the end of the year, the British had also successfully annexed Pegu.[5] These new acquisitions were combined with Arakan and Tenasserim to become in 1862 the Province of British Burma, or "Lower Burma," administered under a chief commissioner with headquarters in Rangoon.[6] The Second Anglo-Burmese War (1852–1853) thus resulted in the loss by the Konbaung dynasty of its outlet to the sea and the rice surpluses from Lower Burma and led to rapid transformations in Burma's political and socioeconomic landscape.[7] For several decades thereafter the British government based in Rangoon made concerted efforts to ensure the dominant economic position of Lower Burma while nominally sharing political power with the Konbaung government. British efforts to develop Lower Burma into a source of raw materials and a market outlet in the decades after the Second Anglo-Burmese War were evident in the unparalleled growth of processing, port, and railway centers, particularly in Rangoon and Bassein.[8]

During the period between the Second Anglo-Burmese War and the third and final one in 1885, European merchants and firms in Lower Burma, seeking freer trade with and access to the resources of Upper Burma and neighboring China, became increasingly vocal in their calls to annex Upper Burma. Another impetus for the annexation of Upper Burma was the signing of the Franco-Burmese Treaty on 15 January 1885. The Burmese government had been cultivating friendlier relations with French, Italian, and other European powers in the 1880s in the hopes of offsetting British encroachment on Burma. Such relations, especially with a competing imperial power consolidating its colonies to the east of Siam, were perceived as serious threats to British interests.[9] The immediate cause of the Third Anglo-Burmese War, however, was a fine of approximately £180,000 imposed by the Konbaung government on the Bombay-Burma Trading Company for logging beyond what its license permitted. The company disputed the charge, and while negotiations between the government and the company were still ongoing, the British India government authorized the chief commissioner of Burma to issue an ultimatum to King Thibaw consisting of four main points: accept a British resident at the court and allow him "free access" to the king, suspend the proceedings against the company until the arrival of the resident, conduct all future foreign relations "in accordance with the advice of the Government of India," and "grant proper facilities for the development of British trade with Western China through Bhamo."[10] On 11 November 1885, two days after the British government received a reply from King Thibaw, which it deemed a refusal or evasion of all the terms outlined in the ultimatum, the war began. The British quickly took control over Upper Burma. On 29 November the last Burmese monarch and his immediate family were shipped off from Mandalay to the town of Ratnagiri along India's western coast, where King Thibaw spent the remainder of his life. On 1 December a proclamation announcing King Thibaw's surrender, dethronement, and deportation was issued.[11] The royal palace in Mandalay was abandoned as the seat of the state—the main halls of the palace turned into an Anglican chapel and the Upper Burma Club— and the British made Rangoon the administrative capital of colonial Burma, consolidating the preeminence of Lower Burma. The last Burmese dynasty had come to an end, and the *colony khit* (colonial era), otherwise known as the *British khit* (era of the British) had begun.

Unlike colonial Malaya, which became "British Malaya" and whose sultanate was not abolished, colonial Burma was incorporated into the British Raj and administered by and subordinated to the government of India. Not until 1897 was Burma given a separate government with a lieutenant governor—no longer just a chief commissioner—as its head. A Legislative Council, consisting of seven British officials and two European representatives of the mercantile community, was also formed. This advisory body, with the sanction of the governor-general, was enabled for the first time to enact legislation concerning Burma without being referred to the Indian Legislative Council.[12] British officials never attempted to create an administration specifically for Burma. They opted to transfer a form of governance that they had developed through their administrative experiences in British India. The most controversial example of this was the Upper Burma Village Regulation Act of 1887, an instrument of martial law enacted to suppress rebellions against the British. The act, based on the assumption that in Burma, as in India, the village was the basic social and political unit, increased the authority and duties of the village headmen, the *thu gyi* or *ywa thu gyi*.[13] It made the *thu gyi* responsible for the maintenance of order in his village and empowered him to deal summarily with those deemed agents and supporters of dacoits and rebels. Chief Commissioner Charles Crosthwaite, who drafted and pushed for the ratification of the act, described it as having been "framed in accordance with the old customary law and with the feelings of the people."[14] In actuality, the most important traditional local-level unit of administration was the *myo*[15]—a town or a district consisting of a main town, a market, and surrounding villages and smaller towns—governed by a hereditary headman, the *myo thu gyi*,[16] whose lineage usually went back to the sixteenth and seventeenth centuries.[17] Crosthwaite acknowledged the existence of the *myo,* yet he considered the village to be the "customary" administrative unit and the *thu gyi* the rightful local administrator, whose power and position had been usurped by the *myo thu gyi.* Incidentally, he suspected that the *myo* functioned as the locus of organized resistance against the British. Under the Village Regulation Act, the *myo thu gyi* gradually lost their jurisdictions and found themselves displaced by the *thu gyi.*[18]

At the same time, the British colonial administration in Burma, however coercive, remained a "skinny" state.[19] Many of its policies and practices are best characterized as laissez-faire even in "Burma Proper," or "Ministerial Burma," comprising the central plains, the Irrawaddy Delta, and the southern archipelagic areas, where the colonial government practiced direct rule.[20] Upon annexing Upper Burma, Lord Dufferin, then the governor-general of India, instructed that "the simplest and cheapest system of administration open to [the British]" be adopted and that "most of the unimportant criminal work and nearly all the civil suits must be disposed of by the native officials, subject to the check and control of the district officer."[21] In earlier phases of colonization, officials were similarly left "to dispense justice and collect revenue according to their own ideas of equity and common sense with very little interference from above"[22] and relied on the *thu gyi* for the maintenance of law and order, the collection of revenue, and general administration. If Furnivall is correct, even up to 1900, local people "saw little of any government officials, and very few ever caught more than a passing glimpse of a European official."[23] The colonial government remained distant from the local population and, in addition, made little headway in actually administering the province even by its own standards. Even after Pegu had been under the British for a quarter of a century, exceedingly few roads had been paved.[24] In his annual report for 1869, the chief commissioner of Burma complained that "beyond the mere fact of our military possession of the country, beyond the existence of a police, most inadequately paid, there is hardly anything in the length and breadth of the Province to testify the presence of any rule superior to the one from which it has been wrested."[25]

In fact, until the early twentieth century, the overriding concern of the British administration was the pacification of the province and the collection of just enough taxes to cover the cost of the enforcement of law and order; trade and other economic activities were to be left to "free private enterprise."[26] This was no mean task. It took the British eleven years and eight years to "pacify" Tenasserim and Pegu, respectively. Resistance, dacoity, and rebellion similarly followed the British annexation of Upper Burma. Upwards of 16,000 troops reinforced the original expeditionary forces in 1886; by February 1887, British and Indian troops deployed to "pacify" Burma numbered 40,500. The cost of the annexation and subsequent pacification campaigns amounted to over £1.27 million by 1888.[27] According to John Nisbet, the conservator of forests in Burma from 1895 to 1900, Burma was not "absolutely free from organized dacoity" until 1899.[28] Crosthwaite described his own administration as "an isolated administration hardly able to look up from our own affairs, and obliged to work in detail, district by district, to establish a beginning of order."[29]

By the turn of the century, the colonial state was devoting more resources to the development of basic infrastructure and agricultural services "in order to support the more rapid development of the country's resources, both human and material."[30] Numerous departments were established, including those of agriculture, veterinary and fishery, public health, cooperative credit, and information. From 1923 the Province of Burma constituted a governor's province, and responsibility for a whole range of functions was transferred to the government of Burma. Yet still, certain functions of government continued to be controlled by the central government of India, notably defense and external relations, currency and coinage, tariffs and customs, civil and criminal law, and communications and transportation controls. In 1937, just over a decade before independence, a fully self-contained constitution for Burma finally came into effect, and Burma was administratively separated from India. Although defense, external relations, and monetary policy remained under the control of the governor of India, who was ultimately under the authority of the British Parliament, in all other areas of national life the Burmese Legislature exercised control subject only to certain reserve powers vested in the governor.[31] For the most part, the British colonial government treated Burma as a remote appendage of British India. Notwithstanding its remoteness from Burma, however, the colonial state managed to transform the social and economic structure of Burma, especially of Lower Burma.

SOCIAL AND ECONOMIC STRUCTURE:
PLURAL SOCIETY REVISITED

Burma was an ethnically plural country before the colonial period. The ethnic antagonism between the Burmans of the north and the Mons, or Talaing people, of the south is well known. Victor Lieberman points out in his study of ethnic politics in precolonial Burma that the Mons felt culturally superior to the Burmese, whom they tended to disparage as "'upcountry rustics,' whereas the Burmese scorned the 'effeteness' of their southern neighbors."[32] Although the Burmans and the Mons shared many cultural traits, they displayed awareness of ethnic difference.

Well before the arrival of the early European traders, Upper Burma had been a destination for male *tayoke* (Chinese) traders and settlers from Yunnan who married local women, learned the local language, and adopted the local practices of Buddhism and *nat* (spirit) worship.[33] Similarly, coastal Burma served as host to male itinerant traders and immigrants engaged in the Indian Ocean trade as early as the thirteenth century, when Tamil merchants known as *nanadesi* (those trading to foreign countries) resided not only in Burma's port cities but also in the Upper Burman capital of Pagan.[34] By the sixteenth and seventeenth centuries, the maritime districts of Mergui, Tavoy, Martaban, Pegu, and Akyab had developed into "the locus of highly complex cultural flows and eddies"[35] and a host to Persian, Hindi, Bengali, Pathan (Afghan Muslim), and Portuguese courtiers, merchants, explorers, and mercenaries, Mon and Thai war captives, and "Dutchmen retired from East India Company service, and permanent English and French residents."[36] In southwestern Burma, the Arakanese polity's pattern of military recruitment, "using much of its sea-derived wealth to employ foreign mercenaries from all over Eurasia . . . even Christian samurai driven from Japan by the early Tokugawa shoguns,"[37] furthermore contributed to the cosmopolitan character of the coastal cities. In the eighteenth century, overland Sino-Burmese trade sustained the inflow of Chinese merchants from Yunnan who were engaged in the profitable silk and tea trade. Maritime commerce, centered around the ports of Pegu, likewise continued to attract merchants from China and India.[38] According to Lieberman, traffic between China and Burma, and between India and Burma, increased during the eighteenth century. Writing in the 1790s, Michael Symes, the British embassy to the court of Ava, described Rangoon as a city crowded with "insolvent debtors" and "foreigners of desperate fortunes," most of whom made their living as petty traders: "Here are to be met fugitives from all countries of the east, and of all complexions. . . . Malabars, Moguls, Persians, Parsees, Armenians, Portuguese, French, and English, all mingle here, and are engaged in various branches of commerce."[39]

The speed and intensity with which the delta region of Lower Burma became an ethnically, linguistically, and socioeconomically diverse urban center under colonialism were unprecedented, however. In the decades following the British annexation of Lower Burma in 1850, the delta region grew into the leading rice-exporting area in the world; the region contained twelve of the thirteen principal rice-growing districts in Burma, a high concentration of rice mills, and the chief ports of Burma's rice export.[40] Burma developed a highly specialized single-product export economy focused on rice, making it heavily reliant on the import of manufactured goods as well as of a considerable amount of simple, essential staples of the Burmese diet such as salt, salted and unsalted fish, and cooking oil. The delta region served as the main entry point not only for foreign products but also for immigrants. Men, and to a much lesser extent women, came from the colonial metropole, British India, and Malaya, as well as China, to fill the numerous administrative, commercial, industrial, and agricultural niches created by industrialization and the expansion and elaboration of the infrastructure, the financial system, and the capitalist market economy in Burma. By 1918, Rangoon had become second only to New York as a port for immigration. For a period in the 1920s, Rangoon was the busiest port in the world, with as many as 360,000 immigrants and 280,000 emigrants in one year to and from Indian ports alone.[41]

Burma hosted Eurasians from India and Malaya who, together with local Eurasians of Portuguese and French descent, dominated certain government sectors—namely, the railways, telegraph and postal departments.[42] The bankers, merchants, and entrepreneurs represented a medley of Baghdadi Jews, Armenians, *chettiar* (a South Indian moneylending caste) from Tamil Nadu, British, and other *bo* (Europeans).[43] Integration into British India triggered a steady stream of seasonal laborers whose journeys were facilitated by the falling costs of steamship travel. Thousands of *kala* (Indian) seasonal traders, workers, and laborers came from the Indian subcontinent annually to work in Burma's paddy fields, rice mills, factories, and docks.[44] Far from being a homogeneous community, the group of *kala* immigrants included a diverse array of people from Hindu, Buddhist, Jain, Muslim, Sikh, and other religious backgrounds: besides the *chettiar* moneylenders already mentioned, sailors and boatmen from Chittagong, coolies from Telegu,[45] and Bengali *durwan* (guards), *dhobie* (laundry washers), tailors, and barbers. The colonial government and companies hired upper-caste Bengalis as clerks, and Tamils from Madras usually became household servants.[46] *Tayoke* immigrants likewise constituted a varied group of Hokkien, Cantonese, and Hakka men and women, most of them having migrated from the Provinces of Fujian and Guangdong, or from the Straits Settlements—a departure from precolonial patterns of Chinese immigration primarily from Yunnan.[47] The traders, bankers, and shop owners—that is, the white-collar workers—among the *tayoke* were referred to as *lak rha* (long sleeve), while the blue-collar workers, mostly craftsmen, carpenters, farmers, and coolies, were known as *lak tui* (short sleeve).[48]

The immigrant population of women paled in comparison to its male counterpart. In 1931, approximately 72 percent of *kala,* 66 percent of *tayoke,* and 68 percent of *bo* were male. Of the immigrant population from India, which constituted roughly 80 percent of the total immigrant population in Burma, females represented only 18 and 16 percent in 1921 and 1931, respectively. Females accounted for 21 percent of the total immigrant population from China and 32 percent of the total European immigrant population.[49]

The colonial capital, Rangoon, where the Burmese themselves were fast becoming a minority, manifested most visibly the magnitude of these colonially determined immigration patterns. According to the 1921 census, the population of Rangoon was 341,962; in 1881, however, the total population of Rangoon had been just 134,176, and in 1872, only 98,745. While Rangoon undoubtedly attracted newcomers from the countryside seeking better employment opportunities in a new environment, the 1901 census shows that fewer than half of the 234,881 residents in Rangoon were born in Burma (125,652 were born in either India or China). By 1931, immigrants constituted 65 percent of the population of the capitol.[50] Females, however, accounted for only 12 percent of the total immigrant population of Rangoon in 1921. In inverse relationship to the male immigrant population, Burmese and in particular ethnic-majority Burmans dominated the population of female residents in Rangoon.[51] Approximately 80 percent of these women, furthermore, were under the age of forty. The presence of Burmese women in urban areas was striking enough for the census commissioner of Burma to remark in the 1931 census report that "apparently Burmese women appreciate the amenities of town life."[52] In fact, from the early twentieth century and at least until the beginning of the 1930s, there were consistently more Burmese women than men in urban areas, whereas there were three times more Indian men than Indian women and twice more Chinese men than Chinese women.

The high rate of "mixed" relations in colonial Burma is therefore unsurprising. The large influx of male immigrants that colonial rule precipitated, and the minuscule population of *bo, kala,* and *tayoke* women in Burma—which composed only 5 percent of the total female population in 1931—made the rapid growth in relations between foreign men and local women inevitable, as evinced by the sharp rise in the "half-caste" population in Burma, especially Eurasian and Indo-Burmese. At the turn of the twentieth century, there were 9,974 Eurasians and 20,423 Indo-Burmese; by 1931, the number of Eurasians had doubled (19,200), and the number of Indo-Burmese had increased almost ninefold (182,166).[53] Although census data do not provide information on the Sino-Burmese population, British travel literature from the late nineteenth century as well as colonial-period court records concerning marriages between "Chinese Buddhist" men and "Burmese Buddhist" women demonstrate that Sino-Burmese unions were similarly widespread.[54] In *Picturesque*

Burma, travel writer Alice Hart portrays Chinese men in Burma as industri-ous, patient, even-tempered, and devoted to family, adding: "He thus becomes a very acceptable husband to the independent, active Burmese woman; and as Chinese immigrants almost always arrive alone, without their womankind, marriages between Chinese and Burmese women are rather frequent, and prove highly satisfactory."[55] The chief justice who ruled in a decisive case on whether Burmese Buddhist law should apply to a Sino-Burmese marriage even asserted that such marriages were the most common form of intermar-riage in colonial Burma: "Again it must not be lost sight of that Chinamen have come and settled in Burma in growing numbers since the first occupa-tion of the country. And more than any other race they have inter-married and joined in the social and religious life of the people of the country."[56]

The influx of largely male immigrants thus triggered a proliferation in mixed sexual relations and marriage. Colonial Burmese society was far from integrated or cohesive, however, as demonstrated by the anti-Indian riots that erupted in the 1930s. The first of the riots occurred in May 1930. Their immediate cause was a strike against the Scindia Steam Navigation Company Ltd., by approximately 2,000 immigrant Indian dockworkers who demanded an increase in wages. Although the company initially refused to comply with the demand, hiring instead some 2,000 Burmese laborers willing to work for less pay, it eventually conceded. On the morning of 26 May the Burmese workers arrived at Lewis Street Jetty, not having been informed of the settle-ment, only to be met by the reinstated Indian workers. A brawl resulted and led to a Rangoon-wide fight between Burmese and Indians that involved looting, burning of homes and shops, and armed attacks. The communal vio-lence lasted four days and left 110 people dead and nearly 800 injured.[57] The second anti-Indian riot, known as the 1938 Burma Riots, began on 26 July 1938 when a mass meeting of Burmese Buddhist monks and laymen at the Shwedagon Pagoda turned into a violent assault on Indians. The meeting had been organized to protest an anti-Buddhist book first published seven years earlier and republished a few months prior to the riots. Those gathered for the meeting marched to the Soortee Bara Bazaar and, upon arrival there, began throwing stones and attacking Indians. As in the first anti-Indian riot, looting and damaging of Indian mosques, shops, and homes spread through-out Burma immediately following the unrest at the bazaar, extending into September 1938 and resulting in 220 dead and 926 injured.[58] In both 1930 and 1938 the Burmese were mostly on the offensive, and the casualties were mostly Indians.

Several factors account for this ethnic antagonism. First, there was an unmistakable ethnic division of labor and economic specialization. The

1931 census report shows that Europeans and Eurasians specialized as "clerical workers," "technical experts," and "professionals" and represented the majority of the upper echelon of colonial Burmese society. While Chinese and Indians born outside Burma specialized in trade and unskilled labor, respectively, the majority of the indigenous population of Burma consisted of agriculturalists; 75 percent of Burmese earners and 87 percent of earners of other indigenous ethnic groups—earners who, combined, constituted more than 80 percent of the total earning population and more than 90 percent of Burma's total population—were engaged in agriculture. Because British colonials found that "it was less trouble and usually cheaper to recruit Indians than to train Burmans,"[59] immigrants tended to fill the socioeconomically desirable positions. The dislocation felt by Burmese men found expression in the popular press. A cartoon published in *Thuriya* (The sun) in June 1938, one month before the 1938 Burma riots erupted, depicts what appears to be four foreign men—Arab, Indian, Chinese, and British—sitting side by side comfortably on a bench on which *mran mā prañ* (country of Myanmar) is carved (figure 1.1). A Burmese man, smaller than the other four, sits uncomfortably on the edge of the bench, as it has almost no room left for him. The caption reads: "Crowded by other guests, such is the lot of the Burmese." Such a pattern of demographics and economic specialization combined with

Figure 1.1 "Crowded by other guests, such is the lot of the Burmese," in *Thuriya,* June 1938.

the administrative practices of the colonial state to give rise to a new awareness of ethnicity, race, and religion. Census and law, two cultural technologies of rule and discipline, were of particular importance in this regard and
facilitated the coalescing and codification of religion and race as categories of
classification and sources of ethnic identity.

As mentioned above, ethnic distinction existed in precolonial Burma.
However, the structure of the society was dominated not by ethnic distinction but instead by class cleavage. Take, for instance, the indigenous *dhammasat* texts. These texts, extant in thousands of palm-leaf and paper manuscript
versions that attest to their popularity in precolonial Burma, served as legal
and ethical treatises that outlined appropriate Buddhist social practices and
methods of dispute settlement. The *dhammasat* categorized men and women
on the basis of their *amyo*.[60] The term literally means "kind," "sort," or "species" and came to refer to groups (such as Shans, Kachins, and Karens) that
constituted the indigenous "races" of Burma under colonial rule and the
indigenous "ethnic minorities" in post-independent Burma. In the context
of the *dhammasat,* however, *amyo* clearly signified class, and people were categorized principally along four class divisions paralleling the four varnas in
Brahmanism (i.e., ruling, Brahman, trading, and agricultural).[61] The sections
in *dhammasat* texts concerning marriage are particularly instructive. The various *dhammasat* evince preference for class endogamy, but nowhere in them is
found a proscription against interethnic, interracial, or interfaith marriage.[62]
The *dhammasat* do not comment upon marriage between spouses of different
"ethnic" groups or "races." A telling example comes from the laws governing
the division of property:

> O great King! The Lord Rishi Manu has decided that the property of a
> man should be thus divided among the four kinds of wives. If the wife
> belongs to the royal family, she shall receive four shares; if she belongs to
> a Brahman family, she receives three shares; if she belongs to a merchant
> family, she receives two shares; and if she belongs to a cultivator's family,
> she receives one share. The sons of such wives are entitled to the inheri-
> tance in the same proportion as their respective mothers. Thus the Manu,
> the Rishi, has decided.[63]

The content of another *dhammasat*'s section on divorce is similarly revealing.
Of the forty-seven laws enumerated in the section, more than half concern the
division of property according to the types of marriage contracted—"when
the husband and wife are both children of nobles," "when the husband is a
noble, and the wife of the wealthy class," "when the husband is a noble, and

the wife a bramin," "when the husband is a noble, and the wife of the poor class," "when the husband is of the poor class and wife noble," and so on.[64] The royal orders, or *amein daw*,[65] are similarly silent on the issue of people of other religions, classifying people primarily according to class and as either freeborn or slaves.

Although class continued to serve as a key source of identity and social status during the colonial period, the British administration developed other categories for classifying its subjects. First and foremost, people were divided into different races—namely, those seen as "foreign" races (i.e., Europeans, Chinese, and Indian) and those seen as "native" races (e.g., Burmans, Shans, Kachins, Chins, Karens, and Mons). Although each race was further differentiated by language and place of birth, the dominant qualifier of race was religion: Buddhist, Animist, Christian, Muslim, Hindu, Confucian, Jain, and so on. The distinctly modern categories of Burmese Buddhist "natives" and European Christian, Indian Hindu or Muslim, and Chinese Buddhist "foreigners" thus crystallized. Because the European and Anglo-Indian population was almost exclusively Christian, the term "European Christian" or "Anglo-Indian Christian" was seldom used. Similarly, the category "Buddhist," unless qualified as "Chinese Buddhist," was taken as synonymous with the "native races"—namely, Burman and Shan, who made up the majority of the Buddhist population.

Why did the British employ these categories? The argument that such census categories served as a useful means of social control and social segregation integral to the colonial practice of "divide and rule" has become something of a truism.[66] In the case of colonial Southeast Asia, Ann Stoler has made a compelling argument that European colonial states deployed racial categories to police and deter the forging of powerful alliances along common class interests not only among disparate colonized subjects but also across the colonizer-colonized divide. Her works have traced the way the colonial state continually readjusted its policies and practices in order to create a falsely homogeneous community of white bourgeois colonials who were in reality separated by discrepant interests and by class and gender asymmetries, thereby naturalizing and hardening the boundary separating the colonizer from the colonized.[67] Yet scholarship by other imperial historians, especially on the constructions of caste identities in British India, has shown that the systematic classifications of colonial societies cannot be reduced to a strategy of "divide and rule" by the Raj.[68] It is conceivable that British colonial officials in Burma employed race and religion to classify their subjects because they believed that they determined an individual's identity. Just as the British officials in India felt that caste and religion "were the sociological keys to understanding the Indian people,"[69] in Burma they saw race and religion as the keys to knowing the natives; not by coincidence, caste was used in the Burma census until 1911, after which the British distinguished Burmese culture and society from those of India and replaced caste with race. Whatever the intention, the census operation, which required the census takers—many of whom were not British colonial officials but Indian, Eurasian, and Burmese—to repeatedly ask colonized men and women questions about their religion, race, and ethnicity, contributed to the heightening of racial, religious, and ethnic consciousness in Burma.

The census was distinctly modern also in its employment of bounded, determinate, and exclusive classifications. The colonial census created an official grid of races that did not tolerate "multiple, politically 'transvestite,' blurred, or changing identifications."[70] Ethnic identity in precolonial Burma was more porous in nature, as Lieberman has argued in the case of the Mons and the Burmese. The categories of "Burmese" and "Mon" in precolonial Burma were not mutually exclusive, and a Burmese could choose to become a Mon, and vice versa. Thus, in the eighteenth century, when the Burmese had established a strong hold over the valley area and subjected the kingdom of Arakan to the west, Mon speakers tended to tattoo their thighs and to acquire Burmese speech because this behavior conferred political and economic advantages.[71] The colonial period introduced a less fluid conceptualization of ethnic identity.

The ethnic boundaries of colonial Burmese society were also reflected and reified by the plural legal system that the British implemented. Because Burma was an extension of the Raj, Anglo-Indian codes and statutes passed by the British governor-general in India—codes and statutes based on English law—were extended to Burma. As in British India, cases related to family relations and religion were exempted from Anglo-Indian law and were made subject to the "personal law" of the individuals involved in the dispute. Therefore, although the immigrant population in colonial Burma never accounted for more than 10 percent of the total population, and nearly 90 percent of the total population was Buddhist, the British institutionalized a plural legal system whereby in cases concerning marriage, divorce, inheritance, and succession, the court administered the Buddhist law in cases where the parties were Buddhists, "the Mohammedan law" in cases where the parties were Muslims, and the Hindu law where the parties were Hindus.[72] In reality, this plural legal system was hardly enforced, as many did not use the courts and many judges failed to apply Anglo-Indian legislations in Burma. Nevertheless, it served as yet another instrument of the state that rendered ethnicity an important basis for affiliation and identification.

British colonial rule had without a doubt produced a set of conditions that made men and women in Burma acutely aware of ethnic divisions. At the same time, however, colonial Burmese society was not torn apart by ethnic strife. It is remarkable that the two anti-Indian riots of the 1930s are the only documented incidents of large-scale communal violence that occurred in colonial Burma. It is also worth noting that ethnic antagonism became pronounced only in the 1930s, during a period of economic downturn and intensifying anticolonial activity. The high rate of intermarriage, notably among Burmese and Indians, also belies the representation of colonial Burmese society as a plural society in which various ethnic groups remained isolated from and in conflict with each other. Similarly, the ethnic stratification of the plural society in colonial Burma was mitigated by the fact that no socioeconomic role was an exclusive domain of a particular ethnic group. Upper middle-class Burmese and ethnic minorities who were educated abroad or fluent in English from missionary schooling worked alongside Europeans and Anglo-Indians in public administration. The indigenous population participated extensively in moneylending and wholesale marketing, in sharp contrast to the comparatively low level of involvement in these activities by indigenous people in other parts of Southeast Asia. For instance, wholesale trade and credit provision were left chiefly to the Chinese minorities and the mixed Chinese population in Thailand, Java, and the Philippines, while in Malaya both Chinese and Indian immigrants filled most of the middleman's niches.[73] Ironically, the British government's annexation of Burma, its brusque abolition of the monarchy, and its imposition of direct administration, although violent, appear to have provided radical economic opportunities for indigenous peoples. Local entrepreneurs flourished following the British cancellation of restrictions on rice exports and the abolition of royal sumptuary laws that had formerly prevented people from engaging in the conspicuous consumption that can follow and sometimes inspire economic success. In the following passage from *The Burma Delta,* Michael Adas vividly describes the widespread diffusion of foreign consumer items, reflecting the prosperity gained by some ordinary agrarians as a result of economic growth accompanying British colonialism:

> Successful agriculturalists often lived in houses made of wood rather than the traditional thatch and bamboo. Corrugated iron roofs, which were considered signs of prosperity, were common in the villages of many tracts. . . . European and Indian textiles and cheap consumer items like kerosene lamps, canned milk, biscuits or sardines, mosquito nets, soap, and European glassware or crockery were found in all but the poorest villages. In the more fertile tracts cultivator-owners' (as well as landlords')

houses commonly contained European furniture, mirrors, artificial flow-ers, gramophones, English lamps, looking glasses, metal safes or chests, and clocks. Their walls were decorated with portraits of Queen Victoria and Kaiser Wilhelm, Christmas cards, and pictures cut from the illus-trated magazines of the day.[74]

British intervention offered socioeconomic mobility for locals, not merely for immigrant foreigners. In fact, the colonial state played a vital role in provid-ing a means of socioeconomic advancement that was of particular importance to women in Burma.

EDUCATION

Prior to the nineteenth century, education in Burma was administered almost exclusively through Buddhist monastic schools. The principal goal of these schools, at least in theory, was to encourage students to study the Buddhist texts thoroughly for their moral and spiritual development and to prepare the students for their ordination. In actual practice, however, the majority of students intended to return to lay life after their study at the mon-asteries, which represented the only place where education was available. From at least the Pagan period (1044–1287) onward, monasteries offered a gen-eral course of study catering to such students that included lay subjects but nonetheless required the study of Buddhist scriptures. Both Pali and literary Burmese were taught, and Buddhist texts included in the *Tipitaka,* together with its Pali and vernacular commentaries, were taught alongside Brahmanical texts, arithmetic, poetry, astrology, medicine, and law. This general course of study was given at primary and secondary levels of education, at the end of which the students decided whether to pursue higher monastic education—that is, a more specialized curriculum devoted to a detailed study of the *Pali nikāya*—available mainly in royal monasteries based in the capital or in large cities.[75] There were no fees for monastic education and no formal examina-tions until the late nineteenth century. Centralized state-sponsored monastic examinations known as *pathama pran,* which involved the assessment of orga-nizational skill and bureaucratic procedures, had existed since the seventeenth century. However, the sangha vehemently resisted the formal examination sys-tem favored by the state until the mid-nineteenth century, and it was not until the nineteenth century under King Mindon (1853–1878) that both the mon-arch and the sangha accepted formal monastic examinations.[76] In precolonial Burma, monastic schools thus exercised extensive freedom in designing their own syllabi and in assessing the needs and desires of the students.

Although monastic education espoused a flexible curriculum open to students of diverse interests and backgrounds, it did not provide for female education. Even in the late nineteenth century, the Cambridge-educated, Sino-Burmese civil servant Taw Sein Ko (1863–1930) noted with regret that "the rigid rules of monastic discipline do not justify the *hpongyi* [monks] to entertain female pupils, and consequently, the carrying on of female education, which is regarded by them as below their holy dignity, and as unnecessary by the people, has hitherto been left to the care of untutored masters."[77] By "untutored masters," Taw Sein Ko appears to have been referring to private tutors or to laymen and -women who taught in what came to be called lay schools during the British period. In 1869 there were 340 lay schools with 5,069 students (3,838 boys and 1,231 girls), whereas monastery schools numbered 3,438, with 43,773 students (27,793 lay pupils and 15,980 novices). The first director of the Department of Public Instruction described the lay schools as preparatory schools for both boys and girls that readied the pupils for any other school that might be within reach. Taw Sein Ko later described them as schools intended primarily for the education of girls. In addition, U Kaung indicates that the subjects taught were more or less the same as those taught in monastic schools and that the schools were run by laymen and -women who taught for merit and charged no fees.[78] Little to no historical records pertaining to lay schools in Burma remain, however, and it is unclear how long they had been in existence prior to the nineteenth century. They are seldom mentioned in either indigenous records or European travel accounts, indicating that they were relatively uncommon and, unlike monastic schools, did not serve as important educational agencies.

Over the course of the nineteenth century, the sangha gradually lost its prerogative as the chief provider of education in Burma as privately and governmentally supported lay and mission schools that offered vernacular, Anglo-vernacular (i.e., English and Burmese), and English education—what was referred to as "modern education" by the Burmese—expanded. The pioneers of modern education were Christian missionaries, who had already set up mission schools in Burma in the eighteenth century. Until 1824 the few mission schools run by the Barnabite Roman Catholic missionaries taught primarily the small Christian community in Burma and the select local converts.[79] After the first British annexation of Burma, missionaries became significantly more active in the area of education. The American Baptist Mission (ABM) opened the first mission schools for Burmese and Mon children of the lower classes—mostly little girls—in Amherst, Moulmein, and Tavoy in 1826, 1827, and 1828, respectively. Burmese was the language of instruction, and the schools taught reading, writing, and arithmetic; in addition, girls were taught sewing and needlework. Similarly, in the 1840s, Roman Catholic missionaries set up Karen vernacular mission schools for Karen adults and children, among whom the missionaries were conducting extensive evangelical work. Catholic missionaries also became increasingly involved in the education of the children—including the Eurasian orphans—of the growing community of Europeans and Indians who had settled in Lower Burma for the purposes of trade. For instance, they established a part-orphanage school for girls in 1840, which later became St. Joseph's Convent, a famous European girls' school for both orphans and paying pupils.[80] Finally, the 1850s saw an Anglican missionary group, the Society for the Propagation of the Gospel, join the American Baptist and Roman Catholic missionary bodies in educational work as they began establishing mission schools throughout Burma.

At their inception, the mission schools were modest enterprises that could hardly be considered rivals of Buddhist monastic schools. For example, the six schools that the ABM had managed to set up in Moulmein by 1835 had only 45 to 50 students; their six schools in Tavoy fared better but still had only 150 pupils in 1836.[81] Yet from these humble beginnings developed a considerable system of day and boarding mission schools encompassing large towns and small villages. By 1900 the government recognized 67 Anglo-vernacular and English mission schools, and by 1927 the number had climbed to 275. By 1920 there were 30,854 students enrolled in these schools, and enrollment had more than doubled by 1930, to 69,242. Most importantly, mission schools had gained a monopoly over Anglo-vernacular and English education and an early stronghold over secondary and tertiary education. All secondary schools registered in 1891 were under missionary management, while most of the primary schools were under indigenous management. Judson College, one of the two colleges in colonial Burma, was an outgrowth of the Rangoon Baptist College and, similarly, was run by missionaries. In 1894, Cushing High School, founded by the ABM in 1872, opened the Baptist College as a department affiliated with Calcutta University. It became a full-fledged degree institution in 1909 and was subsequently renamed Judson College in 1918 in honor of Dr. Adoniram Judson, the first American Protestant missionary in Burma.[82]

Another area in which missionaries made headway was female education, which was no doubt a vehicle for gaining female Bible readers and converts. Because Christian missionaries were not welcomed in Burmese homes, "schools functioned as common meeting grounds for European missionaries and teachers and Burmese."[83] In addition, even missionaries who dismissed the idea that native women might make influential evangelists recognized the important role that women were likely to play in the religious practice of their children—women were informal evangelists.[84] At the same time, the interest of missionaries in educating native girls and women stemmed from their dismay at the perceived "ignorance" of women in Burma. Take, for instance, a 1914 survey by the Christian Literature Society of thirty correspondents involved in education, mainly Christian missionaries, conducted on the impact of modern conditions on the state of Buddhism in contemporary Burma.[85] The respondents portrayed women in Burma as "more ignorant" and "less well educated" than men in Burma and felt that the women knew "nothing else but Buddhism"; they agreed that Anglo-Christian education was the key solution to the problem of "uneducated" women in Burma.[86] Female education also served as an instrument for cultural reeducation through which missionary educators "attempted to shape 'home care' and women as 'good housewives' according to their notions of 'civilized' Christian living."[87] Accordingly, while female students in Anglo-vernacular middle schools took the same courses as their male counterparts, they were required to take domestic economy and needlework in lieu of geometry.[88] Again, the 1914 survey offers insight. When questioned about the effect of Anglo-Christian education on the condition of women in Burma, one interviewee replied that women had become "better home-keepers" and "more intelligent wives and mothers," and another replied that "they make ideal Christian wives, but as mothers are still lacking in firmness."[89] Through education, missionaries hoped to instill Christian and Eurocentric conceptions of femininity, morality, and domesticity in the native female population.

In sharp contrast to the zealous efforts of Christian missionaries, the colonial government displayed little to no interest in educating the native population until the 1860s. Only four government schools opened between 1834 and 1844, and in 1852 the pupils in these schools totaled a mere 316, of whom about two-thirds were "natives."[90] The government formed the Department of Public Instruction in 1867 and an Education Department in 1868, heralding a period of increased state intervention in the area of education. Even during this period, however, the government invested relatively little in education, at least in fiscal terms. State revenue spent on education in Burma between 1910 and 1921 totaled £219,111 whereas expenditures for education in the provinces of Bengal, Punjab, and Madras were £667,023, £427,514, and £795,061, respectively.[91] In addition, at least until 1924, the general state policy towards education was to regulate, inspect, supplement—and thus extend supervision and control of—the existing schools by administering grant-in-aid to all the schools in the province, rather than support or expand its own few government schools. Schools continued to be maintained voluntarily by monks, laypeople, municipalities, and other associations. This grant-in-aid system of public education, aimed at sidestepping an expensive duplication of schools throughout Burma, was conceptualized as early as the 1820s, when the first mission schools in the country began receiving grants in the form of land, books, and supplies from the government.[92] Only in the 1860s under Sir Arthur Phayre, the first chief commissioner of Burma, was it institutionalized as a system of public instruction that included local monastic and lay schools. The government relied on the mission schools it aided via grants for the provision of English as well as secondary education (sixth to ninth standards) and the training and recruiting of local English-speaking clerks and interpreters for the colonial administration and European trading firms. For primary education, Phayre originally envisioned using the already existing and ubiquitous monastic schools, but he also hoped to make the education of the masses more "sound" and "systematic" through the addition of "secular studies"— geography, surveying, arithmetic, anatomy, ancient history, geometry, and astronomy—to the curriculum in the monastic schools.[93]

Unlike the government grants given to mission schools, the grants to monastic schools were distributed only in the form of Burmese-language primers for the "secular" subjects, written with the help of American Baptist missionaries who translated the material from English to Burmese. The predictably lackluster response of the monks to the grant-in-aid system led the government to promote lay schools instead as the vehicles for public primary education. Government grants to lay schools were paid in cash to both the teachers and the students according to the academic performance of each individual student; girls were paid double the amount fixed for boys.[94] Lay schools emerged as attractive alternatives to monastic schools not only because of the lack of enthusiasm on the part of monasteries but also because they accepted female students. In addition, lay schools were amenable to state-regulated educational reforms because, unlike monastic schools, they relied heavily on the government grants as their main source of funding. The educational reforms included, in addition to the study of the supplementary "secular" subjects mentioned above, annual government examinations—instituted in 1880 and held by the Education Department, by Calcutta University, or by the Educational Syndicate (founded in 1881)—at which the pupils had to be present. The course of study at the lay schools also had to correspond to the standards prescribed by the government of Burma or Calcutta University and had to be inspected by the Education Department.[95]

By the turn of the century, colonial Burma had developed a system of public instruction that provided nine standards of education—the first four were primary and the subsequent five were secondary—through two main types of schools, Anglo-vernacular and vernacular, each distinguished by the language of instruction and examination. Although "European," or English, schools were another type of public school among those recognized by the government, they were not in effect open to the general public. The proportion of non-European students admissible in European schools was initially 15 percent. The colonial administration subsequently reduced the proportion to 10 percent in 1913, fearful that "the dilution of the European element by too large an admixture of children whose vernacular is not English would tend to lower the standard of English, already none too high, in the European schools."[96] The government remained committed to the grant-in-aid system, having established only 79 government schools by the 1920s, but public schools under indigenous and missionary management had multiplied significantly. In 1870 only 22 lay schools were officially recognized by the government in Burma, but by 1890 the number had risen to 704, and by 1910 to 2,653. In 1913, of the 1,400 public secondary schools in Burma, 33 were European, 142 Anglo-vernacular, and 1,225 vernacular. Most of the 7,725 public primary schools were vernacular, with the exception of 16 Anglo-vernacular schools and 2 European schools, and received only a small proportion of financial support from the government.[97] According to records of government expenditure during 1910–1921, £249,698 of the £360,718 spent on education—nearly 70 percent—went to secondary schools. In contrast, primary schools received £73,262, or roughly 20 percent of the educational expenditure.[98] The number of monastic schools remained stable until the 1920s, when it began a steady descent. In 1887 there were 3,975 monastic schools in Lower Burma alone.[99] By 1928 the number of monastic schools in all of Burma had decreased drastically, to 1,120, while lay schools had increased to 4,770.[100] The traditional monastic schools were not entirely supplanted by the grant-in-aid system of public instruction, however. Even in early twentieth-century Burma, when monastic schools survived only in towns, many village monasteries still retained learned monks who served as essential vehicles of primary and secondary vernacular education.[101] As late as 1920 the government had managed to extend public instruction to less than a third of rural Burma, where such village monasteries presumably functioned as the chief providers of education.

Coeducation had become by and large the norm in Anglo-vernacular and vernacular schools: 95 percent of the female student population attended coed vernacular schools, and there were three times as many female students in coed institutions as in girls' schools. While both girls' and boys' schools existed, there was no clear distinction between the two types of schools, and the 1912–1917 quinquennial report on public instruction notes that "large numbers of boys are found in girls' schools and very much larger numbers of girls in boys' schools."[102] Female students took the same courses as their male counterparts, but in the early 1920s, "hygiene" had become a compulsory subject of middle school examinations for girls, whereas English as a second language had been made an optional subject.[103]

Despite the expansion of public instruction as well as female education, neither the government nor the local population was satisfied with the educational reforms that had taken place. The government, on the one hand, expressed concerns over the failure of lay schools to provide adequate "moral instruction." As with other European colonial governments, the British administration in Burma regarded schools as institutions to harness the loyalty of its colonial subjects and to instill in them the "imperial idea," that imperial subjects should "work towards the prosperity and strength of the British Empire as a whole."[104] The government was also of the opinion that "secular education" alone could never be "the corrective for vice and crime"[105] and that moral instruction was essential to the creation of disciplined, pliant, and governable subjects. Monastic schools were supposed to furnish such moral instruction through their teaching of Buddhism, and lay and mission schools were expected "to inculcate morality and discipline by moral text-books and primers of personal ethics."[106] However, a committee that was formed to consider religious instruction for Buddhist pupils in vernacular lay schools concluded in 1928 that moral education in both Anglo-vernacular and vernacular lay schools required strengthening.[107] The report prepared by the committee stated that "religious instruction at schools must impart [to] school boys refining qualities, such as sobriety, honesty, industry, truthfulness, fidelity to duty, unselfishness, obedience and respect to superiors," and that "a little memorizing of prayers and precepts" was insufficient.[108] Although the concern of the committee was, in theory, confined to Buddhist religious instruction given in vernacular lay schools only, the committee nevertheless complained about the state of moral instruction in Anglo-vernacular schools: "No one will deny the value of the educational work now being done by Christian Missionaries, but one must doubt the efficacy of moral instruction based on a creed which the child has not accepted and will not accept."[109] Burmese men and women were likewise dissatisfied with the state of moral instruction in the colonial educational system. Some lamented the marginalization of the teaching of Buddhist doctrines in the modern education system and bemoaned that "boys should leave school with as little knowledge of their religion as they had when they were children."[110] Others complained that the elevation of "Western" and "secular" education above monastic education had eroded the moral character of the native youth. In 1884, Taw Sein Ko wrote in an article entitled "Moral Education in Burma," published in the Buddhist journal *Our Monthly:* "Now-a-days, in Burma, old men and women complain that youths in general, who have a smattering knowledge of the English language, and who are not acquainted with Buddhist doctrines, are apt to despise their national religion and their paternal calling, that they are not docile and obedient as they were before, but rash, independent and conceited."[111]

There were other aspects of education with which Burmese people were dissatisfied, such as the influential position that mission schools occupied in the educational system and the spending of large sums of public money "collected from a mainly Buddhist population on institutions with an acknowledged Christian missionary purpose."[112] Also disconcerting was the failure of Calcutta University to make any financial contributions to the support of education in Burma despite its heavy hand in determining and overseeing the educational curriculum and standards.[113] In the early decades of the twentieth century, as Buddhist monks and educated elites involved themselves in political activity and experimented with new forms of collective political organization, they became increasingly critical of the instrumentalist nature of colonial education. Most felt, as Furnivall claimed decades later, that modern educational institutions represented "nothing but factories for the mass production of cheap clerks."[114] Others objected to the "imperial idea" infusing the educational reforms that the colonial government helped put into place. Schools were geared not only towards the economic and efficient production of locally trained subordinates with proficiency in English and accounting but also towards the propagation of the "imperial idea."[115] In the words of the students of Rangoon University protesting in 1920 against the current state of education, "what knowledge we could gain from what is called the government system of [Anglo-vernacular] education in Burma is just enough for us to be their slaves or those of the rich."[116]

These discontents surfaced at the turn of the century, first, with the establishment of the first Buddhist Anglo-vernacular high schools by Burmese elites who were English-trained and often graduates of universities in England. Concurrently, monks promoted the study of Buddhism among the lay population with new vigor. Eminent scholar monks such as Ledi Sayadaw (1846–1923) and Manlay Sayadaw (1841–1920) traveled extensively for the purposes of preaching and capitalized on the development of print technology and its potential to reach large and distant audiences. They authored and printed books on Buddhism—written in simple and easily accessible language and style in the hopes of giving people "good, practical explanations of Buddhist doctrine, in order to enable them to answer the criticisms of people of other religions"—and urged laypeople to study them.[117] Moreover, as in neighboring Sri Lanka, numerous lay associations appeared, united in their concern for the revival of Buddhism in Burma and their vision of Buddhist education as the ideal means to promote morality.[118] Among these lay organizations was the Young Men's Buddhist Association (YMBA), founded in 1906 on the model of the YMCA. The most famous and influential lay Buddhist organization in colonial Burma, it actively promoted the teaching of Buddhism in government schools and endeavored to secure funding for private Buddhist schools equivalent to that given to Christian missionary schools and to have basic education made compulsory in rural areas.[119] In 1920, private "national schools," managed by Burmese instructors, were set up to offer modern education outside of the control of the state. As the discussion of the national schools in chapter 3 shows, they failed to compete successfully against the government system of public education. Nevertheless, national schools contributed to the overall growth of modern education. By the end of 1921, national schools numbered 80, with an enrollment of 15,000 students, many of whom had transferred from public vernacular schools. By 1922 there were 92 national schools—82 Anglo-vernacular and 10 vernacular—that provided English as part of their curriculum, unlike public vernacular schools.[120]

The various problems associated with modern educational institutions notwithstanding, the number of schools and enrolled students continued to increase throughout the early decades of the twentieth century. In 1900 the government recorded 17,620 private and public schools and 307,614 pupils. By 1930 there were 25,524 schools and 738,267 students.[121] Urban Burmese parents were quick to recognize the value of modern education. The centralized British administration represented a bureaucracy that local men and women could access only through educational qualifications. The advent of European trading firms combined with the privileging of English as the language of administration to create a demand for local men with some knowledge of English and accounting.[122] Institutionalized education thus offered socioeconomic mobility and the key to succeeding in the new political and social order ushered in by colonial rule. Referring to missionary schools, a Burmese Buddhist parent declared in a newspaper in September 1919: "If we wanted our children to become *hpongyi* [monks], we should send them to the monastery; but we want them to be men of the world and we send them to your schools."[123] Admittedly, Burmese parents with adequate means sent their sons rather than their daughters to school in order that they might become civil servants and further their career.[124] But girls, too, were sent to school, including Anglo-vernacular schools, though not necessarily to make them suitable bureaucrats. According to a prominent Burmese woman writer, Khin Myo Chit, education for girls was "a final polish for [a] potential husband-catcher." She explains that "whatever opportunities the education system in the colonial days had to offer, sending girls to school to get 'modern education' was popularly considered a part of the grooming to be wife and mother."[125] Modern education held symbolic capital. It was not merely a means to elite status; it had become synonymous with being an elite.

Irrespective of the intentions of the missionaries, lay teachers, and government in establishing modern educational institutions, and regardless of the expectations of the parents who enrolled their children in the vernacular and Anglo-vernacular schools, educational reforms in colonial Burma led to the expansion of the class of educated Burmese. In particular, they provided the necessary institutional structure for extending greater opportunities for education to women and, as chapters 2 and 3 illustrate, enabled the growth of Burmese women intellectuals and cultural intermediaries. The educational reforms also increased the literacy rate of the local population, which was instrumental in the rapid rise and spread of the popular press.

PRESS AND THE PUBLIC SPHERE

As in other parts of Southeast Asia, the printing industry in Burma was pioneered by Christian missionaries. Baptist missionaries brought the first printing press to the country in 1816 to print Christian tracts and pamphlets. In fact, the first Burmese-language newspaper, *Dhamma sa taṅ: cā* (The religious herald), and the first Karen- and Sgaw-language newspaper, *Chā thū vo* (The morning star), published from 1843 and 1842, respectively, were Christian evangelical monthlies.[126] Baptist missionaries managed to retain a virtual monopoly on the technology until the 1830s, when English-language newspapers began printing locally. The earliest among these, and the first newspaper to be issued in Burma, was the *Maulmain Chronicle,* a weekly paper established in 1836 by Edmund Augustus Blundell, then the commissioner of Tenasserim, with his own funds. The paper was to strictly avoid "all political and controversial subjects," concentrate on disseminating information related to British Burma, and contain "advertisements, notifications, statements of arrivals and departures, trade, etc., and items of the latest intelligence from neighbouring countries and provinces."[127] Ironically, the paper grew into a mouthpiece for the English-speaking mercantile community in Moulmein, often critical of colonial officials and their policies and practices.[128] There were, as a matter of course, papers that supported the administration. The *Rangoon Times,* published from 1858 until 1942 and owned by a series of European lawyers, merchants, and doctors, abstained from any criticisms of the colonial government. The *Rangoon Gazette,* established in 1861 and managed until 1942 by a syndicate of lawyers, judges, and merchants, was called the "bureaucrat newspaper" because it faithfully transmitted the offi-cial views of the colonial administration.[129] Nevertheless, the majority of the early English-language newspapers appear to have been commercial in nature, as titles such as the *Maulmain Advertiser* (1846) and *Akyab Commercial Advertiser* (1853–1854) suggest; they were started and funded by merchants and companies and featured advertisements prominently.

In subsequent decades, printing presses set up by European merchants, professionals, officials, and syndicates changed hands. Many were bought by Burmese entrepreneurs and lawyers. Burmese Buddhist monks, who con-trolled much of textual production and reproduction prior to the advent of the printing press, had likewise gained access to printing presses by the 1870s.[130] The communications and transportation revolution of the second half of the nineteenth century—especially the electric telegraph, which began operat-ing in Burma in 1870—also had a resounding effect on the print industry. Through such means as imperial shipping lines, mail and telephone services, and regional and international news syndicates, colonial Burma had become linked to an imperial network of transportation and communication stretch-ing across the British Empire. Through this network, an unprecedented amount of ideas and information circulated—in English, the lingua franca—at an unprecedented rate.[131] Within Burma itself, this traffic of information was made possible through a rapidly expanding railway system that facili-tated transportation to areas not served by the existing inland water trans-port system. The extension of the railway system, and a large supply of paper from India, also made printed material increasingly available and afford-able.[132] Together with the relatively high literacy rate of Burmese people at the time—roughly 70 percent of the male population aged five and over and about 20 percent of the female counterpart—these developments led to the spread of the print media and the Burmese popular press.

The government census recorded only 15 newspapers in circulation in Burma in 1891 and 26 in 1901. The number of newspapers and periodicals published in Burma more than doubled between 1911 and 1921, going from 44 to 103.[133] Between 1870 and 1920, Burmese-language newspapers, maga-zines, and journals appeared alongside English-language periodicals. In 1871, *Mran mā saṃ tau chaṅ.* (Burmah herald) and *Mran mā gejak* (Burmah gazette) began publication.[134] These were the first Burmese-language newspapers to be published in Rangoon and the first vernacular periodicals that were not organs of Christian proselytization.[135] Like many contemporary English-language periodicals, these newspapers reported international events based on information supplied by foreign news agencies, at the same time that they covered local news. Beginning with *Hanthawaddy sa taṅ: cā* (Hanthawaddy weekly review), established in 1889 by an Anglo-Burmese man named Philip Ripley, vernacular papers featured a wider range of contents. Besides news articles, editorials, and the like, they included law reports, letters and comments from the readers, advertisements, serialized fiction, poetry, anecdotes, gossip columns, astrology, and instructions on gardening, recipes for snacks, and guides to tea and tobacco shops. Another shift in Burmese-language newspapers came in 1911, with the publication of the first openly anticolonial vernacular paper, *Thuriya*.[136] By this time, photographs and cartoons, many focusing on current events and carrying distinct social and political undertones, added to the wide-ranging contents of the Burmese press. A later addition was the women's column. Most Burmese periodicals featured routine columns (examined in subsequent chapters) that were written by women writers though not confined to "women's issues," as well as biographies of Burmese women intellectuals and historical figures.

These Burmese print media were meant not only for the English or Western-educated elite but also for a large and diverse popular Burmese readership. Tellingly, the publishers of the weekly journal *10,000,000*, which began publication in 1935, chose a number for its name as a symbol of their commitment to making the journal a straightforward periodical that any reader would find easily understandable.[137] By 1921, vernacular papers overtook the number of those printed in English; there were 47 Burmese-language newspapers with a combined circulation of 70,773, and 36 English-language newspapers with a combined circulation of 44,267.[138] By the end of the 1930s more than 200 newspapers and periodicals were published in Burma.[139] Even in the immediate aftermath of the Second World War, when only eight Burmese-language dailies were functioning in Rangoon, their circulation totaled 25,500 to 28,000.[140] These numbers compared favorably with the publishing statistics in other parts of colonial Southeast Asia. In British Malaya and the Straits Settlements, 173 periodicals appeared between 1876 and 1941.[141] In Indochina 304 periodicals were in circulation in 1934, and 9 of the most popular *quoc ngu* (Romanized Vietnamese script) periodicals had a combined circulation of 80,000 during 1936–1939.[142] The success of the periodicals in Burma was due to their eclectic contents as well as to their low cost. The average cost of a newspaper decreased from six pyas in the early 1920s to three and a half pyas in the mid-1930s, making it even more affordable than it already had been to the average Burmese family: at even six pyas per paper, an average Burmese family would have spent less than 2 percent of their monthly income on buying a newspaper on a daily basis.[143] The popular press had surfaced not only as an inexpensive source of information but also as an avenue of public discourse, art, and entertainment.

That the press had developed into an influential cultural medium that Burmese people widely utilized is made particularly clear from colonial records related to the 1938 Burma Riots, mentioned above. The *Final Report of the Riot Inquiry Committee* lists numerous causes of the riots, including the large-scale Indian immigration into Burma, unsatisfactory conditions of land tenure, intermarriage between Buddhist Burmese women and Muslim Indian men, and the global economic depression. However, it pinpoints the Burmese press as the chief cause of the riots, concluding that, through its publication of wild statements and objectionable photographs, the Burmese press exacerbated and fueled the riots, which could have otherwise been contained and handled by the largely Indian police force. "The effect which these photographs and the exaggeration of the Press generally had," the Riot Inquiry Committee reports, "is most marked in the Districts, where rioting started in many places simultaneously with their receipt from Rangoon."[144] Colonial administrators were keenly aware of the crucial role, highlighted by Benedict Anderson a half century later, that print capitalism played in forming public opinions and "imagined communities."[145] A year before the riots, the government had adapted the Press and Registration of Books Act and the Indian Press (Emergency Powers) Act for use in Burma and had begun imposing limitations on the freedom of the press. Under these acts, owners of printing presses and publishers of newspapers were required to deposit a security to be forfeited in cases where "use is made of any words, signs or visible representations which incite or encourage, directly or indirectly, violence or murder.[146] The 1938 Burma Riots only reinforced the government's conviction that the Burmese press had become too influential in forming the opinions and sensibilities of the public.

Government officials at the time attributed the popularity of the press among Burmese people to the role that it played as a tool of anticolonial organizations. Likewise, scholarship on the relationship between literature and nationalism in Burma has shown that most popular Burmese periodicals at the time did attend to contemporaneous anticolonial developments, espouse to varying degrees a certain political opinion or another, and attempt to sway the political views of the Burmese masses.[147] Yet Burmese periodicals were by no means nationalist propaganda leaflets. For example, the colonial administration in Rangoon labeled the *Myanmar alin* (New light of Burma), established in 1914 by entrepreneur-cum-politician U Tin, as the unofficial mouthpiece of the leading anticolonial organization in the 1940s, the Anti-Fascist People's Freedom League. The same administrators also noted that U Than Tint, the chief editor, "has no particular views or any strong opinion on any particular subject—an ideal editor for a paper that follows the tide."[148] While newspapers, magazines, and journals certainly functioned as ideological tools of nationalists and other politicians, they provided, more generally, a discursive space where people debated the policies and practices of the colonial government. The Burmese press was not unlike the modern public sphere conceptualized by Habermas: a sphere anchored in the principle of critical public debate among private people where a public, united through its use of reason, supervises and keeps a check on political power.[149] In colonial Burma, too, the press was underpinned by the idea that political power must be supervised and checked by a "reasonable" public.

It is worth stressing that only some of the ideas that were discussed and exchanged in the press concerned politics, and only some of the "public opinions" formed in and through the press sought to legitimize or delegitimize the government. Since Anderson's analyses that rightly underscored the role of print capitalism as a catalyst for nationalism, the modern press has come to be understood among scholars of colonialism primarily in political terms.[150] Yet the press has long been situated at the intersection of politics and popular commercial culture. From the very start, the majority of newspapers and periodicals in Burma were set up by merchants and companies and functioned as "advertisers." *Mran mā. tā rā sa taṅ: cā* (Star of Burma), published from 1900 until 1948, devoted thirteen of its eighteen pages to advertisements by the British emporium Rowe and Company.[151] Similarly, one needs only to look at the advertisements in the Burmese-language newspapers and magazines to see that commerce and consumerism were constitutive elements of the press. Take, for instance, *Thuriya,* a paper for which Burma's eminent "patriot-writer" Saya Lun wrote and served as a chief editor.[152] Given that nationalist leaders at the time were advocating the boycott of such foreign, imported products as cotton and canned goods, it is striking that a paper run by a fervently anticolonial editor in chief contained advertisements for products like the "English" perfume powder, the Anglo-Swiss Company's Milkmaid Brand condensed milk and "colonial" traveling rugs and shoes (figures 1.2–1.4).[153] Western shoes, after all, were at the heart of the "no footwear" campaign against the wearing of shoes by foreigners at pagodas and were the source of one of the most publicized disputes between the British and the Burmese, seen by the colonizers and the colonized alike as emblematic of the anticolonial struggle.[154] The decisions of the proprietors and editors were determined as much by their ideological leanings as by their endeavor to ensure and maximize the commercial and financial success of the newspapers and magazines. Potential buyers and readers had to be convinced that newspapers and magazines were well worth their money if the publications were to become an essential part of the everyday routine. The various innovations in

Figure 1.2 Advertisement for Hazlehurst's English Rose toilet powder, in *Thuriya,* 1927.

Figure 1.3 Advertisement for Anglo-Swiss Company's Milkmaid Brand condensed milk, in *Thuriya,* 1927.

Figure 1.4 Advertisement for Colonial traveling rugs, shoes, and so on, in *Thuriya*, 1927.

the popular press such as serialized fiction, pictorials, and women's columns that added to the intellectual, artistic, and entertainment value and appeal of the press were intended to keep print media competitive at a time when other forms of entertainment and popular culture, especially the cinema, were on the ascent, as illustrated in chapter 3. The Burmese press was far more than a public arena for rational and principled debate, and the increasing popularity and relevance of the press were products not merely of nationalist politics but also of a growing consumer culture and the rising demand for new media.

CONCLUSION

Demographic changes brought about by immigration, transformation in the legal system and ways in which identities were classified, and the spread of modern education and the press redefined the face of urban and everyday life in colonial Burma. The ethnic and socioeconomic makeup of urban societies in Burma underwent unprecedented change. Colonizers and colonized alike became more cognizant of ethnic difference and conceived of social and political inequalities in religious and racist terms. Yet even as colonial Burmese society appeared to be pluralizing in the Furnivallian sense, cross-cultural and interethnic interactions continued most conspicuously in the form of intermarriage. Modern education and the press also represented sites of engagement that offered opportunities for complex social and cultural transactions between disparate groups. They opened up new media and techniques for the production and dissemination of knowledge. The press developed into a powerful cultural, didactic, and commercial institution that increasingly defined popular consciousness. As the following chapters illustrate, these developments profoundly influenced how local men and women understood their identities and affiliations, as well as their relationship to what they understood as "modernity." They enabled men and women in Burma to appropriate, experiment with, critique, and fashion various colonial, elite, Buddhist, nationalist, and otherwise contemporary discourses about colonialism and modernity. They enabled and stimulated new ideas and behavior. And nowhere were these changes as visible as in the emergent representations and discourses of *khit kala* women.

2 | Women on the Rise

Education and the Popular Press

Since Anthony Reid reinforced the argument by George Coedès that women in Southeast Asia were conferred important roles by the culture of the region, the notion of the "traditional" high status of women in Southeast Asia has been foundational to paradigmatic understandings of the region as a distinct geopolitical and cultural entity separate from the rest of Asia.[1] Juxtaposed against images of women in South and East Asia that have been inextricably intertwined with and determined by norms and practices such as sati, purdah, polygyny, concubinage, and foot-binding, claims about the freedom and independence of women in Southeast Asia have figured prominently in the revisionist attempt by scholars to (re)center a marginalized Southeast Asia.[2] Yet historians and anthropologists of Southeast Asia have recently problematized the discourses of the "traditional" status of women which, as Barbara Andaya points out, "carry with them implicit messages of gender equality, economic independence, etc., and invoke a kind of golden age when women were different from men 'but in no way inferior.'"[3] They have shown, in particular, that assertions about the purported high status of women, often documented as a resilient, underlying social structure or culture of Southeast Asia, in fact derived from observations of women in the region by early colonialists and Western travelers and scholars who disregarded local and historically specific constructions of gender relations. In Burma, too, representations of "Burmese women" by colonialists and colonial scholars were instrumental in shaping salient notions of the "traditional" status of local women.[4]

Most portrayals of "Burmese women"—whether by Christian missionaries, colonial officials, Indian nationalists, representatives of local and international women's associations, or members of the indigenous elite—underscored their freedom, independence, and power. Writing in 1898, Harold Fielding Hall, a British officer in Burma, stated that a Burmese woman, unlike a European or an Indian woman, "has been bound by no ties." He elaborates:

> You see, she [a Burmese woman] has had to fight her own way; for the same laws that made woman lower than man in Europe compensated her to a certain extent by protection and guidance. In Burma she has been neither confined nor guided. In Europe and India for very long the idea was to make woman a hot-house plant, to see that no rough winds struck her, that no injuries overtook her. In Burma she has had to look out for herself: she has had freedom to come to grief as well as to come to strength.[5]

Similarly, R. Grant Brown, a colonial officer writing in the early twentieth century, observes that the reason it is often said that "the women do most of the hard work of the country" is "not because they are the slaves of their husbands" but rather because "they occupy a position of independence and responsibility."[6] This reputation of women in Burma as independent and equal to men was prevalent not only among British colonial civil service officers. For example, while the respondents in the 1914 survey by the Christian Literature Society, discussed in chapter 1, asserted that Burmese women were uneducated, they were also of the opinion that women in Burma "enjoy already many of the privileges for which their Western sisters are clamoring."[7] They offered the following explanation: "It is probably true to say that whilst the position assigned to women in Buddhism is low, yet in practice the women of Burma have made a place for themselves which is certainly unique in the East; and in some ways in advance of that in the West—if not actually, at least relatively, to the position of men."[8]

This perception of women in Burma as uniquely powerful women of the East and on par with, if not more advanced than, women of the West derived from a number of facts—for instance, that there were no patronymics in Burma and that a woman was not expected to take on the surname of her husband. The most important of these facts, however, was that they already possessed "many of the privileges for which their Western sisters [were] clamoring," in particular the right to own and inherit property and to work outside of the home. Studies of legal texts by British officials and scholars and their ideas of "Burmese Buddhist" or "customary" law placed emphasis on the division of marriage property in divorce and the equal rights of women to inherit.[9] Hall explains that "marriage does not confer upon [a Burmese woman's] husband any power over his wife's property, either what she brings with her, what she earns, or what she inherits subsequently; it all remains her own, as does his remain his own."[10] He adds that women in Burma had always had "freedom from sacerdotal dogma, from secular law," and that "in no material points, hardly even in minor points, does the law discriminate against women."[11] Writing a decade after Hall, Brown reinforced his predecessor's assertion that gender equality underlay norms and practices pertaining to marriage, inheritance, and ownership in Burma:

> Not only do sons and daughters inherit equally from their parents, but a married woman has an absolute right to dispose as she pleases of property acquired or inherited by her either before or after marriage. She is usually a partner in her husband's business, and as such has just as much right to sign for the firm as he; but she may have a business of her own, with the proceeds of which he cannot interfere. Even in matters in which she has no part, she is usually consulted before an important step is taken.[12]

International women's associations seeking to secure equality of liberties and opportunities between men and women justified their requests to have suffrage extended to women on the basis of property rights held by Burmese women. The British Commonwealth League, for instance, explained to the British government that enfranchising women in Burma was "essentially just" since "according to Burmese law and custom, wives are in fact joint owners of the property" and that "[to] distinguish between the joint holders by enfranchising one only is an obvious injustice."[13] The International Alliance of Women for Suffrage and Equal Citizenship similarly wrote to the secretary of India urging that "the franchise to be exercised by owners of property should be on the basis of the vote of both husband and wife as we understand that in Burmese law they are joint owners."[14] Based on Eurocentric notions of suffrage and citizenship premised on property ownership, women in Burma were more "advanced" than women in the West—that is, Christian women—as the interviewees stated in the Christian Literature Society survey mentioned earlier. One eminent Burmese woman writer claimed even in the 1970s that no feminist movement had developed in Burma because "customary laws ensure for women a position suitable to present-day concepts of equality."[15]

Similarly, women in Burma were deemed more advanced than women in the West because of their prominent economic role both inside and outside the home. Women in Burma were no "hot-house plants"; they owned businesses and worked away from home. Even when they didn't, they often still held the purse strings. Sir George Scott, a British officer in Burma at the turn of the century, writes in his "handbook" on Burma that whereas a Japanese wife "treats her husband as an idol," the Burmese wife treats her husband "as a comrade" and "is far ahead of her lord in the matter of business capacity by the way in which she rules the household without outwardly seeming to exercise any authority."[16] A Burmese woman confirmed this view in a talk titled "Englishmen as Seen by Burmese Women," given at a meeting of the Rotary Club of Rangoon in 1937: "Englishmen respect their women, but he will not entrust his pay envelope wholly or solely to her charge. Not so in Burma. The Burmese woman knows how to make money and how to keep it. She sees to it that she is appointed 'Chancellor of her husband's exchequer' and keeper of the 'Family Purse.' "[17] The "new woman" who emerged in Europe, the United States, and Japan in the nineteenth century sought equality before the law, as well as economic and financial independence, and challenged the authority of men in the home.[18] Women in Burma, however, allegedly already asserted these rights for which "new women" elsewhere were struggling.

Last but not least, women in Burma were depicted as liberated and independent because they were free from "degenerate," "barbaric," and "oppressive" "traditional" practices such as sati, purdah, and foot-binding. As scholars working on colonial and nationalist discourses of women in the context of South Asian, subaltern, and feminist studies have revealed, images of Oriental women oppressed and humiliated by traditional "customs" served to legitimize the colonial civilizing mission.[19] Examinations of nationalist representations of "traditional" and "modern" women have likewise contributed important insights into the ways that the "conditions of women" functioned as an index for measuring modernization. In Republican China, for instance, the debate on modernization was premised on the idea that "while China's women remained weak and crippled by foot binding and ignorant, unproductive, dependent, and isolated in the domestic sphere, there was no hope for the nation."[20] Burmese women, however, because they were predominantly Buddhists, were deemed free from such inhumane customs attributed to Hindu, Muslim, and Confucian societies. This intrinsically comparative view was founded upon the works of colonial-period Orientalist scholars of Buddhism who delineated Buddhism as a rationalist religion in direct opposition to Hinduism and Islam, which were deemed irrational.[21] In keeping with this characterization of Buddhism, a British female traveler writing in 1896 remarked that "utterly unlike their miserable Mohamedan and Hindoo sisters," women in Burma "enjoy absolute liberty—a liberty of which, if rumor prove true, they make ample use."[22] Former Burma governor Sir Harcourt

Butler likewise pointed out in an article in *Times of India* that what distinguished Burma from India and made Burma "one of the fairest countries of the British Empire" was that Burmese women did not wear the veil.[23] British Indian subjects who traveled to Burma reinforced the view that women in Burma occupied a higher social position than that of women in India. One of the pioneering leaders of nationalism, democracy, and nonviolent political resistance in India, Lokamanya Tilak, referred to the social condition of women in Burma in speeches he gave in India after a visit to Burma in 1899: "All the reforms like absence of caste division, freedom of religion, education of women, late marriages, widow remarriage, system of divorce, on which some good people of India are in the habit of harping *ad nauseam* as constituting a condition precedent to the introduction of political reforms in India, had already been in actual practice in the province of Burma."[24] Rooted, on the one hand, in a comparison with Orientalist representations of women elsewhere and, on the other, in an emphasis on their "traditional" economic agency and property rights, women in Burma were increasingly described in the twentieth century as possessing remarkable freedom, independence, and equality with men.

The laudatory image of independent and liberated women of Burma was furthermore popularized through its deployment as a strategy in pressing for political and social reforms. For instance, when Tilak spoke of the socially advanced status of women in Burma, he did so to draw attention to the British refusal to grant political reform to Burma in spite of social reforms. He argued that the advice given by European writers "to bring about social reform as a preparation for political reform" would remain suspect "till we see with our own eyes what kind of political reform is given to Burma which is socially in a position to deserve it."[25] In India, nationalists saw the British colonization of Burma, *despite* the freedom and independence of women, as proof that the British colonial state was not genuinely concerned with the "oppressive" treatment of women in India but was merely using it as a justification for refusing to grant political reforms in India. Shobna Nijhawan has more recently revealed that the "conditions of Burmese women" played a key role not only in the political maneuvers of nationalists but also in the feminist-nationalist project in India.[26] For example, the Hindi monthly *Stri Darpan* (Women's mirror), published from 1909 until 1928 and edited by and for women, printed numerous ethnographic accounts of Burmese women who "from birth to death . . . enjoy equal rights."[27] In the same issue, "the Burmese wife" is described as "a true friend and companion of her husband": "Her *pativrat dharma* [unconditional devotion] is not limited to washing his feet or comforting him with cool air; she is on his side in all life-battles, she bears the difficulties of life just the way he does and fills his life with joy and happiness."[28] According to Nijhawan, the motive behind such enthusiastic portrayals of Burmese women was to offer an example of gender equality "that was not modeled on the Western woman and that at the same time went beyond sacrificial and submissive notions of Indian womanhood."[29] The traditional high status of Burmese women provided a path for feminist social reforms that was "progressive yet traditional rather than overtly Westernized."[30]

In Burma, too, the high status of women served as a vital tactic for demanding greater political power. The image of the exceptionally liberated Burmese women, positioned in contrast to the traditionally repressed Hindu and Muslim women in India, was repeatedly cited as evidence of the country's legitimate demand for administrative reforms. Characteristic of this political strategy, the only woman delegate to the Burma Round Table Conference in 1931, Daw Mya Sein, put forward the case for extending the reforms granted to India in 1910 but denied to Burma: "The women of Burma occupy a position of freedom and independence not attained in other provinces. Socially there is practical equality between the sexes. *Purdha* is unknown; women take their full share with men in the economic life of their country and the percentage of literates among women is far higher than elsewhere."[31] Burmese men and women embraced the favorable evaluations of the "conditions of women" in Burma, and administrators, intellectuals, and politicians cited the equality of the sexes as a resilient Burmese tradition and evidence for their legitimate demand for greater local control over the administrative machinery. As in China, where women "became the site for refiguring China's international position relative to the West,"[32] women in Burma had emerged as the site for negotiating prevailing, unequal relations of power. However, unlike in China or India, where foot-binding and widow-burning had to be abolished in order to modernize the countries and refigure their positions vis-à-vis the West, women in Burma did not need to be "refigured" for modernization.

What the positive representation of Burmese women disregards is that practices favorable to women have historically existed side by side with customs and representations unfavorable to women. Although women in Burma had for a long time an influential presence in the economic sphere, as in other premodern Southeast Asian societies, the active role of women as economic agents—the very attribute that gave women their autonomy and power—subordinated them to men socially, spiritually, and politically. Economic prowess enabled women to undertake merit-making activities such as contributing donations to pagodas, but at the same time the worldly sphere of commerce, profit seeking, and monetary affairs was deemed spiritually polluting.[33] Additional regulations that applied to female members of Theravada

Buddhist societies, such as the exclusion of women from the sangha and the shorter history of Buddhist nuns, have contributed to perceptions of women as occupying a secondary position to men.[34] Narrative depictions of women in Pali and vernacular Southeast Asian Buddhist literature, furthermore, have delivered both positive and negative portrayals of women. Buddhist literature has cast women not only in the role of devoted followers of the Buddha, donors, renunciants, and teachers who contributed to the development and spread of Buddhism but also in the role of impure temptresses charged with keeping men from attaining *nibbāna* (*nirvāṇa*).[35] Likewise, stories extolling the female virtues of Princess Yasodhara (the wife of the Buddha) and Queen Mahapajapati (the sister of the Buddha's mother) have long been common parables in Burma, as have stories from the *Tipitaka* of beautiful maidens who "devour the virtue of many [men] with manifold wiles" and of weak, age-weary, and unsightly women who elicit strenuous contemplation on the part of the observer.[36] The female author Mi Mi Khaing thus asserts in her book *The World of Burmese Women*: "There is no doubt in our minds. Spiritually, a man is higher than a woman. This is just not an abstract idea belonging to religious philosophy. Conviction of it enter[s] our very bones."[37]

Furthermore, administrators and communal authorities such as court officials, village headmen, and monks were principally men.[38] Women rulers, while they did exist, "entered a domain where the vocabulary associated with leadership was quintessentially male," and "political consolidation privileged male authority and patrilineal descent."[39] Lower Burma was once ruled by Queen Shin Saw Pu (1453–1472), but she was a rare figure and an exception that proved the norm.[40] Female authority and leadership in the sphere of administration and governance were virtually unknown. And finally, women lagged behind men in the area of education and literacy. In his seminal work on the distinctively Southeast Asian pattern of high female autonomy, Anthony Reid stresses that literacy among women in premodern Southeast Asia was relatively widespread.[41] However, it is quite clear in the case of Burma that, at least until the eighteenth century, most women were denied access to learning to read and write. As in other Buddhist societies in the region, the association of learning with the propagation and preservation of accurate knowledge of the *sāsana* (teachings of the Buddha), and of texts and writing with spiritual potency, made the sangha the primary educational institution and knowledge broker; literati and experts on medicine, arithmetic, and astrology tended to be monks or former monks and were, in any case, male.[42] As we have seen, education in precolonial Burma was managed and delivered almost exclusively by Buddhist monastic schools that did not provide for female education.[43] There were nunneries near Sagaing in Upper Burma that served as centers of female education where Buddhist nuns, or *thila shin* (keepers of the precepts),[44] taught the Burmese language, Pali grammar, and texts from the Buddhist canon to girls from nearby villages, but these educational centers served only a small population of a few hundred *thila shin* at the peak of enrolment at the turn of the twentieth century.[45] Most women acquired "learning" not through formal education but through informal instruction—for example, through sermons or recitations of the *jātaka* (scriptures and the stories of the life of the Buddha) by monks.

Literacy among women of royal and wealthy families was not uncommon, and Burmese court literature was written not only by monks and ex-monks but also by ladies of the court, the most well known of whom is Mya Galay, a queen consort of King Bagyidaw's who wrote primarily for the king and for the court audience.[46] Many of these women were educated by *thila shin,* because female members of the royal family were frequently prohibited from having contact with men outside the court.[47] Yet, even *thila shin* struggled to attain education, their ability to author and transmit knowledge was severely limited by their exclusion from the sangha. Although *thila shin* exist in Burma today, they have not been recognized as part of the sangha since the thirteenth century.[48] As renunciants who abide by monastic rules, they support the sangha in their daily activities—by cleaning the grounds of the monastery or cooking for the monks, for instance—and otherwise participate in and contribute actively to the operation of monastic institutions in Burma, but they lead their religious lives as subsidiaries to the monks. As Hiroko Kawanami points out in her study of *thila shin,* teachers and masters of the scriptures were seldom "open-minded enough to accept the notion of providing women with advanced scriptural education."[49] Even if *thila shin* managed to find a teacher, Kawanami explains, the male environment of the sangha made the pursuit of education difficult. The sangha thus represented the dominant producer and provider of knowledge, and as in other parts of premodern Southeast Asia, there was "a persistent view that writing and reading were inappropriate skills for women"[50] and that female formal education was at best secondary to male education.

Drawing on observations by European traders in Burma, Michael Charney has argued that this pattern changed during the Konbaung period (1752–1885), with a general increase in the importance of literacy and with the development of lay schools that offered education either for both boys and girls or for girls exclusively.[51] "By the end of the eighteenth century," he writes, "Burmese were in the process of becoming perhaps more literate than ever before and literature previously limited to the elite circles of the court had entered popular society."[52] That there were lay schools devoted specifically

to instructing females indeed suggests that the low regard for female education had begun to change by the mid-nineteenth century. Yet the first British
census, in 1891, lists almost 90,000 boys in school but only 3,000 girls, and
the 1901 census shows that approximately 50 percent of the male population
over fifteen years of age was literate whereas the female literacy rate was about
3 percent.[53] The administrative records from turn-of-the-century Burma indicate that significant growth in female education and literacy did not emerge
until the 1910s.

In fact, like the Christian missionaries in Burma, European and native
administrators and intellectuals agreed that Burmese women were "uneducated" and that female education held little social currency. In June 1916
the secretary to the government of Burma asked the deputy commissioner
of Bassein, G. F. Arnold, to present his opinions on the best methods of
expanding and improving primary, secondary, and higher female education
in Burma. Arnold's resoundingly negative response, detailed in a nine-page
letter, claimed that there was little, if any, need, desire, or purpose for reforming female education in Burma at the time, and additionally that there were
no resources to support such an effort. While Arnold concurred with the view
of the Indian government that "it is inadvisable to place restrictions on any
kind of useful education for girls," he vehemently opposed reforming female
education in Burma.[54] According to Arnold, people in Burma were unwilling
to finance the expansion of female education. He argued that women were
considered inferior to men in both Burmese and Buddhist societies—noting
in particular the hostile stance of the sangha towards female education—and
claimed that there was no local interest in or support for female education,
except among Burmese Christians. He explained:

> The [Burmese] desires his sons to be educated to get appointments as I
> have said above. I do not think that he even desires these for his daughters
> nor do I think that many Burmese girls want them. . . . Indeed it is dif-
> ficult to say what should be regarded as the ideal in female education for
> the Burmese. The ordinary Burmese girls seem intent on selling in the
> bazaar, flirtation, wearing jewels and visiting pwes[55] and occasionally the
> pagodas. . . . I doubt if hygiene as an ideal would attract any of them, even
> though made to include nursing. Possibly coeducation might have some
> advantage in giving more scope for flirtation. . . . The fact seems to be
> that most Burmese girls do not aim at anything which the usual educa-
> tion given in school is likely to get for them.[56]

Arnold went on to say that "if any Burmese women become sufficiently
educated to desire to push female education I think it most probable that such

persons would be out of touch with their own people."[57] He added that even if more Burmese women were to receive education, such educated women, unlike educated Burmese men, had no prospect of finding employment. Ironically, the assertion by Deputy Commissioner Arnold about the irrelevance of female education to people in Burma was followed almost immediately by the most transformative two decades in the history of female education in Burma, during which period female education and literacy expanded at phenomenal rates.

CHANGES IN FEMALE EDUCATION AND LITERACY

As noted in chapter 1, early twentieth-century Burma witnessed the expansion of a coeducational system of public instruction that provided primary and secondary education, thanks largely to the efforts of missionary and local men and women. As a result, an unprecedented number of women gained access to education. The population of female students in primary and secondary private and public educational institutions increased by 61 percent (from 74,753 to 120,419) between 1911 and 1921, and by 82 percent (to 219,549) from 1921 to 1931. These statistics may appear unremarkable when compared, for instance, with those of neighboring Siam, which experienced a similar upturn in the trajectory of female education and had a larger population of female students; by 1925, Siam already had 232,120 girls in primary school alone.[58] When compared with trends in other parts of colonial Southeast Asia, however, the expansion of female education and literacy in Burma was hardly modest. In Vietnam, for example, of the 435,782 pupils in primary schools in 1930, only 40,752 were girls.[59]

The number of women among students receiving tertiary education was also on the increase in Burma during this period. In 1911 the students at the two colleges in Burma—Baptist College (otherwise known as Judson College) and Government College, both in Rangoon—totaled only 279, of which 17 were female. The number of male college students had more than doubled (to 581) by 1922, but the number of female college students had more than tripled (to 56).[60] Although female university students constituted merely 12 percent of the total university student population in 1931, the number of women university students had nonetheless increased by tenfold over the first few decades of the twentieth century. The population of Burmese women among college students paralleled the rapid expansion of female education in general. Only 6 of the 56 female students in 1922 were Buddhist, and in 1924 only one Burmese woman had received a bachelor's degree.[61] But by 1928 the number of Buddhist women in college exceeded that of any other religious group: there were 63 Buddhist women, 33 Europeans and Anglo-Indian Christians, and 54 Indian Christians.[62]

The increase in the matriculation of Buddhist female college students is minuscule in comparison with the considerably higher population of Burmese girls in primary and secondary schools. But even in Siam the number of female students enrolled at the tertiary level remained relatively small; in 1925 there were 68 women attending Chulalongkorn University, the only tertiary institution in the country.[63] In order to fully appreciate the significance of the minority of Burmese female students in 1920s Burma, one needs also to consider the various challenges that a Burmese woman faced in pursuing a college education. The cost posed a major problem. In 1922 the average annual college fee per student was ninety-six and a half rupees, or roughly one-seventh of the average annual income of a Burmese family. The average fee for sending a child to middle school, in contrast, was less than two rupees for vernacular schools and twenty-six rupees for English and Anglo-vernacular schools.[64] In addition, beginning in 1920, every matriculated college student was required to reside in a university hall of residence unless she lived with her parents. In order to send a child to a college, the parents therefore had to reside in Rangoon or be able to afford the child's living expenses there.[65] This requirement clearly presented a financial constraint and also a cultural dilemma for the Burmese parents who lived elsewhere; their daughter would effectively be uprooted from her familial environment and moved to a place where they would no longer be able to keep watch over her even as she commingled with a community of similarly unfettered young men and women. Amid these obstacles, the growth of a community of Burmese female college students, despite its modest size, was hardly a trivial development.

The rise in the number of educated Burmese women paralleled the rising appointment and employment of women in the medical, legal, educational, and journalistic professions. Daw Saw Sa, the first Burmese woman doctor, received her medical service diploma in 1911. In 1926, Daw Me Me Khin received her bachelor of law degree—the first Burmese woman to do so—and was appointed registrar of the High Court the following year. And in 1927, Daw Pwa Hmi became the first Burmese woman barrister-at-law. In 1924 Daw Mya Shwe and Daw Mya Yin became the first women educational administrators in Burma, followed by the first Burmese woman vice principal, Daw Hmi, in 1927.[66] Census records from 1921 and 1931 show that the population of women employed in the professions of public administration, law, medicine, education, and journalism increased by 33 percent (from 17,760 to 23,588) during the 1920s. Especially notable were the 96 percent increase (from 3,332 to 6,540) in the field of medicine and the 64 percent increase (from 2,955 to 4,857) in the field of education.[67] The most well known of these pioneering professionals is Daw Mya Sein (1904–1988), who rose to fame as the only woman member of the delegation to the Burma Round Table Conference held in London in 1931. A superintendent of a national girls' high school at the time of the conference, Daw Mya Sein had graduated from secondary school as well as university with distinction, earned a master's degree from St. Hugh's College, Oxford University, in 1927 and a diploma in education in 1928, and continued to have a successful career in education.[68] Admittedly, relatively few women worked in public administration: only 388 of 44,867 public administration workers in 1931 were women.[69] Yet the paucity of women in public administration stemmed not from a shortage of female applicants for posts but from the reluctance of the colonial administration to employ women. The colonial government was inclined to appoint men rather than women in administrative posts and maintained that "the employment of married women should be resorted to as little as possible."[70]

The reluctance of the colonial administration to employ women is also discernible in its adverse reaction to a 1919 legislative proposal to remove the disqualification of women from civil service or from university enrollment on the grounds of sex or marital status. The Sex Disqualification (Removal) Act, otherwise referred to by the colonial government as the Women's Emancipation Bill, put forward for consideration by the legislature in 1919, sought to amend the law that disqualified a woman, especially a married woman, from being appointed to or holding any civil or judicial office, post, or profession.[71] Upon passage of the bill's second reading, the chancellor of treasury sent a confidential letter, along with a memorandum by civil service commissioners and the treasury, to the War Cabinet and the Home Affairs Committee, urging that the bill be reviewed at once "as it raises such grave issues—unforeseen, I think, and certainly unprovided for by the promoters [of the bill]."[72] The memorandum defended the general rule of the civil service at the time that a woman who held any established post therein had to terminate her employment on marriage, arguing that the employment of women as civil servants conflicted with the normal duties of a wife: "Women Civil Servants if married either must deliberately endeavor to remain childless or will be forced to neglect either their children or their duties to the Service or both. Either neglect, it is submitted, is contrary to public policy. The social effects will obviously be undesirable."[73] The civil service commissioners also challenged the bill on the grounds that the demand for "equal pay for equal work" between the sexes was not justifiable, explaining that they did not consider it proved yet "that women in general could do work, [for example,] in Civil Service, equal in value to that of men."[74] "This doubt," they added, "would be much greater in the case of married women, at any rate such as were not deliberately sterile."[75] Government records from the early 1930s indicate that despite this unsympathetic view held by the government, applications for administrative and clerical posts by Burmese women kept mounting and forced colonial officials to reconsider their position on the appointment of women in government offices.[76]

Women also joined men in the ranks of the most prominent and widely read writers. Daw Amar (1915–2008), otherwise known as Ludu Daw Amar,[77] a distinguished and prolific writer-cum–social critic, came from an upper-class family in Mandalay whose fortune was made in the tobacco trade. She went to the American Baptist Mission school from the third to the ninth grade and then completed the tenth grade at the national secondary school in Mandalay, before moving to Rangoon in 1935 to begin her college education at Rangoon University. She began her career as a writer while a university student by contributing to such popular periodicals as *Bama gyanay* (Burman journal), *Tekkatho magazine* (University magazine), *Oway magazine* (Peacock's call magazine), and *Ngan hta lawka* (World of books) under the pseudonyms of Mya Myint Zu and Khin Hla Win. Her breakthrough came in 1935 when she wrote about Nehru in *Kyi pwa yay* (Improvement) magazine. Equally important to her career was the publication of her translation of Maurice Collis' *Trials in Burma* in 1938 in *Thuriya*.[78] She married Ludu U Hla, the owner of *Kyi pwa yay,* in 1939 and wrote for the magazine until the start of the Japanese occupation of Burma in 1942. Daw Amar founded the *Ludu* (The people's) newspaper and journal with her husband in 1945 and worked as the editor of the journal for more than twenty years, during which period she wrote her critically acclaimed social critiques under the pseudonym "Father Aung Naing."[79]

Many other women in colonial Burma not only wrote for some of the most popular newspapers and periodicals but also owned and edited their own papers. The first female-owned newspaper in Burma, *Tharrawaddy sa taṅ: cā* (Tharrawaddy record) was published under the management of Daw Pwa Shin (1878–1957), the newspaper's proprietor and chief editor, in 1919.[80] The first periodical written specifically for female readers, *Kraññ tau chak* (Bridge of friendship), was published in 1922 by Dagon Khin Khin Lay (1904–1981), a literary prodigy only eighteen years of age at the time. Khin Khin Lay received only seven years of formal schooling, five of which were spent in an English school in Magwe. Her knowledge of Burmese history and literature came from her grandfather, a learned *myo sa*[81] who played a formative role in her education. In 1916, when she was only twelve years old, Khin Khin Lay won a literary prize, sponsored by *Thuriya,* for her first short story "Nwe Nwe."[82] She continued to publish fictional works and eventually founded *Kraññ tau chak,* a magazine that consisted of short stories; she wrote, edited, and financed the entire magazine herself.[83] Shortly after *Tharrawaddy* and *Krañ̃ tau chak* were launched, a more popular newspaper, *Independent sa taṅ: cā* (Independent weekly), was founded in 1925 by Independent Daw San (1886–1950). Born into an upper-class merchant family in Mandalay, Daw San and her siblings were raised by parents who were active patrons of the local literati. After finishing the seventh grade in a vernacular school with honors—she was a recipient of the state scholar prize—she became a teacher at the Morlan Lane school in Moulmein. Prior to establishing the *Independent,* Daw San was a teacher at a national school in Upper Burma and wrote political articles for another magazine, *Pinnya alin* (Knowledge). When the British issued a decree that all schoolteachers must apply for permission from the commissioner of education to write in newspapers and magazines, Daw San resigned from her teaching post and set up the *Independent.*

As these brief biographies suggest, education, even after significant expansion, remained concentrated among the daughters of affluent families, and only a minority of those who were formally educated achieved successful careers. Nevertheless, educational reforms had produced, within decades, many thousands of literate women in Burma. Approximately 620,000 women, or 10 percent of the total female population, were literate by 1921. The proportion of literate females increased by 60 percent between 1911 and 1921 and by 47 percent between 1921 and 1931.[84] By the mid-1930s a clear literacy and education gap between women under and over the age of thirty was apparent. The younger generation of literate men and women formed the basis of an expanding reading public. They also facilitated the flourishing of the publishing industry, which, in an effort to capitalize on the growing reading public and to boost readership, disseminated and promoted the image and the aspirations of educated men and women of the *khit kala.*

PRINT MEDIA, LADIES' COLUMN, AND THE YOUNG WOMEN OF THE *KHIT KALA*

Although the first "women's magazine" published in Burma was Khin Khin Lay's *Krañ̃ tau chak,* the periodical that brought the female voice into the world of popular literature and spearheaded the creation of publications specifically for women was *Dagon Magazine,* the first illustrated magazine in the country. Published monthly from 1920 until 1948, *Dagon* was started by a successful department store company called Myanmar Aswe for the purpose of advertising the company's goods, but it soon turned into a literary magazine under the management of its chief editor, Saya Lun (1876–1964).[85] A playwright, poet, teacher, and journalist, Saya Lun has been described as "the single most revered literary figure in modern Burma."[86] Best known as a "patriot-writer" who ardently supported Burma's nationalist movements, Saya Lun derived his pen name, "Mr. Maung Hmaing," from a notorious libertine character in U Kyi's "Khyaṅ poṅ rvak sañ ñ moṅ mhuiṅ: vatthu" (Story of Maung Hmaing, the roselle seller, 1902). Together with the prefix "Mr.," which was used to refer to Burmese people who adopted the prefix as an honorific to their names, the pen name represented his attempt to ridicule Burmese anglophiles.[87] The most famous of his literary innovations was his *tika* (commentary) published in the *Thuriya* newspaper. Derived from a genre of Pali commentarial texts, his *tika* presented political satire in mixed verse and prose. In these commentaries, Saya Lun often portrayed himself as a wise and holy man who was addressing his female disciples, and he included poems by the female disciples that were presented as their own compositions.[88]

Aside from its illustrations, what distinguished *Dagon* from other contemporary periodicals in Burma was the serialized column "Yuwadi sekku" (Young ladies' eyes),[89] which featured female writers exclusively. Published intermittently from 1920 on, the column consisted of correspondence between two women: "Yangon" Khin Swe in Yangon (i.e., Rangoon) would write a letter to "Mandalay" Khin Toke in Mandalay, who would provide a reply in the following issue. The letters discussed various subjects ranging from gossip, arts and letters, and histories of their hometowns to commentaries on Burma's current political, economic, and social affairs. Ironically, "Yuwadi sekku" was in reality written entirely by male authors. Although it's probable that Saya Lun contributed to the creation of the column, it was the brainchild of his friend Ledi Pandita U Maung Gyi (1878–1939), the author of the column and subsequently an editor for *Dagon*. A famed editor, writer, and novelist from Upper Burma, U Maung Gyi spent most of the first thirty years of his life in the sangha, many of them in Monywa at the monastery of Ledi Sayadaw.[90] U Maung Gyi had been taught the *Tipitaka* by Ledi Sayadaw himself, and already at the young age of twenty-three, he had become an erudite scholar of Buddhist scriptures as well as *lokī* (mundane) texts such as the Sinhalese chronicles *Dīpavaṃsa* (The island chronicle) and *Mahāvaṃsa* (The great chronicle), and the Pali verses on ethical conduct *Dhammanīti* and *Lokanīti*.[91] After leaving the sangha, U Maung Gyi began writing short stories and historical novels and worked as an editor for *Myanmar alin* and *Pinnya alin*. He became an editor for *Dagon* in 1923.[92] That U Maung Gyi wrote the letters in "Yuwadi sekku" entirely by himself, using the two female pseudonyms, was not disclosed to the readers. Instead, the letters were published along with pictures of the invented female authors in an effort to convince the readers that the letters were indeed written by women (figure 2.1).

The decision by U Maung Gyi to invent these young women writers may simply reflect the rarity of female authorship at this time. Even so, it elicits other and even conflicting interpretations. One might suggest that by writing as women, U Maung Gyi was circumscribing, rather than endorsing and facilitating, public and literary expressions by women. Lorrayne Carroll, who has examined the rhetorical impersonation of female-gendered subjectivities by men in captivity narratives of early American women, has argued that male authors "sought to establish constraints or limitations on female authorship and, more particularly, on women's agency in *interpreting* for readers the

Figure 2.1 Portrait of the pseudonymous writer "Mandalay" Khin Toke, in *Dagon,* December 1926. Reproduced by permission of the family of U Tin Nwe (of A.1 Film).

meanings of their own experiences."[93] The Tagalog moral guidebook *Urbana at Feliza* (1887), by the Filipino priest Modesto de Castro (1819–1864), likewise demonstrates that male-to-female authorial impersonation may represent attempts by men to co-opt, instead of foster, the voices of women. Regarded as the first Filipino best-seller, *Urbana at Feliza* was written in the epistolary style and revolved around the correspondence between Urbana, studying at a religious school for women in Manila, and her younger sister Feliza, who remained at home in the provincial town of Paombong, Bulacan. The letters amounted to a book of conduct in which Urbana gave her sister advice on religious duties, Christian devotion, and proper social behavior, with emphasis on a woman's submissiveness, passivity, obedience, sexual purity, and duty as a nurturer of her husband and her family.[94] Men's writing as women does not necessarily encourage women to act as autonomous, authoritative, and interpretive subjects, nor offer women an alternative to prescriptive texts written by men for women.

U Maung Gyi did aim to advance female authorship, however, by integrating female voices into his writing. In her autobiography, Dagon Khin Khin Lay revealed that U Maung Gyi lamented the need to fabricate the women authors in "Yuwadi sekku." He solicited her for short stories and articles to be published in *Dagon* and asked her to contribute to his ladies' column, which she did under the pseudonym "Yadanaboun Hteik Tin Hlaing."[95] In all likelihood, then, U Maung Gyi used female pseudonyms in an effort to cater to and mobilize the increasingly literate generation of young women as both authors and readers. By casting women in the role of writers, he associated with women the authority long ascribed to male writers and intended to foster the interest of women in what were formerly considered inappropriate skills for them. Take, for instance, a letter from Khin Toke to Khin Swe in the December 1926 issue of *Dagon*.[96] Referring to Yangon Khin Swe's letter published in the previous issue (November 1926), Khin Toke praised her for her bold and brilliant criticism of the sangha's transgression. The transgression she speaks of, it appears, is the increasing discord among the politically active members of the sangha—namely, between *yahan* (young monks) and *sayadaw* (elder abbots).[97] While the *yahan* continued to pursue a boycott movement against tax collection and against the Legislative Council (begun in 1920), the *sayadaw* became involved in legislative politics, thus forsaking the boycott.[98] Khin Toke indicates that some unidentified newspapers had feverishly denounced Khin Swe's criticism of the sangha and the failure of the monks to unite in their anticolonial effort, declaring that "those who pass judgment on the sangha are digging their own graves."[99] Some readers of such newspapers, Khin Toke adds, had mindlessly reiterated this view without any reflection upon the matter. She, however, commends Khin Swe's forthright assessment of the sangha's actions and her readiness to assert her own opinion, citing a Buddhist proverb in which a monk, speaking to the Buddha, conveys his view that one ought to criticize the sangha, as long as the criticism is legitimate. In the second half of her letter, Khin Toke responds to Khin Swe's statement in her previous letter that "young women of the times[100] end up in offices because of their novel and peculiar[101] ways."[102] Khin Toke explains that because the statement could be interpreted in many ways—for instance, that young women end up in a police office because of their unruly behavior—she would like to clarify her own interpretation. She first asks that if "young women end up in such 'offices' as legislative, parliamentary, or press offices, because they have obtained bachelor's degrees, isn't that an encouraging development?"[103] She then asserts that, "as Ma Khin Swe has already agreed," young women's place in society is not located solely in the home and that women with professional careers should not be confined by marital, parental, or other domestic duties. After further elaborating on her interpretation, Khin Toke concludes her letter to Khin Swe with the following word of warning to young women in Burma:

> Don't waste your afternoons taking naps,
> Chitchatting and larking about just waste your time,
> Use your time to gain much knowledge of the present and of the past,
> So that you may perceive the world around you as informed, intelligent
>   women.[104]

This letter illustrates what U Maung Gyi was trying to accomplish through his ladies' column. The most obvious of his concerns was to embolden young women in Burma to freely express their opinions, even against the sangha. The letter likewise defends and promotes the intellectual and vocational aspirations of young women in Burma, even if this entails their renunciation of conjugal duties—a radical stance for the time. It also emphasizes the importance of education. In this era, the *khit kala*, knowledge (*pinnya*)[105] ceased to be a desirable quality and a prerogative of men, monastic or lay; women and men alike needed to cultivate knowledge in order to make sense of the world around them. In addition, the merits of a person and her words and deeds depended on her *pinnya*, not her social status. Tellingly, in a 1919 article in *Thuriya,* a male author claimed that educated Burmese women "would be more suitable for elections as members of the legislative assembly than village headmen,"[106] the position of village headman traditionally being hereditary. Although formal schooling constituted a fundamental part of the pursuit of knowledge, Khin Toke advises her readers to pursue education not merely for the sake of degrees, for it is not enough that a contemporary Burmese woman, or *khit hmi thu,* has a degree. She must educate and inform herself about what is happening in the world. What better way to stay informed than to read newspapers? U Maung Gyi does not expressly point to the popular press, but the implication is unmistakable: a young woman must not waste her afternoons taking naps or making conversation, because she should be using that time to educate herself by reading newspapers and magazines. While the column was, not unlike *Urbana at Feliza,* prescriptive, the values and practices it sought to prescribe were subversive.

By writing as two young ladies, U Maung Gyi sought to legitimize and popularize female education, readership, and authorship. To a certain extent, this mission must have been driven by a desire to give *Dagon* a broader appeal and to enable it to reach a wider audience. U Maung Gyi appears to have been equally motivated by a quest to elevate the position of women as knowledge brokers. Evidently, Ledi Sayadaw's campaign for the education of the laity, which specifically included women among those he sought to reach and educate, had made a lasting impression on U Maung Gyi. As Eric Braun has shown in his intellectual biography of the renowned scholar monk, Ledi Sayadaw advocated, in response to the declining political and educational roles of the sangha, a new vision of modern Burmese Buddhism that placed utmost importance on the participation of the entire laity, not just the monastic elite or men, in the preservation of the Buddha's teachings.[107] Yet Ledi Sayadaw looked upon women as spiritual and intellectual inferiors who required more moral and doctrinal guidance than men.[108] As the opening passage of the "Yuwadi sekku" column in the September 1929 issue indicates, U Maung Gyi diverged from this view: "Today, worthy and empowered women are on the rise. . . . They are now being offered rights and opportunities they were previously denied. Young women, this is your time to come to the forefront, so take the offer with dignity; seize the moment without hesitation."[109] The reference to "empowered women" who "are on the rise" also suggests that U Maung Gyi may have been engaging in a broader, translocal, and contemporaneous discourse about the "conditions of women" and the related "woman question"—that is, the issue of whether and which conditions of women needed reform, questions undergirding feminist movements elsewhere that fought for women's suffrage or sought to alter women's subordination within the patriarchal structure of family and to increase the presence and participation of women in the public sphere. U Maung Gyi understood education to be the condition of women most needing reform. Not unlike pioneers of women's magazines elsewhere in Southeast Asia that were similarly instrumental in debates about the woman question,

"Yuwadi sekku" was adamant that young women of the era receive education and gain knowledge. The exemplary *khit hmi thu* such as Khin Swe and Khin Toke echoed the trend in the region whereby the "new woman" was necessarily represented as educated.[110]

What is also striking about U Maung Gyi's representation of "worthy and empowered" women of the *khit kala* is his reference to Buddhist parables. The strategy of citing the Buddha was his preferred writing style, undoubtedly shaped by his monastic background, in particular his experience as a *cā khya pugguil* (a teacher of Buddhist texts) at the Ledi monastery.[111] As a *cā khya pugguil,* he would have been required to explain Buddhist texts to students in the form of a *nissaya:* a word-by-word translation of a Pali text often followed by more elaborate vernacular glosses by the translator. Having mastered this skill as a monk, U Maung Gyi employed it in "Yuwadi sekku," an example of which is found in the March 1927 issue of *Dagon.* In this column the subject that occupies Khin Swe's letter to Khin Toke is a demonstration by more than a hundred women, led by Independent Daw San and Daw Mya Sein among others, that took place on 3 February 1927. This particular demonstration concerned a legislative proposal, debated and defeated in the Legislative Council that morning, to abolish the law that prohibited women from running for office in parliamentary elections.[112] Khin Swe describes the prohibition as pure chauvinism: "Men chastise women. They try to intimidate women. . . . Men aspire to oppress women. Like vultures, they safeguard their parliamentary seats. They lock women in. They kick women out . . . so I write because I cannot bear to put up with their harassment."[113] The "harassment" about which Khin Swe writes refers to the various demeaning remarks about women by some of the Legislative Council members who opposed the proposal.[114] Among the most biting comments made, according to Khin Swe, were those by U Kyaw Dun and U San Pe, who contended that women with excessive *awza* (influence)[115]—such as Queen Supayalat, who exercised great influence over her husband, King Thibaw—would spell disaster for the country.[116]

As one of her main arguments against the discriminatory ban on women from seeking parliamentary posts, Khin Swe cites from the *Lomasakassapa jātaka.*[117] "In the *jātaka,* as you know," she writes to Khin Toke, "the Buddha himself lectured on the great strength and ability of women."[118] She then quotes the following passage from the *jātaka:*

> The strength of the moon, the strength of the sun,
> The strength of a wandering ascetic,
> The strength of a seashore,
> The strength of a woman is stronger than these.[119]

Khin Swe translates the passage, cited in Pali, into Burmese, consistent with the *nissaya* commentarial tradition. Her interpretation of the passage is straightforward: the might of the moon and the sun, which bring light and darkness to the human world, is great; the power of the pious ascetic is also great; the force of the ocean's waves and tides are equally great; but the strength of the womenfolk—women who have been castigated, put down, and harassed for rightfully demanding their right to run for parliamentary offices—is the greatest.[120]

U Maung Gyi tapped into Buddhist discourse to encourage readers to broaden their outlook. This was a logical rhetorical choice, not only because of his knowledge of Buddhist texts, but also because this genre of literature was considered uncontroversial reading material for young women.[121] He used Buddhist narratives as ideological support for his potentially controversial representations of Burmese women. He cast women as *nissaya* authors in words and in illustrations, such as a portrait captioned "Translating *theri*" (figure 2.2).[122] It is unclear whether the term *theri* (Buddhist female authorities) refers to the group of young women in the illustration or to the ninth book of the *Khuddaka nikāya, Therīgathā,* which contains seventy-three "verses of the elder nuns" and is possibly the text that is being translated. Either way, the young women are depicted as engrossed in the act of translation.[123] *Nissaya,* which are found throughout Theravadan Southeast Asia, are written in a great variety of styles and function more as commentarial texts than as simple translations of a Pali source text.[124] As Justin McDaniel points out, a *nissaya* author's mere knowledge of Pali terms and his or her ability to memorize, translate, and explain Pali words gave the author great prestige. He elaborates: "Moreover, despite the fact that *nissaya* authors believed they could directly translate Pali words without loss of meaning, some Pali terms were given much more than a direct gloss. The expanded glosses and comments edified the audience, displayed the skill of the author and provided a platform from which to offer a lecture on more general subjects."[125] For U Maung Gyi, therefore, the sources for his young ladies' discussion were located in "traditional" images, texts, and practices. He used Buddhist texts as testament to his suggestion that women of the *khit kala* were "worthy and empowered." They were fully capable of serving as knowledge brokers not only because they held university degrees but also because they could interpret, explain, and spread the words of the Buddha—words that, incidentally, claimed that women were worthy and powerful. Women of the *khit kala* combined knowledge acquired through formal education with knowledge gleaned through reading newspapers and magazines, on the one hand, and more traditional forms of knowledge—namely, that of the *sāsana.* They displayed an attachment to and a desire to preserve the past, even as they heralded a future of change. Reinforced by images of young educated women placed purposefully in the magazine, the ladies' column by U Maung Gyi did more than encourage young women to imagine themselves as part of a growing literary community. The column both fashioned and gave credence to the ideal of the educated *khit hmi thu.*

U Maung Gyi's "Yuwadi sekku" was an immediate success, and in 1925 it became a featured column in which many fictional young women from other towns joined in the correspondences. U Maung Gyi wrote as Tharrawaddy Tin Oung, Pyinmana Su Su, and Ketumadi Mya Mya, in addition to Mandalay Khin Toke and Yangon Khin Swe. Many other renowned contemporary male

Figure 2.2 "Translating *therī*," in *Dagon,* April 1927. Reproduced by permission of the family of U Tin Nwe (of A.1 Film).

writers, all writing under female pseudonyms, also contributed. According to Dagon Khin Khin Lay, some readers were aware or at least suspected that the writings purportedly authored by women and published in *Dagon* were actually the creations of male writers. Yet she adds that the real identities of the authors remained unknown to many readers. At one point, a couple of male readers enamored of some romantic poems published in *Dagon* took their author, Shin Than May—who was in fact a monk—to be a real woman and wrote love letters to "her."[126]

Another widely read periodical, *Deedok gyanay* (Deedok weekly), began publication in 1925 of a column entitled "Yuwadi kye hmoun" (Young ladies' mirror),[127] which virtually replicated U Maung Gyi's "Yuwadi sekku." In all likelihood, the pseudonymous author of the column was Saya Lun, who not only edited *Dagon* but also wrote for *Deedok.* The author of *Deedok*'s "Yuwadi kye hmoun" frequently opened her article with a passage from a Pali text concerning women, such as the following lines that began the 7 November 1925 column:

> The earth is contained by the ocean,
> A house is enclosed by its walls,
> A country is run by her king,
> A woman is controlled only by her will.[128]

Like U Maung Gyi, the author translates the passage into Burmese in the *nissaya* style before providing an extended exposition of her interpretation. The remainder of the column critiques well-known texts that, according to the author, portray Burmese queens and historical figures negatively, such as the "Magghadeva pyo," a nineteenth-century commentarial verse about the *Magghadeva jātaka*,[129] written by Ashin Zawana Manlay Sayadaw, a prominent nineteenth-century monk known for his deprecating depictions of women.[130] Through the repetitive strategy of cite-translate-explain-elaborate, the author endeavored to emulate the most common didactic method of *nissaya*. Repetition, McDaniel explains, was a well-known trait of Buddhist texts in general, used "to emphasize a particular point, develop a convincing argument, establish the authenticity of a particular lineage, or for worship."[131] McDaniel goes on to say that repetition served as a method to teach vocabulary and to express new ideas using traditional forms: "Just as apocryphal *Jātaka*s used translocal literary practices to express local values, beliefs and practices, *nissaya*s introduce new ways of reading and teaching a classical Pali source text through the seemingly benign and non-creative practice of translation and repetition."[132]

The *yuwadi* columns clearly represented didactic instruments for inculcating readers with what the authors saw as new, *khit kala* gender sensibilities through the use of traditional literary forms. The educational purpose of the *yuwadi* columns dovetailed with the commercial interest of inspiring female readership.

The strategy proved to be groundbreaking. By 1927 two periodicals that had only recently begun publishing, *Independent Weekly* and *Kavi myak mhan* (Scholars' eyeglasses), contained copycat serialized *yuwadi* columns.[133] The *yuwadi* column had become a widespread phenomenon and a standard feature of the Burmese popular press by the end of the 1920s. By the mid-1930s, actual female writers (not only male writers who employed female pseudonyms) flourished in the Burmese press, and the majority of competitive newspapers and periodicals such as *Independent Weekly, Daung Weekly,* and *Dagon* had prominent female editors on board. Although the *yuwadi* column itself became less prevalent towards the mid-1930s, columns devoted to the opinion of female writers remained popular. The January 1940 issue of *Journal gyaw* (Weekly thunderer), for instance, published a letter from a female reader, Tin Tin from the town of Let Pan Than, expressing her wish that *Journal gyaw* augment its existing editorial column entitled "Ū le: pro may" (Uncle says) with a feminine counterpart, "Dau dau pro may" (Auntie says). "In my opinion," Tin Tin writes, *"Journal gyaw* would benefit from such a column as 'Auntie Says' that gives guidance to *yuwadi* like myself."[134] Even newspapers and periodicals that did not have women editors routinely featured columns exclusively written by women writers, as did *Myanmar alin* (written by Ma Ma Lay), *Kyi pwa yay,* and *Toe tet yay* (Efficiency magazine).[135] Rather than confine themselves to discussions of women in Burma, columnists wrote about women abroad, particularly in other parts of Asia. The 7 January 1937 issue of *Thuriya* provides a captivating example of such articles. In that issue, "Modern Women in China Take the Lead"[136] states that *khit kala* women in China are empowering themselves by paying increasing attention to education, higher-paying employment (in hospitals or in bureaucratic positions), health care, and demands for equal education and inheritance rights. As a testament to the modernization and empowerment of women in China, the article contains a photo of a woman, whom the caption describes as Chinese, walking on a beach in a bathing suit, which was considered to be revealing in 1930s China and Burma.

Editors and writers experimented with techniques to stimulate female readership by publishing such things as *yuwadi* columns, biographies of Burmese women intellectuals and historical figures, and women's portraits. By catering to female readers as the subject of collective reception, popular print culture gave women public literary representation and irrevocably increased their importance as readers and writers. Ladies' columns did not immediately engender a homosocial literary community for women. Khin Khin Lay's *Krañ tau chak* discontinued publication after just two years, and no other women's magazine appeared until after the Second World War.[137] Nevertheless, ladies' columns enabled young women to imagine themselves as part of a growing community of women readers and writers. They served to discredit sexist views about the impropriety of female education, literacy, and authorship and to establish opinions and experiences of women as appropriate subjects for public discussion by women, not only men. Innovative writing techniques used by columnists, reformist ideas about female education, and sales strategies served as catalysts to the production of images of women. At the same time, old parables expressed new ideas and old representational practices were disseminated through new media in the popular press, making it a fertile public forum for fashioning new understandings of femininity and giving rise to the first of many heterogeneous idealized images of the women of the *khit kala* that were to appear in colonial Burma: the educated young woman.

THE EDUCATED MODERN WOMAN AND VISIONS OF PROGRESS

Recent scholarship on the "new woman" or "modern woman" has shown that she was not always synonymous with feminism or a movement for women's rights. Louise Edwards has argued, for instance, that in the case of Republican China the modern woman "had less potency for the women's movement than she did with the nationalist project of state building."[138] Scholars of women's suffrage movements in Asia have similarly revealed that nationalists promoted feminism and, in particular, female education in order to mobilize women for the anticolonial struggle and to advance nation building.[139] In British India, too, the appeal of the nationalist movement to women rested on its construct of the new respectable woman as one who sought "cultural refinement through education."[140] In Burma, as in neighboring Siam, China, and India, intellectuals and politicians were no doubt aware that women needed to have the same educational opportunities as men if they were to be expected to contribute to the nationalist struggle.[141] If there were any questions about the importance of education to nation building, the colonial government made clear in no uncertain terms that education was requisite to political participation. In 1927 the British colonial administration defeated legislation that would have allowed women to vote, explaining its decision as follows: "[The Home Member of the Legislative Council] was sorry to say Government had to oppose the resolution which they considered premature. He would be a rash man to say that the Burmese woman had progressed as far as her sister from the West both politically and in education as to take her place in representative institutions."[142] Women in Burma were deemed unfit for enfranchisement because they lacked education.

Three years later, amidst growing demand for women's right to vote and eligibility for election by women's associations in England, as well as British India and other British colonies, the British government faced yet another proposal to modify existing constitutional regulations to qualify more female voters. While recognizing "the growing influence in India of educated women," the government again rejected the proposal on the basis that the majority of the female population had "received no education of any kind" and could not be "expected to have the slightest grasp of the political problems with which the country is likely to be faced during the next generation."[143]

For native men and women engaged in discussions about modernization, education represented the one "condition" of women that rendered Burma "backward" and unprepared for political modernization. To the extent that the "conditions of women" had become, in Burma as elsewhere, the scale for measuring the readiness of a country for national self-determination, the gender disparity in literacy and education represented a national problem. Burmese and Indian politicians drew attention to the high status of women in Burma to discredit the British colonial project and its professed goal of implementing needed social reforms, and the Burmese tradition of gender equality figured as an imperative element of the anticolonial discourse. Yet the lack of female education made this line of argument untenable and placed Burmese women in the same category as the "oppressed" women of "Hindu," "Muslim," and "Confucian" societies. It was not lost on people in Burma that even if "the Burmese woman" possessed those very rights denied to women in supposedly more advanced countries, she had not "progressed as far as her sisters from the West." Education was essential to distinguishing the women of the *khit kala,* who, unlike women of times past, would be the equal of not only the men of Burma but also their "sisters from the West." Burma itself would thus be made equal to the modern nations of the West. Embedded in a discourse about modernization, debates concerning the education and progress of women were also about the empowerment and advancement of the nation.

In fact, as early as the late nineteenth century, members of the indigenous elite viewed education as the key to nation building. In a lecture delivered to the Rangoon Teachers' Association in 1896, Taw Sein Ko claimed that education in Burma needed to be handled with utmost care "if Burma is ever to take her place among the nations of the world."[144] He explained: "It is education that differentiates the European from the Asiatic and has made the nations of Europe great in human achievements, and it is education that has enabled Japan to assert her power against her powerful neighbor."[145] While both men and women were charged with the task of getting educated to enable Burma "to take her place among the nations of the world," women were assigned the work of educating children. Taw Sein Ko's message was echoed in the 1930s by such women writers as Khin Myo Chit, a contributor to *Dagon Magazine,* and Khin May and Mya Gale, who wrote for *Toe tet yay.* These women urged Burmese women, as mothers responsible for the future generation, to gain education. As in the Philippines, where elite Filipino women insisted as early as 1909 that "women get an education for the benefit of the country,"[146] and in the Dutch East Indies, where Kartini made the unprecedented request for female education for the betterment of Javanese society at large,[147] native elites in Burma asserted that women had to receive formal education if Burma was to become an equal among nations.

The support for the education of women that emerged in the 1920s was thus not without connection to Burma's national advancement. As chapter 3 shows, however, neither the ideal of the educated and educating mother, nor an explicit call for women to seek education as part of a nation-building effort, entered popular discourse until the mid-1930s. The concern with the education of women was not only about the welfare and advancement of the Burmese nation. U Maung Gyi presented various justifications for urging the young women of the *khit kala* to pursue education, none of which he identified with the interests of the nation. This of course does not rule out the possibility that he understood the education of women to be ultimately beneficial to the nation. U Maung Gyi, like Saya Lun, was sympathetic to the nationalist movement. His historical novels such as *Nat Shin Naung* (1919) and *Tabin Shwe Hti vatthu* (Tale of Tabin Shwe Hti, 1924) were anticolonialist and written "to remind [the Burmese youth] of their great leaders of the past, to awaken national consciousness and pride and to give the Myanmar people a militant courage to fight against foreign rule."[148] Yet the content of *yuwadi* columns reveals that U Maung Gyi was motivated by other factors, such as the reformulation of the importance of lay education. In the *khit kala,* colonial rule, Christian missionary activities, and European science and technology forced leading scholar monks such as Ledi Sayadaw and his disciples to rethink the role of the laity in the preservation of the *sāsana* and to emphasize the cultivation of *pinnya* for laymen and laywomen. The prominence of Buddha's teachings in the "Yuwadi sekku" indicates that U Maung Gyi, like Ledi Sayadaw, viewed education as the key to making laywomen, alongside laymen, fitting protectors of the *sāsana.*

U Maung Gyi may have also been influenced by emerging gender sensibilities and reformist discourse about the "woman question." The claim that women with *pinnya* were as qualified as men to engage in activities that were traditionally male dominated, particularly in the area of knowledge production, profoundly challenged the status quo in gender relations in Burma. No feminist cause can be securely attributed to the *yuwadi* columns, as they never provided a systematic critique of gender relations in Burma. It is important, furthermore, to bear in mind the commercial nature of the *yuwadi* columns. As this chapter has shown, the columns were part and parcel of a marketing strategy; they served as a major force in expanding female readership and proved instrumental to the success of the burgeoning publishing industry. Nonetheless, and irrespective of the intentions behind the creation of the *yuwadi* columns, the effect of encouraging young women to aspire to attain *pinnya* and seize "rights and opportunities they were previously denied" was to encourage women to reinvent themselves and to perceive themselves as equals of their male counterparts. The discussions about women in the *yuwadi* columns demonstrate that the figure of the educated *khit hmi thu* had as much potency for the feminist struggle as she did for the nationalist struggle.

This discourse on women and education also shows that the educated *khit hmi thu* was a product of a growing consciousness of global events and trends among men and women in Burma. The frequent pleas to keep up with women in more advanced countries such as China and Japan were premised on a cosmopolitan frame of reference that required an awareness of debates about the Modern Woman that were taking place in other societies. As studies of nationalist representations of "traditional" and "modern" women elsewhere have revealed, visions of modernization expressed in various parts of the world and in disparate contexts nonetheless converged on the imperative of improving the conditions of women.[149] Nilüfer Göle has even argued, in the case of Turkey, that the construction of women as public citizens and of women's rights was even more cherished than the construction of citizenship and civil rights, due to the importance of the conditions of women to the project of modernity and to political reforms.[150] The ideal of the educated woman was fashioned by men and women in Burma who partook of such discourses about modernity that were emerging and circulating simultaneously and globally. Yet even as they enjoined young Burmese women to pursue formal education in unison with modern women elsewhere, they reminded the young women that without traditional forms of knowledge such as that of the *sāsana,* they would not be truly cultivated. Those who espoused the ideal of the educated woman in Burma maintained that, by seizing new rights and opportunities, women of the *khit kala* would be heeding the teachings of the Buddha. The *khit hmi thu* that cosmopolitan men and women in Burma envisaged bridged the local and the global, and the past and the present. She imbued tradition with new life even as she symbolized changes already under way.

This is not to suggest that she was a construction by cosmopolitan intellectuals, politicians, writers, and publishers experimenting with new ideas. The "young ladies" in the media and the young women who composed a major share of the educated population and literary community were mutually constitutive. Young women in Burma were not only inspired by the discursive *khit hmi thu;* as they pursued higher education alongside men and wrote publicly for and on behalf of female readers, they also inspired Burmese young men and women to form new self-identities and to contemplate the meaning of the *khit kala.* The 1920s marked a period in Burmese history when women began to play more visible and active roles in politics as well as cultural production, functioning in the capacity of producers, arbiters, and transmitters of knowledge. These were groundbreaking developments. U Maung Gyi's "worthy and empowered" women, the subjects of the *yuwadi* columns, were real-life women such as Daw Mya Sein and Daw San. These women, no less than the "lady" authors of the *yuwadi* columns, were responsible for the appearance of the educated *khit hmi thu.* They, like their discursive counterpart, represented Burmese women "on the rise" who reconfigured existing gender norms and practices.

3

Between Patriotism and Feminism

Politicized and Organized Women

Following on the heels of *yuwadi* columns were articles and featured columns that focused less on the emergent class of educated young women and were written by and for women in general (*amyothami*).[1] A growing number of articles for and about women were published as regular features of newspapers and magazines in the 1930s. *Toe tet yay,* for instance, printed a column entitled "Women's Advancement"[2] from the start of its publication in 1933. *Youq shin lan hnyun* (Screen show weekly), which also appeared in 1933, featured a regular "Women's Guide."[3] In 1935, *Independent Weekly* changed the title of its *yuwadi* column, "Young Ladies' Mirror," to "For the Housewives."[4] What was noticeable about these articles, the majority of which were written by women or by men writing as women, was their attention to the role of women as wives and mothers.[5] They gave useful information, advice, and guidelines on matrimony, child care, and housekeeping to the women of the *khit kala,* even featuring recipes for Burmese dishes. The articles presented an elaborate image of the home and family and of the duties of wives and mothers.

This shift was no doubt a strategy to maximize circulation, by catering to a broader audience and by keeping up with the population of female readers who were growing older. The entertainment value of subjecting the image of housewife-and-mother to public scrutiny, discussion, and consumption must also be considered. Take, for example, a cartoon entitled "The Loving Kindness of a Stepmother,"[6] published in *Deedok gyanay* in 1927. It juxtaposes an image of a woman with her "real," or biological, daughter and an image of the same woman with her stepdaughter. With her own daughter, the woman is depicted as a loving mother who reads to her daughter. In contrast, she maltreats her stepdaughter, putting her to work in the kitchen like a servant. The caption for the cartoon is a warning to widowed men: "Beware, widowers!"[7] While it is possible that the purpose of the cartoon was didactic, the sensationalist portrayal of the evil stepmother suggests that the cartoon was intended to amuse as much as to educate the readers about remarriage or motherhood.

The emergence of the discourse on housewifery may also have been an attempt to update domesticity and thus make it more acceptable to modern women who might otherwise find a career and independence more appealing than marriage and motherhood, as Adrian Bingham has argued in the case of interwar Britain.[8] The women's columns tended to stress the importance of the domestic role of women. Khin May wrote in her October 1933 editorial in *Toe tet yay* that a woman's beauty and character lay in her loving treatment of her husband, implying that a woman could not be beautiful independently and outside of matrimony.[9] The next month, the columnist propounded that the most meaningful way in which Burmese women could make progress was in their capacity as mothers, especially of young children.[10] In "About the Need to Improve Women's Cultivation,"[11] also published in *Toe tet yay* in 1934, Mya Galay asserted that mothers, not fathers, were responsible for disciplining their children because a *ya khu khit*[12] (present-day) father was the breadwinner of the family and therefore was unable to give adequate attention to his children.[13] Precisely because mothers were now in charge of raising their children, women had to prioritize the study of Buddhist teachings over modern education, though the latter was also important to women's development.[14] Illustrations of motherhood, such as that on the cover of the December 1937 issue of the literary and educational magazine *Ngan hta lawka* (figure 3.1), served as visual aids to articles that detailed the duties of Burmese women as mothers responsible for the health and education of the future generation. The discourse on the *ya khu khit amyothami* drove home the imperative of domesticity for women. It also provided consolation for women with reservations about marriage and motherhood. The prolific woman writer Khin Myo Chit was known for her articles that gave advice to young wives, such as "The Mother-in-law," in which she counseled her female readers on how a woman could overcome ill feelings, jealousies, and hostilities between herself and her mother-in-law, with whom she lived.[15]

Also distinctive about the articles for and about the *ya khu khit amyothami* was the emphasis placed on her devotion to her *amyo* and her *taing pyi*[16] (her kin and her country). The use of the term *amyothami*, a compound of the word *amyo* and *thami* (daughter), is itself indicative. Like the term *meinma*,[17] *amyothami* refers to a female person and can also mean "wife." Unlike *meinma*, however, *amyothami,* which literally means "a daughter belonging to an *amyo,*" can additionally mean "member of a nation or ethnic group" and "fellow countrywoman."[18] The word *amyo* actually refers variously to race, kin, breed, lineage, family, rank, caste, kind, sort, and species. It is unlikely that the term *amyothami,* which dates back to at least the sixteenth century always denoted

Figure 3.1 Depiction of mothers as nurturers and educators, on the cover of the educational magazine *Ngan hta lawka* (World of books), December 1937. Reproduced by permission of John Ady, grandson of J. S. Furnivall.

"daughter of a nation or ethnic group."[19] Yet, in colonial Burma, *amyo* took on the meaning of "a nation or ethnic group," and the word *amyothami* reflected a conceptualization of a woman who was closely tied to the notion of the Burmese *amyo*.

For instance, Mya Galay proclaimed that a truly cultivated *amyothami* paid attention to the prosperity and advancement of her *amyo*.[20] What determined the character of an *amyothami,* she added, was "her love of her country and her ability to reform herself in such a way that benefits and dignifies her country."[21] One of the most vital capacities in which a woman looked after the interest of her people and country, according to Mya Galay, was in the role of a mother who dutifully nurtured her children. In particular, the writer warned that women must not mingle with men of questionable character and intelligence because such men would damage not only the women themselves but also the children begotten through such relationships and, ultimately, would ruin the future of her *amyo*.[22] Khin May was likewise of the opinion that the modern *amyothami* should make an effort to raise her children to be valiant men and women who were proud of their country. In her November 1933 "Women's Advancement" article, for example, Khin May advised her readers to choose wisely the kinds of stories they told their children. "You should not tell your children Western fairy tales nor purposeless stories," she counseled. She recommended instead that mothers tell their children legends about intellectuals, literati, and gallant men and women from Burmese history. A mother should acquaint her children with stories "that make them aware of the great and noble past of their *amyo*" and "instill pride in their country and heritage."[23] Mirroring the political realities of the 1920s and 1930s, a period in Burmese history widely recognized as the era of political awakening and the emergence of the *wunthanu* (protector of national interests), the archetype of the modern patriotic woman had emerged in the figure of the wife-and-mother conscientious of her duties to her *amyo*.[24]

The often exalted depiction of women as hearth and home and self-sacrificial protector of the nation has been established as a salient feature of nationalism.[25] In Burma, too, nationalist discourse aimed at naturalizing and valorizing the role of women in the family and defined the home as the primary responsibility of a woman. Men were not excluded from the domestic sphere, but in order for women to be able to devote themselves to the family, men needed to support them financially through work. That women should not be distracted from their domestic duties is evident not only in the categorization of men as the breadwinners but also in the absence of servants from discussions of the home and family. The disappearance of the servant was probably also due to the increasing inability of Burmese families to afford household help. Yet what was at stake in the erasure of servants and non-middle-class women was the ideal of the modern wife-and-mother, who was expected to care for her *own* home and family, not caring for other men and their families.[26] She was, furthermore, a custodian of her *amyo* and *taing pyi*. Through sufficient and wise care of her husband and children, she biologically and culturally regenerated and sustained her people and country. The values and stories associated with the glorious days of Burma's past, which the idealized *amyothami* was encumbered with transmitting to her children, marked Burma off from other countries and conversely guaranteed a sense of national identity. They also helped foster patriotic children primed to serve their *amyo* and *taing pyi*. Implicit in the linking of the home to the nation was the demarcation of family as a functional unit, a part of the national whole that was entrusted with guarding the security, morality, and well-being of its members and of the nation at large.[27] In this manner, the affairs of the family were designated as public matters rather than private ones, and women were cast as wives and mothers of the nation.

Burmese women were not encouraged to confine themselves to the domestic sphere, however. They were expected to show their patriotism both privately and publicly. Articles about the wife-and-mother circulated hand in hand with historical accounts of the *myo chit may* (female patriot),[28] most popularly the French national heroine and martyr, Joan of Arc. While such articles were meant chiefly to edify the concept of *myo chit may*, they also suggested that a woman could demonstrate her patriotism outside the home.[29] The popular press also featured commentaries that prompted Burmese women to actively pursue professional careers. A 1936 editorial in *Myanmar alin*, "Some of Burma's Problems,"[30] is a case in point. In the editorial's section entitled "Burmese Women," the editor exhorts Burmese women not to fall behind women in other independent and rapidly modernizing countries—such as China, Japan, Turkey, Persia, and Egypt—who are taking up professions as journalists, doctors and nurses, police officers, teachers, lawyers, and judges. "Burmese women," he says, "are you going to keep standing still? . . . Are you going to let your time-honored reputation as exceptionally liberated women of the East be ruined?"[31] But why was it "Burma's problem" if the country's women did not keep up with professional women elsewhere? Perhaps the editor was concerned with sustaining the image of Burmese women as independent and progressive (discussed in chapter 2). More striking, however, was his choice of professions. He urged Burmese women to heed the examples of women elsewhere who had taken up professions that contributed to public life. The visible participation of women in public life was integral to visions of modernization and national progress. Contrary to the impression given by the editor, however, educated Burmese women were wasting no time pursuing careers as teachers, lawyers, journalists, administrators, and so on, as previously shown. They were also quick to acquire visibility in the public sphere through another venue: participation in organized political agitation.

WOMEN'S ASSOCIATIONS AND THE POLITICAL MOBILIZATION OF WOMEN

Organized politics in Burma began, as in colonial Lanka, in the form of Buddhist revivalist movements and the related campaign for Buddhist education (described in chapter 1).[32] The Young Men's Buddhist Association (YMBA), the voice of the revivalist movement in Burma, was established by middle-class, educated Burmese elites who were beginning to experiment with new forms of collective political, social, and cultural organization. Originally, it was a nonpolitical group that organized conferences on social and religious issues and served as the nodal point connecting disparate lay organizations in Burma. In 1917, however, the group passed, for the first time, resolutions of a political and anticolonial nature that ranged from the decision to send a delegation to Lord Montagu—the secretary of state to India, who was preparing a report on proposed constitutional reforms in Burma—to a strong protest against Europeans' wearing shoes in pagoda precincts, contrary to Burmese custom.[33] In the same year, the YMBA split into two factions, and in 1920 the faction led by the younger members formed the General Council of Burmese Associations (GCBA), the first organization with explicitly political goals that focused on securing representative political rights. Within a few years, the GCBA had twelve thousand branches throughout Burma.[34]

The year 1920 was a political turning point for other reasons, not least the 1920 University Boycott and the ensuing national education movement. The boycott began on 5 December of that year in protest of the University of Rangoon Act, also known as the University Act, which had gone into effect on 1 December. The act, whose stated object was "the establishment and incorporation of a centralized teaching and residential University at Rangoon," entailed three basic measures: it unified the existing Rangoon and Judson colleges; required all matriculated undergraduate students of a constituent college, unless they lived with their parents, to reside in a university hall; and implemented a mandatory one-year preliminary course for students who had not shown proficiency in English in their School Final Examination. The main objection of the boycotters to the act was that higher education would become prohibitively expensive for the college students whose parents or guardians were not sufficiently well-to-do to afford the luxury of residing in Rangoon.

The addition of a year-long "preliminary course" for students who failed to show proficiency in their School Final Examination similarly added significantly to the cost of a Burmese student's college education. The boycotters expressed concern that many Burmese college students were unable to follow the lectures on account of insufficient proficiency in English, causing them to fail examinations, but argued that the solution to this lay in the employment of more capable faculty and staff and the adoption of better teaching methods.[35] On 5 December, approximately five hundred students who lived at the residence halls of Rangoon and Judson colleges left their dorms to undertake a university strike. An additional number of students, estimated at about one hundred, who lived elsewhere joined the boycotters the following morning by refusing to attend classes. Of the forty-eight female college students enrolled at Rangoon University in 1920, eight participated in the boycott. Altogether, between 60 and 75 percent of college students in Burma participated in the strike.[36] The boycott spread to all government schools and even missionary schools. Students in girls' schools such as St. Mary's and the American Baptist Mission school in Rangoon joined the strike, forcing the schools to close temporarily beginning on 6 December. Despite the boycott, the authorities refused to modify the University Act, which remained in force in its original form and was not revisited until the second University Boycott in 1936, when college students renewed criticisms of the educational system. Nevertheless, the 1920 student boycott marked the first organized display of defiance of the colonial administration and served as a landmark in the Burmese anticolonial movement. It also yielded one important outcome, which was the setting up of private "national schools."

As evinced by the rhetoric of the boycotters who claimed to be emulating Bengal's example, these schools were clearly inspired by the National Council of Education (NCE) movement in Bengal, which was spearheaded by pioneering Indian nationalists such as Raja S. C. Mullick, Sri Aurobindo, and Rabindranath Tagore.[37] It was no coincidence that one of the largest financiers of the national education movement in Burma was the Burma Committee of the Indian National Congress, founded in 1908 by a close friend of Gandhi's.[38] The GCBA, another staunch supporter of the movement, also had connections to the national education movement in Bengal. The most prominent member of the GCBA at the time was U Ottama, a widely traveled Buddhist monk associated with the Bengal National College and a member of the Indian National Congress (INC) of Bengal from 1918. Known as the "Gandhi of Burma," U Ottama had spent many years in India imbibing the political ideas and strategies of the INC, and he is credited with the politicization of the Burmese sangha. He introduced the slogan "Home Rule or Boycott" to Burma and served as the main liaison between the Burmese and Bengali nationalists.[39] As with the NCE in Bengal, the objective of the National Education Committee and the Council of National Education in Burma, formed in 1920, was to create alternative and independent educational institutions where "love of country and love of nation are no less assiduously cultivated and nurtured" through "the invaluable services of Burmese literature and Burmese history."[40] Many of the teachers at the national schools had participated in the 1920 University Boycott. The national schools were poorly funded, however, and some eventually opted to seek financial assistance from the government. In 1926, 44 national schools with a student population of 7,936 received government aid. Only a few national schools—notably the Myoma National Boys' High School in Rangoon—developed into respected and prestigious institutions. The national education movement in Burma, as in India, failed to flourish, but it nonetheless "increased the popular awareness of the potential of local organization in the face of state opposition."[41]

Buddhist monks formally involved themselves in political activity in 1920 with the establishment of the General Council of Sangha Sammeggi (GCSS). Under the leadership of U Ottama, the GCSS founded a group of political monks known as *dhammakathika,* who played a key role in the formation of *wunthanu athin,*[42] or village-level "patriotic associations." *Wunthanu athin* advocated noncooperation with the British government in various forms, such as refusal to pay taxes, defiance of orders of the village headmen, boycott of foreign goods, and use of indigenous goods. By 1924, *wunthanu athin* were found in almost every village in Burma, reflecting not only the organizational ability of the political monks sent out by the GCSS to the villages but also, as Robert H. Taylor points out, "the peasants' perceived need to have a voice in the growing nationalist movement."[43] The success of the political monks was such that the government arrested and imprisoned them throughout the 1920s and turned one *dhammakathika,* U Wisara, into a martyr. Arrested repeatedly by the government for seditious activities, U Wisara undertook a hunger strike each time he was imprisoned, to protest the ill treatment of political prisoners. He, like other monks, had been disrobed, physically abused, and kept in solitary confinement. He died in jail in 1929, on the 166th day of a hunger strike.[44] In spite of the government's attempts to suppress the activities of political monks, *wunthanu athin* developed into influential political institutions in the countryside, as demonstrated by the central role they played in the Saya San Rebellion of 1930–1932. The largest peasant uprising in Burmese history, the Saya San Rebellion was aimed at the expulsion of the British. It began on the night of 22 December 1930 and set off a series of uprisings that came to be known collectively after the prime mover behind them, Saya San—described variously as an ex-*hpongyi* (ex-monk), a folk doctor, and sometimes a nationalist. The colonial administration failed to bring the rebellion under control until 1932, by which time the fatalities attributable to the rebellion totaled nearly 1,700.[45]

The Saya San Rebellion was followed by the second University Boycott. On 25 February 1936, between 600 and 800 day students and resident students from the two colleges began a strike during the last week of the term, when examinations were taking place. The immediate catalyst of the strike was the expulsion of U Nu, the president of the Students' Union, and the suspension of Aung San, the editor of the *Union Magazine;* both men were leaders of a growing leftist anticolonial student movement at the time and later became respectively the first democratically elected prime minister of Burma and a nationalist martyr.[46] Harkening back unmistakably to the 1920 boycott, the protesters denounced what they believed to be a continued non-Burmese control of higher education that financially and systematically prohibited Burmese students from gaining access to modern education.[47] In this second boycott, 36 female college students publicly protested on the slopes of the Shwedagon Pagoda hill in downtown Rangoon, where they camped with more than 450 male resident students from the two colleges who had left the university hostels.[48] Other female students likewise picketed the university premises in a nonviolent protest by lying down on every entrance to the examination halls and inviting bystanders to tread on them, a strategy that had rendered the university inoperative (figure 3.2).[49] As the peaceful picketing by the female boycotters suggests, the students in the second University Boycott, like those in the 1920 boycott, continued to emulate strategies of Indian nationalists, specifically Gandhi and his anticolonial resistance based on ahimsa (nonviolence).

At the same time, student activism in Burma was also inspired by Irish nationalist publications and leftist—mainly Fabian and Marxist-Leninist—literature from Britain. The most important political organization to emerge out of the efforts of student activists, the Dobama Asiayone (Our Burma Association, or Our Burmese Association), was modeled after the Sinn Féin Party in Ireland.[50] Though founded in 1930, the Dobama Asiayone rose to prominence only after it was taken over by the student leaders of the second University Boycott, such as Aung San. Known popularly as the Thakin Party, the members of the Dobama Asiayone titled themselves *thakin* (master)[51] as a symbol of the idea that the Burmese people, not the British, were the rightful masters of Burma and as an expression of their goal to transform Burma into a classless society of only masters. Dobama Asiayone served as the umbrella organization that linked the rapidly expanding number of nationalist youth

Figure 3.2 Female students who participated in the 1936 University Boycott. Photograph courtesy of Bo Bo Lansin.

groups in urban and rural Burma.[52] By 1938 the number of voluntary youth organizations—either student unions or branches of the Dobama Asiayone—reached 230, of which 160 were considered explicitly political by the government.[53] The activities of the Dobama Asiayone were not confined to student activism, as demonstrated by the vital role *thakin* played in 1938 in the 1300 Revolution, named after the Burmese calendar year.[54] The final act in the political upheavals in prewar Burma, the 1300 Revolution began with an oil-field workers' strike and culminated in a countrywide general strike of students, factory workers, office clerks, dockworkers, and bus drivers that was organized by the Dobama Asiayone. While the strike by the workers for the Burmah Oil Company in Chauk in January 1938 had not been planned per se, *thakin* had helped since 1937 in the setting up of workers' unions and had organized meetings and mass rallies at Yenangyaung and Chauk to urge the workers to protest low wages and other oppressive measures taken by the oil companies. *Thakin* had also gathered support among members of the police force, the army, and the civil service. By 18 January 1938 the Dobama Asiayone had coordinated a general strike by the entire workforce in Burma, and within a month there were 34 strikes involving an estimated 17,645 workers in foundries, dockyards, public transportation, civil service, and the oil, rice, cotton, match, rope, and rubber industries.[55]

Varied political strands and activities thus characterized the politics of the 1920s and 1930s. The YMBA, the GCBA, the GCSS, and student activists were all influenced by the ideas and strategies of the INC, though some were reformists while others were revolutionaries. At the same time, as Robert Taylor has argued, the noncooperative forms of behavior by *wunthanu athin* were based on "traditional patterns of avoidance of unjust or exorbitant demands by the state and its officials."[56] Still, *thakin* were swayed by the ideas of secular progress and Marxist revolution. Together, these disparate political developments—party politics, university boycotts, labor strikes, and nonviolent protests—signified the emergence of a new kind of *nain ngan yay* (politics),[57] involving predominantly, though not exclusively, middle-class individuals who fashioned new political vocabularies and widened the competition for power. It was against this background of changes in ideas and forms of *nain ngan yay* that the organized and politicized contemporary Burmese woman appeared.

In 1919 the first women's organization in Burma, the Burmese Women's Association (BWA), was formed.[58] An elite women's organization with approximately three hundred members—mostly educated women, wives of officials, and prosperous women entrepreneurs—the BWA was established to reinforce the activities of the GCBA as well as to protect and advance the intellectual and spiritual growth and well-being of fellow Burmese women. Also in 1919, Young Women's Buddhist Association (YWBA) and Wunthanu Konmaryi Athin (Patriotic Women's Association)[59] were formed as subsidiary branches of the YMBA and *wunthanu athin*.[60] The appearance of these early women's organizations, whose objectives were explicitly linked to the growing anticolonial struggle, generated no controversy even though, prior to the 1910s, *nain ngan yay* belonged to a fundamentally masculine domain.

Several factors account for the favorable reception of the early women's organizations in Burma. First, they were ancillary associations whose primary goal was to help Burmese men gain access to political power. Whereas the members of contemporary British, American, and European women's organizations entered the political sphere as suffragettes and campaigned against gender discrimination and patriarchy, members of Burmese women's associations were politically mobilized as patriots. As the next section shows, the BWA did develop into an autonomous women's organization with a strong legislative and feminist agenda, but no clear feminist cause emerged from either the YWBA or the Wunthanu Konmaryi Athin. Moreover, the BWA, the YWBA, and Wunthanu Konmaryi Athin all played supporting roles to the GCBA, as illustrated by their early activities. One of the prime targets of the GCBA in particular and the *wunthanu* movement as a whole was the

British government's economic policy, which undermined local industries and impoverished the Burmese common folk. The GCBA advocated the use of local goods, the boycott of imported products, and the picketing of stores that sold imported items. Accordingly, one of the first organized actions of the members of the women's associations was to condemn the use of imported goods and to wear blouses made of *pinni* (light brown, homespun cotton)[61] and *longyi* with local *yaw* designs originating in the western hill tracts of Burma. Members of the YWBA and Wunthanu Konmaryi Athin attended demonstrations organized by the GCBA, organized and gave patriotic speeches throughout the country, and supported antigovernment protests such as the university boycotts and the Saya San Rebellion by providing food, clothing, weapons, and other supplies. On numerous occasions they attempted to stop the police from detaining fellow male patriots for seditious activities, by lying down in front of vehicles transporting the arrested men—actions for which the women themselves were arrested. Women were supporters, not leaders, of the *wunthanu* movement.

The formulation of the *wunthanu* movement as a matter of protecting Buddhism also facilitated the politicization of women as well as monks. From the moment of their founding, the BWA and YWBA urged women in Burma to defend the *sāsana* and to abstain from marrying men of religious faiths other than Buddhism. The BWA in particular campaigned assiduously for legislative reforms that would ensure that a Burmese woman did not lose her Buddhist spousal rights as defined by customary law, especially those pertaining to divorce and inheritance, through her marriage to a non-Buddhist.[62] The members of the early women's organizations were thus protectors not only of religion but also of tradition. To signify their role as bearers and wearers of tradition, they wore scarves woven with a design of a peacock, the symbol of the last Burmese dynasty, on top of *pinni* and *yaw longyi*. The members of Wunthanu Konmaryi Athin furthermore cast themselves in the role of moral guardians in a nonviolent civil disobedience campaign that placed utmost importance on sacrifice, self-constraint, and discipline as the basis for its critique of unrestricted governmental power and all other technologies of coercion. For example, at a 1921 antigovernment demonstration organized by the GCBA to protest the imprisonment of U Ottama, YWBA members defied an order issued by the police that women must not attend the meeting. Consequently, the women were assaulted by the policemen and imprisoned, becoming the first female political prisoners in colonial Burma. Precisely because of the concurrent depiction of woman as mother and protector of her *amyo,* the figure of the politicized woman served as a poignant political icon. Her acts of transgression were more intense than those of her male counterpart; as she crossed the imagined boundary of the domestic into the public, she put at risk Burma's heritage and future. The self-sacrificial political woman was no doubt also influenced by Gandhi's idea that women were better suited than men for the explicitly ethical, ahimsa-based anticolonial struggle. Women were thus cast as fitting participants in an ethical approach to politics.[63]

The subsequent participation of women in politics continued along the same lines, in auxiliary roles and as keepers of religion, tradition, and morality. As noted above, female students took part in the University Boycott of 1936, though the leaders of the boycott were their male peers. Exactly three years later, female university students undertook a hunger strike in protest of the colonial government's imprisonment of their fellow college students who were actively organizing labor union protests throughout Burma. Also in the 1930s, female counterparts to the *thakin* appeared as women joined the Dobama Asiayone. Known as *thakinma*,[64] the women led the effort in 1938 to collect donations for striking Burmah Oil Company workers, about 100 to 150 of whom were women. Also among the workers who joined the 1300 Revolution were 200 women from Yaykyaw Ma Sein Nyunt's cheroot factory and approximately 1,000 more from rope and match factories in Rangoon.[65] That more of the women involved in political agitation came from the working class rather than the upper middle class was a noticeable difference, as was the direct endorsement of equality of the sexes by the Dobama Asiayone. In its six-page manifesto published in 1940, the Dobama Asiayone proclaimed the "emancipation of women from all economic and social shackles" and "equal opportunity for women in all walks of life" as among its goals.[66] *Thakin,* like other contemporary nationalists, recognized that any serious anticolonial struggle was more likely to succeed if women were actively involved, a recognition that must have contributed to their decision to espouse women's emancipation. As Marxist-Leninists, they also attributed all forms of oppression and exploitation to the same source—colonialists and capitalists—and supported, though more so in rhetoric than in practice, the liberation of all those oppressed.

The mounting *wunthanu* efforts in the 1920s pushed for the political inclusion of Burmese men as well as women, and the YMBA, the GCBA, and *thakin* all urged the participation of women in the anticolonial movement, albeit in supporting roles. Although all nationalist organizations encouraged the formation of women's associations, these associations were not autonomous; they were subsidiary branches of the main political organizations under male leadership. Biographies of the presidents of the BWA, the YWBA, and Wunthanu Konmaryi Athin delineate a clear pattern of gendered divisions of patriotic duties: leaders of women's associations all wore *pinni* and *yaw longyi,* collected donations, transferred their children from government or missionary schools to the "national schools," gave public speeches attacking colonialism, and protested through nonviolent means the detention of Burmese male political agitators.[67] While men led the *wunthanu* movement, women followers supported and embodied it. This characterization resonates even in the most progressive renditions of patriotic Burmese women in contemporary literary works. Here, the writings of the well-known leftist writer-cum-politician Thein Pe Myint (1914–1978) offer instructive examples.[68] Thein Pe Myint made his debut in the literary circle in 1933 with "Khin Myo Chit," a short story about a Muslim schoolteacher named Khin Htway and her lover, Htein Lwin, who happens to be a Buddhist and the leader of a nationalist youth activist organization. Khin Htway, convinced that Htein Lwin cannot wholeheartedly devote himself to the independence movement as long as they remain together, breaks off their relationship and adamantly refuses to see him, confining herself to her home. She is, however, overcome emotionally as well as physically by the grief she suffers as a result of the breakup. In her dying words, Khin Htway implores Htein Lwin not to follow in her footsteps if he loves her, and to carry through with his struggle to liberate Burma from colonial rule. For him to see Burma an independent and prosperous country, she says, would make the anguish she endured worthwhile.[69] Khin Htway never takes an active role in the nationalist movement, but she nevertheless dies a *myo chit may.*

Following the publication of "Khin Myo Chit," Thein Pe Myint wrote two books, *Min: ma sū rai koṅ:* (Heroine) and *Sapit mhok kyoṅ: sā:* (The student boycotter). Published in 1934 and 1938, respectively, they featured patriotic female college students as protagonists. *Heroine* follows the life of Khin Myint, a well-read and spirited young woman who, as a result of a moving patriotic speech she hears a fellow college student deliver, repudiates her acquiescent life and becomes a passionate anticolonial activist.[70] Htar Myint in *The Student Boycotter* is a more radical version of Khin Htway and Khin Myint and is presented as a pioneer among politically active Burmese women. She is among the few dozen female students who participate in the 1936 University Boycott and camp out on the Shwedagon. Unlike her female peers, she shows little interest in fashion or makeup and is concerned instead with the independence struggle. She is no less instrumental than her male peers to the student movement. She delivers speeches to disgruntled factory workers on strike in Yangon, actively raises funds for workers' and students' strikes, and distributes leaflets on the student boycott. An avid learner, she searches for a copy of George Bernard Shaw's *Intelligent Woman's Guide to Socialism and*

Capitalism (1928). She is, furthermore, a vocal advocate of women's equal rights and views socialism as the most effective solution to sexism. She rejects marriage, despite her deep affection for Nyo Tun, the main character of the novel, who, like Htar Myint, devotes himself selflessly to the student boycott movement. Htar Myint refuses to divulge her feelings for him, renouncing her personal fulfillment for the sake of her country. The avant-garde yet dutiful Htar Myint who puts her country above all else personifies all the qualities of the idealized revolutionary woman in prewar Burma.[71]

Yet, however revolutionary Hta Myint may seem, she remains a follower and supporter of the *wunthanu* movement. All the student nationalist leaders who appear in "Khin Myo Chit," *Heroine,* and *The Student Boycotter* are men. Insofar as men retained authority and leadership in the domain of *nain ngan yay,* the development of women's organizations and female protesters in antigovernment demonstrations did not represent a break from the past. What did change in the early twentieth century was the meaning and significance of the participation of women in *nain ngan yay.* The involvement of women in political struggles was not simply a matter of demonstrating collective and patriotic consciousness or of promoting the *wunthanu* movement. As shown in chapter 2, both men and women in Burma were well aware of the centrality of the "conditions of women" to the modernization project. They understood that complacent attitudes towards gender inequalities seriously undermined any claims to civilization and modernization. As noted above, women in Burma were urged not only to obtain an education but also to take on public roles as teachers, journalists, lawyers, doctors, and administrators because the visibility of women in public life signified the advancement of a society. Participation in politics was a logical and necessary step towards the modernization of women and Burmese society.

This is not to suggest that politically active women simply served to champion the male-led *wunthanu* movement or to present Burma to the world as a modern and progressive country. The connection between the women's movement and a predominantly male-dominated nationalist movement should not lead us to underestimate the feminist content of the women's movement, as Mrinalini Sinha has argued in the case of early women's organizations in colonial India.[72] The intricate relation between feminism and nationalism must be acknowledged in Burma as elsewhere, but we must also take seriously the feminist content of early Burmese women's organizations, in particular the BWA, a reformist group that used legal and institutional channels to bring about change. The BWA lobbied for legislative reforms that ensured spousal rights of Burmese Buddhist women, as mentioned above, as a result of which the colonial government drafted the Buddhist Marriage and

Divorce Bill in 1927; the BWA continued to push for the bill until it went into effect in 1939. The association was also an advocate of female education. It shared the conviction of reform-minded men and women in many contemporary societies in Asia that "women's rights" had less to do with suffrage and more to do with education.[73] In support of its educational mission the BWA had opened a library—one of the few in the country—for its members immediately upon its inception.[74] Aware of the reluctance of Burmese parents to send their adolescent daughters to school unaccompanied, the association advocated successfully for women-only sections in city trams for the transportation of female students to school. Members of the BWA chaperoned young women to and from school, accompanying them on the trams, in their endeavor to reassure the wary parents and encourage them to allow their daughters to pursue higher education.[75]

The 1927 demonstration for women's right to vote and to stand for parliamentary elections also reveals that the feminist struggle was no less pressing than the *wunthanu* movement for politically active Burmese women. On the morning of 3 February 1927, Independent Daw San and Daw Mya Sein (introduced in chapter 2) led a demonstration by more than a hundred women on the premises of the Rangoon Municipal Hall and the Legislative Council to show support for a legislative proposal—scheduled to be debated in the council the same morning—to abolish the law, known as the sex-disqualification clause, that prohibited women from running for parliamentary posts. The demonstrators gathered at the municipal hall and shouted out the following chant:

> Burmese women, don't be afraid
> Wait and see what will become of the act
> Banning us women from ministerial positions
> Burmese women, be watchful and active
> In Britain, women have attained seats in the parliament.[76]

This endeavor to engender legislative reforms might be attributed to similar initiatives of Burmese male politicians to establish a firm footing in electoral politics and to obtain greater Burmese representation in the Legislative Council. According to Daw Mya Sein, the women demonstrators were well aware that any attempt by Burmese women to be elected to the Legislative Council would be construed as nationalist. In fact, she does not deny that women who sought election "were bound to back the nationalists." As she points out, however, the demonstrators objected to the sex-disqualification clause primarily as feminists who were "amazed to discover that the British officials were not very keen about women getting into the Legislature."[77] In addition, and as their chant suggests, the protesters likened their demonstration for women's right to be elected in the Legislative Council to concurrent struggles in England and India by women trying to remove sex disqualification on voting and attaining posts in respective supreme legislative bodies. The demonstrators strove in unison with international feminist associations such as the International Alliance of Women for Suffrage and Equal Citizenship (IAW) and the British Commonwealth League, which urged the British government "on behalf of the women of the Empire" to grant to Burmese women the right to run in elections for the Legislative Council.[78]

The connection between these early women's movements in Burma and similarly urban, elite, and middle-class international feminist movements, while poorly documented, is not surprising, given that the 1920s and 1930s represented "the high tide of internationalism" for the women's movement.[79] In fact, Daw Mya Sein and Independent Daw San were both members of the National Council of Women in Burma (NCWB). Established in 1926, the NCWB was an affiliate of the National Council of Women (NCW) in India and a local branch of the International Council of Women (ICW)—"the first lasting multipurpose transnational women's organization," founded in 1888 and claiming to represent thirty-six million women by 1925.[80] And the 1927 demonstration at the Legislative Council was featured in *Stri Dharma* (Woman's duty), a well-known women-run journal in India that had emerged in the 1920s and 1930s as "an international feminist news medium targeted at Anglo-Indian, Indian, and British women readers."[81] Anticolonial theosophist-feminists such as Annie Besant, Margaret Cousins, and Dorothy Jinarajadasa—women who played central roles in the development of the first women's organizations in India—had visited Burma as early as the late nineteenth century.[82] Burmese delegates, including Daw San, attended the All Asian Women's Conference in 1931, which was planned and organized by prominent feminists in India such as Sarojini Naidu, Rameshwari Nehru, and Margaret Cousins.[83]

Recent scholarship on international feminism has revealed that there were various axes for international connections among women's movements, especially "South-South connections," that went beyond the more familiar "Western–non-Western axis."[84] Such "South-South connections" were integral to nationalist developments in Burma, as this chapter has shown. They appear to have been likewise instrumental in linking Burmese women to the network of international feminism and exposing them to the ideas and practices of "international solidarity" and "universal sisterhood." An Indian feminist who was particularly keen in establishing such connections was Rameshwari

Nehru (1886–1966), a member of the politically influential Nehru family and among the pioneers of Indian nationalist-feminists.[85] A writer, editor, and political activist, she was behind the publication of *Stri Darpan* (mentioned in chapter 2) and had established a local women's organization, the Prayag Mahila Samiti (Women's Assembly, Allahabad). She traveled to Burma in the 1910s to help establish women's associations in Rangoon and delivered three public speeches to women's organizations, at least one of which was an Indian organization. That Nehru "imagined a community of upper class Indian and Burmese women who, she hoped, would mobilize women to jointly struggle for women's political emancipation," as Shobna Nijhawan points out, is evident in her speeches: "Sisters, it is absolutely necessary that we recognize our state in the world, in our country and in society, before we can set out to progress. We need to understand women's social position."[86] Nehru, like theosophist-feminists such as Besant, Cousins, and Jinarajadasa, envisioned stretching the "imagined boundaries of sisterhood towards the Southeast Asian parts of the British empire."[87]

To be sure, the notion of "universal sisterhood," rooted in the white woman's—and the white feminist's—burden to save Indian women, was fraught with problems.[88] Many of the Euro-American women who dominated the international feminist organizations such as the IAW and the ICW supported the idea of imperialism, and their priority was the emancipation of women in the metropole, not the emancipation of women in the colonies.[89] Though the limited records left by the NCW in Burma do not permit scrutiny of the internal politics of the organization, some tensions and divisions, not least pertaining to the composition of the executive committee of mostly British women, must have existed among its mixed membership of British, Indian, Anglo-Indian, Anglo-Burmese, and Burmese women. For instance, the Burmese Women's National Council, formed in 1931, has been described by some scholars as a splinter organization established by Burmese members of the NCWB such as Daw Mya Sein and Independent Daw San who "had come to feel that the NCWB was too international in outlook, and did not adequately address the nationalist aspirations of its Burmese members."[90] At the same time, the interests of these women did converge on the subject of the "conditions of women." They worked together, for example, to document the lives of women and child laborers in Burma at a time when the existence of such groups went publicly unacknowledged—neither government documents nor press material from the period discussed women or child laborers in Burma—and well before *thakin* and other politicians turned their attention to the plight of the working class.[91] Also worth noting is that many women who were involved in international feminism, such as

Rameshwari Nehru and members of the Theosophical Society—a progressive anti-imperialist religious group established in India around the turn of the century—took explicitly anticolonial stands. The international feminism with which women in Burma became familiar was mediated through figures like Besant, Cousins, and Jinarajadasa, as well as Indian feminists such as Pandita Ramabai and Sarojini Naidu, who jointly shaped the early feminist movement in India.[92] Thus, on the one hand, women in Burma must have been sensitive to the challenges posed by their affiliation with international feminism, spotlighted by the highly publicized claim by Naidu that Indian women's movements were unlike feminist movements in the "West." On the other hand, they must have drawn inspiration from and emulated the Western and non-Western feminists in India who struggled to define feminism in their own terms.

That leaders of Burmese women's organizations might have modeled themselves after feminists elsewhere can be discerned from the striking similarities between the BWA and early women's organizations in India. One such resemblance is the preoccupation of the BWA with legal avenues for reform. In India the women's movement coalesced around the campaign for the passage of the Child Marriage Restraint Act, which raised the age of consent for girls and boys and penalized child marriages.[93] Gail Pearson has also noted that in their campaign for female franchise, prominent feminists in British India demanded a series of constitutional reforms through targeted lobbying that eventually resulted in "an administrative evolution"—that is, the passage of new laws.[94] The BWA likewise pressed the colonial administration to enact legislative reforms that would ensure the Buddhist rights of a Burmese woman upon marriage to a non-Buddhist. Similarly relying on legalistic channels, the BWA helped repatriate, at government expense, Burmese women who were cheroot rollers and had been taken to Penang and then abandoned there by their Burmese employers. As these examples illustrate, the members of the BWA sought to intervene on behalf of victimized women who were unable to help themselves. British imperialist-feminists and Indian nationalist-feminists too endeavored to rescue their powerless—and mostly non-Western—sisters who were depicted as ignorant and enslaved. They fought to emancipate women who, unlike themselves, suffered from lack of education as well as employment in prostitution, polygamy, and child marriage. For all such women, their role and authority as feminists rested on the suffering and then salvation of exploited and "helpless" women.[95]

Ultimately, what is important is not that Burmese women's activism was modeled after British imperial feminists or Indian nationalist-feminists, but that Burmese women perceived the need to mobilize against gender discrimination and took organized action. There is widespread belief even today that Burma has simply never needed feminism and that "no legislation in modern times has been considered necessary, as customary laws ensure for women a position suitable to present-day concepts of equality."[96] According to Daw Mya Sein, only under British colonial rule were Burmese women denied political equality and made to fight for political equality with men.[97] Contrary to such views, and despite the prevalent image of Burmese women that extolled their autonomy and influence, BWA and NCWB members worked to improve the lives of Burmese women. BWA and NCWB activists understood that there were international and nationalist dimensions to the issue of "women's conditions" and used them to advance their particular goals. While they explicitly connected their struggle to those of feminists elsewhere, they were not mindless imitators of Western feminists. Nor were they pawns of male-dominated *wunthanu* movements.

AS FEMINISTS AND NATIONALISTS

The patriotic Burmese woman who gained increasing visibility in the 1920s and 1930s represented the dual obligations that women of the *khit kala* bore to the private and the public spheres of home and nation. As wife-and-mother, she was charged with safeguarding her *amyo* and *taing pyi* through the careful cultivation of a respectable Burmese family. At the same time that the nationalist discourse aimed at domesticating women, it required them to contribute actively to public life. Seeking to have their country recognized as a member of the community of civilized nations, as measured in terms of the status of women, nationalists encouraged the entry of women into the public sphere. Many Burmese women in the 1920s and 1930s did in fact do so, particularly through their participation in organized politics: legislative and party politics, university boycotts, and labor strikes. They participated in antigovernment rallies alongside men, formed women's organizations, and fought for the right to run for legislative positions. As Khin Myo Chit explains, it was due to the growth of nationalist movements in the 1920s "that women were encouraged to come out from the narrow precincts of their homes and contribute towards the national cause."[98] *Wunthanu* movements in the early decades of the twentieth century took manifold shapes and forms, but they all provided an ideological framework for expressing grievances with and contesting the varied political and social asymmetries that characterized colonial Burmese society.

Yet the growing visibility of politicized and organized women must be understood as having been shaped by both *wunthanu* and feminist efforts to mobilize women. There is little evidence to suggest that the *wunthanu* movement sought to alter the position of women. Although "equal opportunity for women in all walks of life" was a self-proclaimed goal of the Dobama Asiayone, in practice, *thakin* were leaders, and *thakinma* were supporters and followers. Scholarship on third-world feminism has suggested that nationalism thwarted the feminist aspirations of women's movements in the third world and that although women's movements in many Asian countries achieved official political and legal equality, they were unable to alter women's subordination within the patriarchal structure of family and society.[99] The case of Burma reinforces this argument. Nevertheless, the task of spreading a feminist nationalist program was paramount to many patriotic women. Members of the early women's associations promoted liberal reforms such as female education and suffrage alongside political tactics that relegated women's activism to morally bound and symbolic critiques of colonialism. Under the nationalist banner, they pursued agendas that benefited Burmese women—especially their less privileged Burmese sisters—and confirmed their feminist identity. The modern politicized woman was a patriot and a feminist, jointly and simultaneously, and intervened in the sufferings of others as patriotic feminists. The patriotic and feminist Burmese woman who emerged was also a product of local and international movements to mobilize women. This chapter has shown that ideas and practices of *wunthanu* were formed not in isolation but rather in conjunction with similar developments elsewhere; so too were women's associations and movements. Burmese women, at the same time that they served as exemplars of emancipated women to be emulated by their sisters in other parts of the world, modeled themselves after feminists who reached out to women in Burma within the framework of global feminism. The modern patriot and feminist thought and acted locally and globally and expressed particularistic and cosmopolitan concerns about equality.

4

Modern Woman as Consumer

Fashion, Domesticity, and the Marketplace

The educated, patriotic, and politicized women were joined by another incarnation of the modern woman who was less of an icon of social and political reform than were the other archetypes: the consumerist woman. The epitome of the *khit hmi thu* as consumer was the fashionista. Referred to most often as *khit hsan thu* (fashionable woman) or *tet khit thami* (girl or daughter of the era of advancement), the trademark of the fashion-conscious *khit hmi thu* was her adoption of *khit hsan* clothing, footwear, accessories, and hairstyles—that is, fashion that *hsan* (resembles) the *khit kala* (era). A less eye-catching icon of consumerism was the housewife-and-mother, whom we have encountered in chapter 3 in a different guise. Unlike the *myo chit may* (patriotic women), however, the *ein shin ma* (housewife)[1] received her share of media attention as the subject of articles on housekeeping and as a fixture in advertisements, particularly for medicine and for child care and household products. On the surface, the two feminine figures seemed to occupy opposite ends of the spectrum of representations of women. The fashionista was fresh, youthful, and unattached. In contrast, the housewife-and-mother was an adult and a thoroughly domesticated woman. The former appeared on covers of magazines and journals, as leading characters in short stories, novels, and films, and in sensationalist discussions in the press on the merits and demerits of women's fashion. The latter was never in the spotlight and was relegated to women's sections of periodicals. These differences notwithstanding, the fashionista and the housewife-and-mother were both closely linked to new bodily practices and conspicuous consumerism. Modern apparel, cosmetics, hygiene and other health-related products, and household items allowed women to refine their own bodies as well as the health and appearance of their loved ones. Through commodity consumption, these women transformed themselves and improved everyday life at home. The fashionista was associated with frivolous consumption and "technologies of the self," whereas the housewife-and-mother was associated with wise consumption and dutiful care of her family.[2] Yet the continuum between the seemingly opposing figures is difficult to ignore: the housewife-and-mother may best be understood as an older and more mature version of the young fashionista who no longer consumed for self-indulgent reasons. Both women identified commodity consumption as a way of being in the *khit kala*. Both were enmeshed in the vigorous advertising campaigns mirrored by the period newspapers and periodicals.

The rise of consumer culture and the consumerist woman in colonial Burma has not been given much scholarly attention, although from the late 1920s and throughout the next two decades writers, intellectuals, and politicians expressed fascination with *khit hsan* clothing, hairstyles, aesthetics, and habits in the press. The spread of illustrated printed material—especially advertisements, the quintessential promoter of consumption—the advent of the cinema, and the ascent of celebrities as arbiters of style all ensured the proliferation of the fashionista and the housewife-and-mother alike. As this and subsequent chapters reveal, the sartorial and consumer choices of Burmese women were topics of intense—and at times violent—confrontations involving both men and women and both monastic and lay communities. In Burma, as elsewhere, fashion served as a powerful trope for modernity, and critics feverishly debated women's bodily practices as though the future of their *amyo* and *taing pyi* hinged on the clothing or hairdo of Burmese women.[3] As historical scholarship on dress, or what Emma Tarlo has termed "the problem of what to wear,"[4] has revealed, dress codes embody larger social and cultural ethics and norms and make powerful statements about identity. Clashes or changes in the fashioning of the body often signify larger social and cultural conflicts and transformations. For instance, studies on the subject of cloth and clothing by historians and anthropologists of South Asia have shown that early Indian nationalists polarized Western(ized) and Indian types of dress, especially *khadi* (homespun cotton cloth), as sartorial symbols of British colonial rule and the independence movement.[5] Although the field of Southeast Asian history has been slow to see dress as a part of political history, recent scholarship on Indonesia and the Philippines has shed light on the centrality of the semiotics of dress to various debates and political strategies on both sides of the colonial struggle in Southeast Asia.[6] The lack of scholarship on "the problem of what to wear" in colonial Burma is particularly surprising given the controversy generated by the "no footwear" campaign, which opposed the wearing of shoes by foreigners at pagodas—the source of one of the most publicized disputes between the British colonizers and the Burmese.[7] Women's dress was likewise central to the problem of what to wear in Burma, as the condemnation of imported clothing by Burmese women's associations demonstrates.

Interestingly, while the adoption of *pinni* and *yaw longyi* by members of women's associations has been described as an organized movement and thus something formulated, structured, serious, and substantial, the bodily and consumer practices of Burmese women in general have been represented as merely trendy and thus fleeting, unpredictable, immaterial, and superficial. To be sure, the choices made and represented by fashionable and consumerist Burmese women belonged in a realm of life considered private and mundane; they did not carry any intentional political connotation in the manner that the sartorial choices of the members of the women's associations did. Neither the *khit hsan thu,* nor the *tet khit thami,* nor the *ein shin ma* symbolized radical change or social reform in the same capacity as the educated or the nationalist and feminist *khit hmi thu.* In fact, the fashionable *khit hmi thu* was eventually castigated for choosing personal fulfillment over pressing collective social and political concerns. Yet, as Barbara Sato has persuasively argued, the personal and everyday qualities of the actions and decisions of these women "do not diminish the importance of the fledgling steps taken by women to map out new possibilities for self-fulfillment, or the role consumerism played as an agent of change."[8] Other scholars have similarly drawn attention to "the complex forms of subjectivity, agency, pleasure, and embodied experience" that are involved in modern consumer practices.[9]

In this chapter, serious consideration is given to the material conditions heretofore dismissed as "fashion," in order to examine what the bodily and consumer practices of the fashionable woman and the housewife-and-mother suggest about how Burmese women imagined themselves to be *khit hsan* or *khit hmi*—that is, to resemble (*hsan*) or to be within (*hmi*) the times. Changes in presentations of the self signify not only changes in wealth, religion, government, and availability of goods but also transitions in "understanding of the self" and social roles and expectations.[10] Take, for example, bobbed hair. It served to distinguish the "new woman," an icon of the increased presence and participation of women in the public sphere, from the "old woman." It was a symbol of the political, economic, and sexual emancipation of the modern female, "the vanguard of a changing age to battle old customs."[11] Yet if bobbed hair was synonymous with serious purpose or feminism in some contexts, in others it was the telltale sign of the ascendancy of a new commercial culture that threatened to remove women from radical politics and enmesh them, instead, in frivolous consumerism.[12] Chapter 6 investigates the varied and often contradictory meanings that critics of *khit hsan* fashion assigned to the bodily and consumer practices of *khit hmi thu*. In the present chapter, however, I look at the aspirations of Burmese women that the fashionista and the housewife-and-mother embodied. This chapter also complicates the image of the patriotic wife-and-mother presented in chapter 3. Even though the Burmese wife-and-mother was indeed tasked with the protection and nurturing of her *amyo* and *taing pyi,* such interpretation takes into consideration only her location within the ideological framework of nationalism. If we are to believe Furnivall's emphatic assertion that the colonial encounter exposed Burmese men and women to unrestrained market forces, then the Burmese housewife-and-mother needs to be understood through her relationship not only to the nation but also to the marketplace.

THE SELF-WILLED *KHIT HSAN THU*

Beginning at the turn of the twentieth century, changes in sartorial norms and practices became visible among upper-class Burmese men, who began to wear belts with their *longyi,* and shoes instead of slippers (figure 4.1). The most noticeable change in men's fashion, however, was in their hairstyles, which went from long hair usually coiled into a pile at the top of the head, customary among both men and women, to hair cropped short in a style referred to as *bo ke* (English cut)[13] (figure 4.2).[14] Women's fashion did not dictate new hairstyle trends but did witness a similar process of trimming. The white extensions of women's *longyi* were cut off altogether, and *longyi* in general were shortened so that they reached down roughly to the ankle instead of to the feet. The length of the *eingyi* (blouse),[15] likewise, decreased and revealed more of the waistline. The most revolutionary development in women's fashion, however, was the *eingyi pa,* an extremely sheer muslin blouse fastened at the neck and down one side with detachable ornate buttons.[16] The signature characteristic of the blouse, also known as *shinmyi eingyi* (chemise blouse)[17] when made of silk or satin, was its gossamer quality that exposed a corsetlike lace bodice called *zar bawli,*[18] which closely resembled European lingerie (figure 4.3).

It was the sheer blouse that distinguished the *khit hsan thu* and made it the most controversial aspect of *khit hsan* fashion. Yet there were many other components, some indispensable and some optional. Some women wore waist-length *kut eingyi* (coat blouse). The *khit hsan thu* coiled their hair into the customary chignon called *sadohn,*[19] but the *sadohn* was positioned higher in the 1920s and 1930s (figure 4.4). The most avant-garde among the *khit hsan thu* placed the *sadohn* on the back of the head instead of at the top and styled the front in the *amauk* (crest hair),[20] as worn by the woman on the left in figure 4.3. The "crest" referred to curly bangs piled high on the forehead, made possible by the nascent development of the perm. Other stylistic choices that were de rigueur for a *khit hsan thu* included high heels and a wristwatch, accoutrements of a woman living in a world that scorned the public display of bare feet or the ignorance of exact time, and cigarettes replaced cheroots. As figure 4.3 also suggests, appearing in public with a "naked" face—a face that had not been "painted" with such cosmetics as tinted powders, blush, and lipstick—had also become unbefitting for the *khit hsan thu.* By the 1930s

Figure 4.1 Changing men's fashion, from the cover of *Thuriya,* 2 January 1926.

an overwhelming majority of photos or illustrations of women in the press featured them with makeup on. The attitude of the *khit hsan thu* towards the function and the propriety of clothing (and underclothing), and her conception of feminine versus masculine hairstyle and skin tone, refashioned the contours of femininity and masculinity.

But whose idea of the feminine did the *khit hsan thu* personify? Such elements of *khit hsan* fashion as high heels, wristwatches, and cigarettes were definitely Western, and the English cut and the crest hair were certainly influenced by the Western association of long hair with women and short hair with men. Long hair had, however, been prized as an essential component of womanly beauty in Burma since well before the twentieth century, and permed

Figure 4.2 The *bo ke* (English haircut) as a new fashion, from the cover of the weekly *Youq shin lan hnyun*, 1934.

Figure 4.3 *Khit hsan* (fashionable) women. Photograph from author's personal collection.

Figure 4.4 Rangoon University students wearing the *mran so sadohn* (high chignon), circa 1935. Photograph courtesy of Bo Bo Lansin.

hair was still coiled into the *sadohn*. The identification of bodily curves and fair skin tone with women, furthermore, was in no way foreign to Burma. In fact, the modern fashionable women elsewhere in the world at this time—the flapper or the *garçonne* (tomboy)—had an androgynous look: with her svelte body, slender legs, and bobbed hair, she even elicited fears of the masculinization of women.[21] The modern woman in Burma, in contrast, continued to emphasize feminine sexual characteristics of bust and buttocks. While underclothing was itself a novel concept, women wore the lace bodice to reveal it, not to conceal it, and the combination of the sheer blouse and the lace bodice closely resembled the already existing custom of wearing an unfastened jacket over an exposed corsetlike undergarment. The use of the word *lady-thami* or *lady-kanya*[22] to refer to the fashionista is also instructive. The combination of the English word "lady" and the Burmese word *thami* or *kanya,* meaning a young maiden, indicates that the *khit hsan thu* was at once local and foreign, or somewhere in between. It is no wonder that a Burmese poem about the flimsy quality of the sheer blouse and the lace bodice expressed uncertainty in locating the cultural origin of the *khit hsan thu:*

> I'm dressed with a sweet face and in a sheer blouse
> as though foreign [*kala*], as though Burmese.
> Of course it tears my *zar bawli,*
> should you so pull my hand![23]

The twofold description of the sheer blouse and/or the woman wearing it as *kala* and as Burmese aptly captures the ambivalent relationship of *khit hsan* fashion to the new and to the traditional, to the foreign and to the local. On the one hand, "as though *kala,* as though Burmese" suggests that the sheer blouse and/or the female subject of the poem were simultaneously *kala* and Burmese and therefore assimilated. It implies, alternatively, that whether the woman/ blouse was *kala* or Burmese depended on which specific aspects of the woman/ blouse were highlighted and which were suppressed. On the other hand, "as though *kala,* as though Burmese" may be interpreted as "not quite *kala* and not quite Burmese," in which case the woman/blouse was neither *kala* nor Burmese—at least not completely. These various interpretations of the *khit hsan thu* and/or her clothing shared the assumption that she/it contained both foreign and local understandings of femininity and resisted fixed definitions.

By and large, *khit hsan* fashion referred to such intermixed and multivalent outfits and paralleled the development of hybrid clothes elsewhere in colonial Asia, where foreign and imported articles of clothing had become increasingly available and affordable. Tarlo points out that "the adoption of a mixture of European and Indian clothes was extremely popular and also relatively uncontroversial in Indian cities, where European garments were readily available for purchasing or for copying."[24] Similarly, in colonial Indonesia, "mixtures of 'old' and 'new' ways of dressing [were] not an exception but a normal way of life."[25] In Burma, too, imported items of clothing were no longer exotic goods, and hybrid clothes were not only popular but the standard for *khit hsan* fashion. A large portion of the Burmese population was buying machine-made clothing or textiles imported not only from British India but also from Japan. Because of its rice-based export economy, Burma imported a great many manufactured goods, a significant proportion of which were related to the apparel industry: cotton yarn, thread, textiles, and finished items of clothing. While the cheap labor provided by the rural female weavers (for whom weaving was a subsidiary, seasonal occupation) allowed the industry of coarse but inexpensive and strong cotton *longyi* and blankets to survive, the local cotton industry could not match its foreign competitors in producing a cheap and yet higher-quality product.[26]

The *khit hsan* outfit was not only a sartorial choice necessitated by changes in the clothing industry but also one that appealed to Burmese men and women. For one thing, the culturally mixed fashion of uncertain origin provided reassurance to those who endeavored to modernize their image without imitating their colonizers. The *khit hsan thu* could be stylish without altogether abandoning the familiar or adopting the foreign.[27] In addition, the development of the cinema as a popular avenue of entertainment and the emergence of celebrities as influential fashion leaders helped popularize the *khit hsan thu*. Within decades of the opening of the first movie theater in Burma in 1908, the industry had flourished with large companies—including the Madan Theatres, the pioneer of the cinema industry in British India—operating throughout the country. There were fifteen to seventeen movie houses in Rangoon alone and sixty-five in other urban areas by 1928. Initially, the industry appears to have been dominated by theaters that catered exclusively to Europeans, Eurasians, and the indigenous elite. Soon thereafter, people of various backgrounds patronized the cinema: Burmese, Europeans, Eurasians, Indians, and Chinese; the educated and the "semi-educated"; and the working and the middle to upper middle classes. The managing director of Globe Theatres, the leading cinema company at the time, noted that "the illiterate classes who would not have otherwise cultivated the cinema habit are now becoming almost regular patrons in increasing numbers." He also remarked that Burmese women were one of the most dependable customers of the theaters.[28] By the mid-1920s the most popular films were local Burmese productions, and incomes from cinemas dedicated to showing Burmese films were proportionately larger than from the cinemas featuring "up-to-date Western pictures" and imported Chinese and Indian films. In 1927, for example, seventy-four Burmese films were shown in Burma, along with thirty-six Chinese and forty-five Westerns films.[29]

Also by the mid-1920s the film industry began to produce a succession of Burmese movie stars, beginning with Khin Khin Nu, who launched into fame around 1921 with the hit film *Yatanabon* (East Lynne) and, for the first time, made acting on-screen a respectable and sought-after career for women.[30] By the 1930s, magazines such as *Youq shin lan hnyun* and *Journal gyaw* were releasing biographies of and interviews with the stars to build and maintain loyal fans. While the media followed the lives of all celebrities closely, documenting, as a matter of course, what they wore, one actress in particular emerged as the trendsetter of *khit hsan* fashion: Khin May Kyi. A Sino-Burmese actress, Khin May Kyi was a divorced mother of two when she entered the movie industry, unlike most Burmese actresses at the time, who began acting as teenagers. Nevertheless, in the film *BA Girl,* she was cast in the role of a glamorous *khit hsan* college student. Decked out in *shinmyi eingyi* and *longyi* that had colorful trimmings, a *"BA sadohn"* that was tucked away on the back of the head and wrapped in a ribbon, and dangling earrings instead of studs, her *khit hsan* outfit incorporated small but striking modifications.[31] According to Saw Moun Nyin, the entire country went into a frenzy over Khin May Kyi's looks and emulated her style.[32] Magazines from the period corroborate the enormous power that film stars wielded as arbiters of fashion. Khin May and Mya Galay, the authors of the "Women's Advancement" columns in *Toe tet yay,* frequently commented on what they described as the obsession of *ya khu khit meinma* (present-day women) with their (and *ya khu khit* men's) appearance. Mya Galay claimed that *ya khu khit* women followed every move of actors and actresses and idealized the attractive heroes and heroines in movies, adding that the cinema was partially to blame for what she perceived as *ya khu khit* women's preference for good-looking men over intelligent or patriotic ones.[33] According to Mya Galay, the reason looks took precedence over character was because *ya khu khit* women wanted to be like actresses and to be with men who were like actors.

Advertising also contributed to the fashioning and popularization of the *khit hsan thu.* As already mentioned, items of *khit hsan* fashion were primarily imported commodities. However, Burmese people were prominent in the retail dimension of textile, toiletry, and apparel businesses.[34] Indian firms and representatives of other foreign companies had no advertising personnel, marketing strategies, or showrooms and left the advertisement of their products entirely to local agents and retailers.[35] Local agents and retailers, in turn, relied on the press as their major advertising medium. An advertisement for Vel-Cord velvet coat-*eingyi* in a 1937 issue of *Thuriya,* for instance, declared that the latest, most fashionable, and best-looking coat-*eingyi* had just arrived in assorted colors for the *lady-kanya.* Similarly, the Chit Pan Nwe Beauty Lotion Company announced the arrival of Chit Pan Nwe powder—the powder of "beautiful face and charming body" that Burmese women "have been yearning for and will never tire of" (figure 4.5). These advertisements were, almost without exception, in Burmese or in both Burmese and English and were intended to shape the taste of Burmese consumers and to make the emerging hybrid *khit hsan* style palatable and thus marketable.

The most arresting aspect of the advertisements is the preponderance of cosmetic and hygiene products, and the equation of beauty with health. The preferred fashion of using makeup entailed a skin regime of cleansing with soap and moisturizing with lotion. The advertisement for Emisan's Powder—touted as "the powder for the *tet khit amyothami*"—insisted that the product would leave the user's skin feeling light and natural (figure 4.6), while the advertisement for Fanchon powder claimed to eliminate unpleasant body odor and result in smooth, velvety skin. Advertisements for numerous soaps, however, reminded women that makeup, if left unremoved, would damage healthy beautiful skin. The ad for Pears Soap asserted that for a woman to be beautiful, she must maintain soft, bright, and radiant skin; using soap, she must clean and remove dead skin and dirt from her skin on a regular basis (figure 4.7). Yet another soap, Telephone Brand, was marketed as a safe

Figure 4.5 Advertisement for Chit Pan Nwe powder, in *Youq shin lan hnyun,* 1934.

Figure 4.6 Advertisement for Emisan Powder, in *Thuriya,* 1937

Figure 4.7 Advertisement for Pears Soap, in *Kyi pwa yay magazine,* 1941. Reproduced by permission of U Po Than Joung, son of Kyi Pwa Yay U Hla aka Ludu U Hla, publisher and editor of *Kyi pwa yay magazine.*

and effective product of state-of-the-art experiments by Western and Japanese expert scientists, specially crafted with rare and beneficial herbal and fruit extracts to produce soft, beautiful, and healthy skin (figure 4.8).

No doubt to spur potential buyers to give the products a try, all the advertisements insinuated that men and women of the *khit kala*—not only in Burma but elsewhere, particularly in industrialized and rapidly modernizing parts of the world such as Japan and the West—cared (and should care) about fashion, hygiene, and health and that those not using the advertisers' products were falling behind the times. The advertisement shown in figure 4.8, for example, stressed that "everyone loves Telephone Brand Soap" and that it was already being used all over Burma. Fortunately for Burmese men and women, all that they needed to do to keep up with the *khit kala* and with

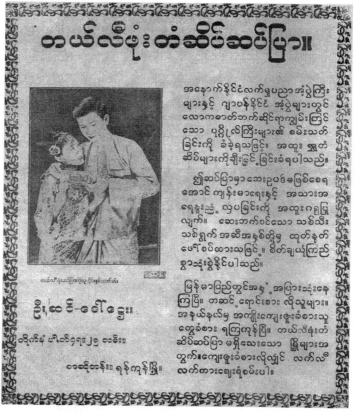

Figure 4.8 Advertisement for Telephone Brand Soap, in *Youq shin lan hnyun*, 1934.

khit hmi people the world over was to use the newest commodities. Everyone could achieve style, beauty, and refinement through the consumption of the latest bodily goods and practices. The advertisements thus promised instant self-transformation. They also implied that a *khit hmi thu* could better her lot in life through consumerism.

This understanding of consumerism was the subject of a 1936 short story by Thein Pe Myint entitled "Lady Khin." The story revolves around Thway, a street vendor who blames her unprepossessing appearance for the fact that, at twenty-six years of age, she is still single and unhappy. In an effort to impress the male students who frequent her stall, Thway bedecks herself in *shinmyi eingyi, zar bawli,* a wristwatch, and a pair of *lady-khin,* the high heels in vogue. While these fashionable items certainly serve to display her wealth, that is not Thway's concern. She wants above all else to alter her appearance to be more attractive to men. Looking at herself in the mirror after she caked her face with makeup, she says: "If I keep my face like this, who would be able to say that I'm ugly?"[36] Her attempt at self-transformation, however, is an utter failure. Her *lady-khin* cause her to fall down, and she finds herself disheveled, covered in dirt, and embarrassed in front of the young men she had intended to impress. Thein Pe Myint depicts Thway and her attempt to gain happiness through fashion and conspicuous consumption as pathetic. Thein Pe Myint's view must not have represented the opinion of the majority, even though social critics such as May Khin and Mya Galay also expressed concerns over the preoccupation of modern Burmese women with physical appearance. After all, if being fashionable was widely seen as pathetic, then there would not have been so many people preoccupied with fashion and beauty. What the criticisms of fashionable women suggest is precisely that there were large numbers of people in Burma who viewed fashionable women as something to be coveted and who associated fashion, beauty, and consumption with self-fulfillment.

Khit hsan fashion provoked public disquiet and accusations of a varied nature—of conspicuous consumption, frivolity, and decadence, sacrificing the "pure" and "authentic" self for an imitation of the foreign and thus the betrayal of one's *amyo*—throughout the 1920s, 1930s, and 1940s. For example, in October 1927 the editor of the newspaper *Bandoola* published a classical Burmese four-stanza verse blaming Burmese women who wore sheer blouses for inciting men to be excessively lustful.[37] His criticism of the sheer blouse stemmed from his opinion that it was titillating and provoked men to be immoral; women who wore such clothing were themselves depraved and the source of moral degeneracy. A boycott of the sheer blouse and a revival of indigenous clothing would thus restore the moral integrity of Burmese men and women. Accusations of the immodesty of the sheer blouse bear a striking resemblance to the criticisms by Sinhala Buddhist nationalists in colonial Ceylon of the short, sleeveless jackets made out of transparent cloth and worn with saris.[38] Between the late 1920s and early 1930s, many Sinhala newspapers and journals published a barrage of articles and poems critical of the short dresses and skirts and the tiny transparent jackets worn by anglicized, Christianized, bourgeois Sinhala women. These writings compared such apparel to the "garb of prostitutes and actresses, the epitome of moral degradation in such discourses."[39] Sinhala women who wore the sheer jacket were likened to "shameless white hussies" and, like women in Burma who wore the sheer blouse, were accused of simultaneously provoking and satiating the lecherous glances of young men.[40] Likewise, the Sinhala critics of the sheer blouse advocated a "respectable," alternative outfit—comprising a long and preferably white sari and a jacket that covered the shoulders, midriff, back, and legs—as more befitting their Sinhalese heritage.[41]

Whereas in colonial Ceylon such criticisms were effective in convincing Sinhalese women to reject European styles and to adopt the "respectable alternative" instead, the *pinni* blouse and the *yaw longyi* failed to attract a popular following in Burma. Shwe Khaing Thar notes that the *pinni* blouse and the *yaw longyi* were passé by the late 1910s and that, as an old Burmese adage points out, they were considered to be good only for "profuse perspiration."[42] Even Mya Galay, who, as we have seen, was an indefatigable pundit of the duties of women towards the nation, declared that wearing the *pinni* blouse and the *yaw longyi* hardly counted as patriotism.[43] The predominant response to the expressions of disdain for the bodily and consumer practices of the *khit hsan thu* was simply to keep being fashionable, as depicted in a 1927 cartoon entitled "Won't Say It Again"[44] (figure 4.9). The husband in the cartoon realizes the futility of his efforts to curb his wife's fixation with her appearance and concedes that the more he complains, the more extravagant her style gets. He finally gives up and tells her to go ahead and follow her *chanda* (desire). The *khit hsan thu* had become firmly established as a model for women to emulate.

THE *EIN SHIN MA*: THE SCIENTIFIC AND HYGIENIC HOUSEWIFE AND MOTHER

As the cartoon "Won't Say It Again" (figure 4.9) suggests, not only young single women but also married women in Burma were aficionados of *khit hsan* fashion. In fact, hygiene and cosmetic products were often marketed in such a way that the intended consumers were only vaguely defined; the *khit hmi thu* could have been a teenager or a woman in her thirties. Furthermore, advertisements tended to portray housewives as attractive women who, even as wives and mothers, remained fashion conscious. At the same time, the primary concern of the housewife-and-mother was not her looks, as indicated by the content of advertisements that specifically targeted mothers and wives among the readership. These included advertisements for other "feminine" products such as fertility drugs or contraceptives for women; baby products such as milk powder and baby food, as well as children's clothing; furniture and household goods; and hygienic products and medicine. The distinctly twentieth-century commodification of a woman's role as wife and mother is unmistakable in these advertisements, which only rarely featured fathers, husbands, or men at all, for that matter. A *khit hmi* mother was an enterprising consumer, "under great pressure to acquire all the commodities necessary for the satisfactory performance of motherhood."[45]

The captions in the advertisements for baby products unfailingly suggested that "everyone knows" that mothers should bottle-feed, not breastfeed, their infants and should nourish their children with condensed milk and malted biscuits; even in Burma's tropical climate, they should clothe their children top to bottom, and precisely because of the hot climate, they should use refrigerators to keep groceries fresh and safe. If Western medicine had endowed mothers with the tools to alleviate their children's everyday illnesses such as coughing and constipation more swiftly than ever before, soaps had

Figure 4.9 "Nok thap ma pro to. bhū:" (Won't say it again), a cartoon depicting modern women's *chanda* (desire) to be fashionable, in *Deedok*, 26 February 1927. Reproduced by permission of Ma Khin Myint Cho, granddaughter of Deedok U Ba Cho.

equipped mothers to prevent their children from getting sick. A 1937 advertisement for Angier's Emulsion, for example, claimed that the emulsion was used widely in hospitals and that doctors recommended its use (figure 4.10). Modern medical technology had also given hope to women who had hitherto failed to conceive, as a 1929 advertisement for the Universal Female Pills—made in Germany, according to the advertisement—suggested (figure 4.11). Although the census report of 1931 states that "there is no evidence of the practice of western methods of birth control among the indigenous races,"[46] advertisements for contraceptive products abounded, informing women that they could control when and how many children they had and could avoid thus excessively large families.[47] Advertisements for the treatment of sexually transmitted diseases and impotence, as well as lotions and tonics to enhance the pleasures of lovemaking, usually accompanied the advertisements for

Figure 4.10 Advertisement for Angier's Emulsion, in *Thuriya,* 1937.

contraceptive products. G. Impoten Pills, for instance, guaranteed to restore virility to that of a younger man, and Wondio avowed to instantaneously give women the sexual drive of a pure virgin and make them inseparable from their husbands.[48] Akin to the "wise mother" of Meiji Japan who performed her domestic duties, child rearing in particular, "in accordance with the latest scientific knowledge and practice,"[49] the *khit hmi* housewife-and-mother modernized the home as a scientific consumer and acquired the technologies and commodities necessary for the upkeep of a sanitary home, a healthy family, and conjugal bliss.

The dominance of hygiene and health-related products as markers of the *tet khit* and the *khit thit,* seen in the advertisements for soaps, is striking in these advertisements as well. In all likelihood, the designation of "hygiene" as a required subject for female students in public and Anglo-vernacular schools contributed to the association of hygiene and medicine with progress and modernity. The implementation of hygiene as a compulsory subject for girls reflected concerns about the medicalization and sanitization of pregnancy, childbirth, and child rearing that emerged around the turn of the century as colonial states initiated the effort to bring "reproduction under state control."[50] Good health was an imperative of the empire, and ill health a problem.[51] These two aspects of the imperial concern about health became apparent in Burma through discussions surrounding the inadequacy of indigenous birthing and nurturing practices and the incompetence of native mothers. The Society for the Prevention of Infant Mortality in Mandalay reported in 1913 that there were nine towns in Burma where the infant mortality rate

Figure 4.11 Advertisement for Universal Female Pills, in *Dagon,* 1929. Reproduced by permission of the family of U Tin Nwe (of A.1 Film).

exceeded 40 percent and that of the approximately five thousand children born every year in Mandalay, about two thousand died before the age of twelve months, and another one thousand before the age of ten.[52] The infant mortality rate remained "excessive" and "deplorable" in 1921, according to the annual report by the Public Health Administration of Burma.[53] European as well as native administrators were dismayed by the high incidence of infant mortality in the country and directly linked the improvement of health to the improvement of women's education. Writing in 1914, a Burmese official in the Judicial Service proclaimed that "it would be better for the [Burmese] race" if the Burmese mother were educated and "taught to take better care of her children; for then we have some hope that there will be a material reduction in the death rate of infants in Burma, which at present is too horrible to contemplate."[54] Similarly, in the Public Health Administration's 1921 report, the lieutenant governor of Burma emphasized the dire need for serious efforts to instruct not just midwives but women more generally on sanitary childbearing and child-rearing methods.[55] In the attempt to intervene in the health of the Burmese subjects, female students were given courses in domestic science and hygiene, and handbooks were published that contained instructions on first aid for mothers during childbirth and on the rearing of infants from the time of birth. Such handbooks asked Burmese women to read them "with the country's welfare at heart, and in view of the appalling loss of life," and "to at least make a study of European methods of treating confinement cases and of rearing infants from birth, and give them a fair trial in their homes and surroundings."[56] Missionaries, doctors, and colonial officers all actively sought to instruct, discipline, and reshape maternity to be scientific and hygienic.

The association of housewifery and motherhood with medicine and instruments of sanitation was at least in part a result of the modern education system, which aimed to inculcate cosmopolitan notions of scientific progress. Another reason for the appeal of medicine and hygienic products was that they made scientific progress readily available. Advertisements for medicine and hygienic goods guaranteed that their products were recommended by doctors and that their effectiveness and safety had been proven by the latest scientific tests. Most importantly, they came with comprehensive instructions for usage (or so the advertisements stated) so that even women who had never taken a course in hygiene or received formal education could achieve scientific progress through the consumption of "scientifically produced" commodities. Like the advertisements for cosmetics, these alluded to instant benefit. They also conjured up the possibility of immediate attainment of social mobility and status, as an advertisement for Lever Brothers' Sunlight Soap suggested (figure 4.12). The ad shows a group of men speaking scornfully about a father and a son:

"Look at the father and son; they are totally stained and dirty. It's disgusting."
Upon returning home, the son tells his mother that people avoid him and his
father and asks why he is so filthy. The parents are both at a loss: they agree
that the whole family looks unclean, even though the mother spends all of her
time cleaning. The husband, acknowledging that she works hard, thinks the
solution is to hire a domestic helper, but they cannot afford to do so. As luck
would have it, a friend advises the wife against getting a helper and instructs
her to start using Sunlight Soap to bathe her children as well as to wash their
clothes and to clean her house. Within days of following her friend's advice,
the home and the family have become immaculate, and the grateful husband
comes home with the gift of a ring for his wife. The consumption of Sunlight
Soap has made the family and their home cleaner, healthier, happier, and more
respectable. Even an average family that could not afford a maid could therefore gain refinement and respectability through cleanliness.

Finally, as the various advertisements discussed in this chapter illustrate,
consumption promised self-actualization and swift gratification. The simple

Figure 4.12 Advertisement for Lever Brothers' Sunlight Soap, in *Journal gyaw*, 1941.
Reproduced by permission of U Moe Hein, son of Journal Gyaw U Chit Maung and Journal
Gyaw Ma Ma Lay.

act of buying and using a particular brand of soap enabled a woman to be an exemplary wife and mother and to transform a scorned and miserable family into a radiant and joyful one. The ring the *ein shin ma* received as her reward likewise symbolized the immediate gratification Sunlight Soap delivered. Other advertisements similarly linked consumption to self-fulfillment and pleasure. Contraceptive products, for example, were not only meant to control family size; they were also explicitly marketed for women "who want a break from the hardship of pregnancy and child rearing" and "who do not want to be disfigured by childbirth and the exhausting demands of motherhood."[57] Even *ein shin ma* and mothers deserved to look and feel their best. Contraceptives must have also allowed Burmese women to explore their sexuality in new ways, as did medication and lotions advertised specifically as being formulated for enhancing sexual intercourse. Consumption of *khit hmi* commodities was both practical and pleasurable. The smiling faces of the men, women, and children in the advertisements evinced the triangulation of consumption, modernity, and fulfillment.

The advertisements that focused on women's domestic life thus projected an idealized conceptualization of the *ein shin ma* and her *khit hmi* home and family. They fashioned an elaborate image of a *khit hmi* private sphere for the public to consume and covet, highlighting in the process the necessary relationship between home and marketplace. The housewife-and-mother depended on the marketplace to provide the scientifically produced commodities from the West and, to a lesser degree, Japan, without which she would be unable to ensure the health and happiness of her family. The representation of the *khit hmi ein shin ma* and her home was deeply informed by Eurocentric notions of scientific progress, and Western hygienic and health-related products served as dominant markers of modernity and development. Yet, like *khit hsan* fashion, the *khit hmi* home in Burma was thoroughly multicultural, not an imitation of the Western home. Penny Edwards has shown that many colonial residents of Burma lived in homes with "cross-cultural interior" and that, "far from rejecting all manifestations of indigenous milieu, fashionable colonial homes . . . embraced a plethora of fabrics and styles, domesticating the indigenous spaces and cultures of the colony."[58] Likewise, the *khit hmi* home was imagined as Burmese at the same time. Advertisements for Western commodities were printed alongside articles that, as discussed in chapter 3, elaborated on the duties of a wife-and-mother to create homes suitable for the Burmese *amyo* and *taing pyi*. Accordingly, the *khit hmi* wife-and-mother had to know how to prepare Burmese dishes and what Burmese stories to tell her children; she needed to have a firm foundation in Buddhist instruction, not just modern education.

Articles that gave advice on how to live harmoniously with in-laws also demonstrate that the modern Burmese family remained an extended one that valued Buddhist ethics of deference to parents. While mutual respect between husband and wife was portrayed as an important Burmese value, the husband and father was the uncontested head of the household. This by no means meant that a husband could treat his wife as he pleased. Khin Myint, whose description of Burmese women as keepers of the family purse was noted in chapter 2, also pointed out that though Burmese men "delight in playing the part of 'Lord and Master,'" the Burmese "wife beater" was a rarity.[59] A letter to the editor by a woman named Nyi Nyi in a 1938 issue of *Ngan hta lawka* resonated with Khin Myint's view of domestic violence. In the letter, Nyi Nyi expresses her disapproval of a decision made by a judicial commissioner of Lower Burma. The commissioner had handed down a sentence of fifteen days of "rigorous imprisonment" to a husband who struck his wife on the head with an ironwood club, cutting open her scalp. The woman's "offense" was that she had failed to have food ready for her husband upon his return home. Responding to the magistrate's remark that "the chastisement of wives should be effected by means of a small cane or bamboo, but in the present instance the accused has transgressed the ordinary system of chastisement," Nyi Nyi stated: "In my opinion husbands have no right whatever to chastise their wives, *even with small canes or bamboos,* and the magistrate must be careful to disabuse his *own* mind of this most erroneous notion of a husband's privileges."[60] According to Nyi Nyi, Burmese families did not tolerate domestic violence. Also "un-Burmese"—according to "Ein shin ma," the author of the "Women's Guide" column in *Youq shin lan hnyun*—was gardening. In a 1934 issue, she waxed lyrical about the art of gardening but acknowledged that Burmese housewives simply had no interest in potting plants or growing flowers.[61]

What is unmistakable in the examples cited here is an articulation of a modern Burmese domesticity. The *khit hmi* Burmese home benefited from scientific and technological advancements such as soap, medicine, and the refrigerator, but it was governed by Burmese Buddhist ethics and codes of conduct. The housewife-and-mother, therefore, modernized her home without necessarily Westernizing it. She, like the young women in *yuwadi* columns who combined in themselves traditional scholarly knowledge and knowledge gained through formal education and printed media, was to (re)learn and (re)appropriate foreign and local—and *khit hmi* and traditional—activities, behaviors, values, and commodities. The message embodied by the housewife-and-mother was that Burmese customary home and family relations could live on in updated forms.

THE ALLURE OF CONSUMPTION

As the fashionista and the housewife-and-mother have illustrated, the allure of consumerism was manifold. The consumption of fashion, cosmetics, medicine, and other commodities examined in this chapter not only functioned as the symbol of *khit hsan* and *khit hmi* women but also held the promise of instantaneous self-transformation, self-actualization, and (self-)gratification. It made progress and modernity easily available to everyone. Anyone— irrespective of her race, class, religion, or educational background—could be *khit hsan* and *khit hmi* and achieve social status through consumption. *Khit hsan* habits and practices served to distinguish the *khit hsan thu* as someone who pursued her ambitions through self-advancement rather than birth. In a sense, then, what was on sale was social mobility and liberation; a woman could escape or at least better her lot through the right kind of consumer practices. The fashionable and consumerist *khit hmi thu,* like the educated *khit hmi thu,* symbolized self-improvement. The consumer practices of the fashionista and the housewife-and-mother were also appealing because they allowed women to be at once *khit hmi* and Burmese. Scientific and technologically savvy mothers still managed to protect and propagate perceived Burmese traditions and Buddhist morality. Wise, economical, and dutiful consumption was perfectly legitimate and necessary for the homemaker, who was tasked with ensuring a hygienic and healthy home for the sake of her *amyo* and *taing pyi.* Although the housewife-and-mother, like the fashionista, was concerned with the care of the self (and not only of her home and family), she epitomized the fusion of utility and enjoyment, duty and pleasure.

In reality, however, the iconic modern consumerist Burmese woman was largely a fantasy. Although a 1934 advertisement proclaimed that "a wedding in the town or the countryside is not complete without merchandise from the Bombay Burma Furniture Mart" (figure 4.13), the people in the countryside who were suffering from the Great Depression of the 1930s could only have dreamed of purchasing such items. Most women and men did not possess the means to acquire all that had been marketed as requisite to a *khit hsan thu* or a *khit hmi* home. In addition, and as the next chapter shows, the *khit hsan thu* did not escape accusations of self-indulgence or of betrayal of her traditions, *amyo,* and *taing pyi.* Being both *khit hmi* and Burmese was not as effortless or uncomplicated as the advertisements suggested. As might be expected, advertisements do not tell us how ordinary men and women lived their everyday lives.

Yet even if Burmese women (or men) could not afford the entire repertoire of commodities required of the *khit hmi thu,* they could partake of consumer culture through magazines, the cinema, and the occasional or token purchase of perfume, clothes, high heels, and cosmetic products. That advertisements did not reflect the realities of everyday life does not mean that consumer culture was irrelevant to ordinary Burmese women. On the contrary, the defiance of the *khit hsan thu* in the face of public accusations of immodesty and self-indulgence attests to the relevance of consumerism to Burmese women and reveals the impact the marketplace had on their taste, sensibilities, and expectations and their decisions about how to care for themselves and their loved ones. In colonial Burma, as elsewhere, what it meant to be modern was shaped by the attendant culture of consumer capitalism. Global commodity flows and discourses concerning beauty and aesthetics, homemaking, and child rearing helped determine the contours of the Burmese fashionista and housewife-and-mother and how Burmese women envisioned themselves to be *khit hmi.*

Figure 4.13 Advertisement for the Bombay Burma Furniture Mart, in *Youq shin lan hnyun,* 1934.

5

Mixing Religion and Race

*Intermarriage, Miscegenation, and the
Wives and Mistresses of Foreign Men*

Once increasing numbers of young unmarried British males
began to arrive in India from the start of the seventeenth century
a mixed race population of British and Indian descent, small at
first but later to grow rapidly, was inevitable.

—*C. J. Hawes, Poor Relations: The Making of a Eurasian
Community in British India, 1773–1833* (1996)

The rapid growth in *kabya* (mixed) population was an inevitable outcome of colonization.[1] In Burma, relationships between foreign men and native
women persisted, and the *kabya* population continued to expand throughout
the first few decades of the twentieth century in spite of the British imperial
policies of racial segregation.[2] Yet the same period also witnessed mounting disdain towards intermarriage and miscegenation among the European
expatriate community in the country and among the local population. As the
British administration noted in its report on the 1938 Burma Riots, "one of
the major sources of anxiety in the minds of a great number of [Burmese] was
the question of the marriage of their womenfolk with foreigners in general
and with Indians in particular."[3] The following year, the recently established
left-wing, nationalist *Kyi pwa yay* press published what is probably the most
extensive and elaborate Burmese-language diatribe against intermarriage and
miscegenation. The 350-page book, entitled *Kabrā: prassanā* (The problem of
mixed people) and written by U Pu Galay, claimed that marriages between

Burmese women and Indian men, and the *kabya* children of such unions, threatened a spiraling destruction of Burmese race, culture, and society.[4] In a country described by early European travelers and by historians as tolerant and even supportive of mixed marriages, U Pu Galay's *Kabrā: prassanā* may seem like an aberration. Yet his polemic against intermarriage and miscegenation was representative of the sociocultural milieu of the 1920s and 1930s in Burma, when intimate relations between Burmese women and "foreign"— i.e., non-Buddhist, non-Burmese—men, and not only "Indian" men, became a topic of heated public discussion and, often, denunciation.

At the center of the discussion were two distinct types of unions: Anglo-Burmese (European man–Burmese woman) and Indo-Burmese (*kala* man–Burmese woman). Burmese women in the former category were referred to as *bo gadaw.*[5] The word *bo* signified the military ranking of a general in precolonial times. The word *gadaw* literally means "wife" but is associated only with a wife of an official or a dignitary; the term for the wife of a high-ranking government official, for example, is *min gadaw. Bo gadaw* thus alludes to the envied status of a military general's wife. As already mentioned, *bo* came to mean "European" during the colonial period, and while *bo gadaw* could refer simply to the wife of a European man, it also took on a pejorative connotation: "a European's mistress."[6] The double entendre of the term *bo gadaw* embodied the nuances of a Burmese woman's relationship with a European man, which was at once prestigious and undignified: her source of prestige was simultaneously the source of her ill repute. No special term was coined to refer to Burmese women who married *kala,* or Indian, men—the term used for this group of women literally meant "Burmese women who married *kala* people"[7]—although they were at times called *kala ma* (*kala* female).[8] That the equivalent of the term *bo gadaw*— *kala gadaw*—never developed is significant. Even during the brief Japanese occupation of Burma during the Second World War, Burmese people coined the term *Japan gadaw* to refer to Burmese women who married Japanese men. This disparity probably resulted from the fact that unlike the *bo gadaw,* who was depicted as marrying up the social and class hierarchy, Burmese wives of *kala* men were portrayed as marrying down. In addition, while both types of women married foreign men and had *kabya* children and both forms of intimacy were discussed as recent developments and problems, the latter were more consistently identified with the "*kabya* problem."

Why were the wives, mistresses, and *kabya* children of foreign men viewed as problems? In what follows, I consider multiple factors that explain shifting attitudes towards intermarriage in colonial Burma. The intensifying nationalist appeal for women—as keepers of tradition—to safeguard the purity of Burmese (that is to say, Burmese Buddhist) culture, the codification of religion and race, the entrenchment of cultural racism, and the growing indebtedness and poverty resulting from the Depression of the 1930s all led to the stigmatization of mixed unions. The discourse on intermarriage and miscegenation also stemmed from the gendered nature of colonial rule. The unprecedented influx of single male immigrants from England and British India, and the displacement of Burmese men from political and socioeconomic positions of power and authority, significantly enhanced the opportunities for, as well as the allure of, intermarriage. The point is not simply that intermarriage was an avenue of social mobility unavailable to Burmese men, but rather that Burmese men were often unable to offer socioeconomic advancement to Burmese women through marriage.

My use of the term "Indo-Burmese marriage" instead of "Burmese-Muslim marriage," the term the British administration used, to refer to a marriage between a Burmese woman and an Indian man requires a brief explanation. The description "Burmese-Muslim marriage" misleadingly suggests that only unions between a Burmese woman and a *mvat ca lan* (Muslim) man had been the target of public castigation, when in fact criticisms were directed at a Burmese woman's marriage to a *kala* (Indian) man rather than a *mvat ca lan* or a *kala mvat ca lan* (Indian Muslim) man per se. For instance, during the 1938 Burma Riots, the rioters shouted "assault Indians!" and "Burmese women who marry Indians! Are husbands scarce in Burma?"[9] They attacked not only Muslim Indians but Hindu Indians as well, leaving 139 Muslims and 25 Hindus dead and 512 Muslims and 199 Hindus injured.[10] According to the government reports on the riot, even Roman Catholic Indians did not escape the violence.[11] Many critics of the Indo-Burmese marriage were indeed more critical of the "Burmese-Muslim marriage" than the "Burmese-Hindu marriage" but, as U Pu Galay did, perceived both to be constitutive of the "*kabrā: prassanā.*" Similarly, critics only rarely singled out *zerbadee,* the progeny of a Muslim father and a Burmese Buddhist mother, and railed against *kala kabya* people.[12] While it may be correct, as the British administration claimed, that the "Burmese-Hindu marriage" was less prevalent than "Burmese-Muslim marriage," the term "Burmese-Muslim" focuses too narrowly on the interfaith aspect of the marriage, whereas the term "Indo-Burmese" allows for a consideration of the interclass and interracial dimensions.[13]

THE PROBLEM OF WHOM TO MARRY: OFFICIAL DISCOURSE ON "TEMPORARY UNIONS"

Although no scholarship exists on relations between Burmese women and European men and historical studies of Burma make practically no mention of such relations, records show that European men and Burmese women frequently entered into a range of intimate relations. A search through less than

10 percent of the biographical information available in the India Office Records shows that at least 419 European/Eurasian–Burmese marriages were formalized between 1880 and 1947.[14] Of these, only six occurred between a Burmese man and a European or Eurasian woman. All others represented a registered marriage between a European or Eurasian man and a Burmese woman or a *kabya* woman with some Burmese ancestry.[15] We can safely assume that a comprehensive examination of records pertaining to marriage in colonial Burma would reveal much higher numbers for the period than these. More common were relations described variously as illicit connections, irregular unions, and prostitution. In confidential circulars from the turn of the century, colonial officials readily admitted that "there has long been a considerable number of cases in which European officers in Burma have entered into temporary connections with Burmese women."[16] Charles Crosthwaite, the aforementioned chief commissioner of Burma, claimed that "the temporary marriage" between a British officer and a Burmese woman was almost universal at one point and remained common.[17] Colonial officials also acknowledged that marriages between European officials and Burmese women were on the rise. In 1885 there was only one officer, Major Parrott, with a Burmese wife; the number had increased to thirteen by 1903, and many more officers were contemplating marriage to Burmese women.[18] John Furnivall himself married in 1906 a Burmese woman, Margret Ma Nyun Toungoo, and the couple had two daughters.[19]

Crosthwaite was of the opinion that the government had no right to dictate to its officers whom to marry, and he did not "see why it should be assumed that every Burmese woman must be dishonest and intriguing." As he pointed out, "Major Parrot who was married to a Burmese lady was an excellent officer and I never heard anything against his wife."[20] Crosthwaite appears to have been in the minority, however, and many colonial officials agreed that marriages involving British civil servants and Burmese women needed to be discouraged, "both on account of their prejudicial effect on the administration, and on account of the unhappiness and social ruin which they not infrequently bring on the officers who contract them."[21] A 1903 memorandum regarding marriages between European officers and Burmese women explained the harmfulness of such marriage as follows:

> A Burmese wife of an English official is usually the centre of intrigue, or is so regarded by the people. She is credited with influence in official matters and whether she has this influence or not people are quite willing to make it worth her while to pretend to it. The freedom of social intercourse which Burmese women enjoy and their usual habit (among their own people) of taking an active part in their husband's affairs tend to accentuate the evil.[22]

Many among the colonial administration may have believed that as long as a Burmese woman was not given official recognition as a wife, she would not or could not cause any "intrigue." Or the tendency of Burmese women to meddle in "their husband's affairs" may have served as a pretext to discourage Anglo-Burmese marriages for other reasons. Studies of interventions by the colonial government in "matters of intimacy"—such as sex, sentiment, domestic arrangements, and child rearing—have uncovered varied political, social, and fiscal motivations behind the promotion of cohabitation over marriage among its personnel. Marriage entailed additional costs for the colonial state: at the very least, higher salaries for married soldiers and officials, expenses for the passage of their wives and children, and provision of suitable housing for married couples and education for the children. Cohabitation reduced these costs, for female companions functioned as servants who conveniently also provided cheap and relatively safe sexual services for imperial personnel; unlike prostitutes, concubines kept incidences of venereal disease in check. Company authorities and government and plantation administrators also claimed that "white prestige" would be jeopardized if European men were made to finance the bourgeois lifestyles expected of European wives and, consequently, impoverish themselves. Cohabitation was instrumental in delineating and maintaining—rather than blurring—the boundary between the European community in the colonies and the colonized people.[23] There is no reason to believe that this was not also the case in British Burma.

For whatever reason, the administration encouraged "irregular and temporary unions" over marriage.[24] An officer was dissuaded from marrying a Burmese woman on the basis that it would "almost certain[ly] result in destroying his official prospects."[25] Those who could not be dissuaded were transferred out of the country before they could get married. Those who managed to secretly legalize their unions to Burmese women were also liable for transfer out of the country and were denied promotion to "any post of independent authority."[26] These policies affected not just the British men in the Indian Civil Service, as the story of Gordon H. Luce, a prominent archaeologist and epigrapher of Burma and a founding member of the Burma Historical Commission, reveals. A fresh graduate of Cambridge at the time, Luce was appointed as a lecturer in English literature at Government College in Rangoon in 1912. He soon developed a close friendship with U Pe Maung Tin, an eminent Burmese and Pali scholar (and later the professor of Oriental studies, the principal of University College, and the chairman of the Burma Historical Commission), and in 1915 married his sister Ma Tee Tee, with whom he had two children.[27] Around 1920, as Rangoon University was in the process of being established, university chancellor and lieutenant governor Sir

Reginald Craddock, informed Luce that "because of his 'Burmanization,' he would not be considered for appointment as its first Professor of English."[28]

Administrative records concerning prostitution in Rangoon in the 1910s offer another picture of the nature of Anglo-Burmese relations in colonial Burma. During the 1910s, Burma witnessed a surge in activities by international abolitionist groups that were involved in what other scholars have documented as a "vigorous campaign to abolish regulated prostitution throughout the [British] empire."[29] The main target of the abolitionist movement were the Contagious Diseases Acts, or CD Acts, of the 1860s—legislation that sought to protect members of the British armed forces from sexually transmitted diseases through compulsory medical examinations of prostitutes. While the CD Acts showed concern for the health of the army personnel, they at the same time revealed that the government tacitly condoned, if not encouraged, prostitution.[30] With the repeal of the acts in 1886, the abolitionist efforts in Britain turned overseas, especially to British India, where the CD Acts remained in force. The colonial administration found itself under attack by various supporters of the abolitionist movement in Burma—the Association for Moral and Social Hygiene (AMSH), the National Vigilance Association (or the Vigilance Association), the YMCA, the Women's Christian Temperance Union, and the American Baptist Mission—that accused its regulation and thus sanctioning of prostitution.[31] The administration was concerned in particular with the activities of John Cowen, a close affiliate of the AMSH, the YMCA, and the ABM, who was employed as a teacher at the Rangoon Baptist College from April 1914 until May 1915. Shortly after his arrival in Rangoon, Cowen addressed a letter to the lieutenant governor, declaring that the Christian teaching was clear and emphatic that no compromise with prostitution was possible, that brothels were completely mischievous and unnecessary, and therefore all known brothels should be immediately closed, every foreign prostitute deported, and every Indian, Burmese, or other British subject working as a prostitute dealt with as seemed appropriate.[32] The commissioner of police, prompted by Cowen's letter, began an investigation into the situation while Cowen himself embarked on what the chief secretary to the government of Burma, W. F. Rice, reported was "an active campaign on the streets and in brothels, attempting to prevent persons from entering such houses or from remaining therein."[33] Rice described Cowen's strategy as "more zealous than discrete" and observed that, rather than interfere with his tactics, the police had to take special measures both to protect Cowen and to prevent serious disturbances that his methods were inclined to arouse.[34]

Cowen's criticism of the colonial administration concerned not only the CD Acts but also what was then referred to as the "segregation policy," wherein the government regulated prostitution by allocating sections of towns for prostitution. Cowen claimed that the "segregation policy" of the colonial administration produced an extraordinary prostitution problem in Burma. In a report to the AMSH, based on his findings from a one-year inquiry conducted in the city, Cowen described the condition of prostitution in Rangoon:

> At Madras we [Cowen and a colleague] found nothing objectionable, even after seeking for it. At Rangoon, in the heart of the town, in the midst of the district occupied by Government offices, banks, shipping offices, business premises, large stores, and principal churches, six or eight colleges and schools, etc., were five long streets officially marked off as thoroughfares in which brothels might be opened and prostitution carried on under special Government sanction. . . . If it had been desired to select an area from which vice and disease might be disseminated throughout the city, no more commanding position could have been chosen.[35]

Cowen noted that whereas Madras and Colombo were generally free from segregation and from known public brothels of any sort, Rangoon had not only the largest segregation area of public brothels in British India but also the largest number of brothels outside the segregation area. The report also documented in detail the abundance of extra-segregation brothels, as well as venereal disease in Rangoon and other major cities in the country such as Mandalay, Moulmein, and Maymyo, and indicated that the clients of the brothels were British troops and sepoys from the Indian subcontinent, not the local male population.[36] Cowen furthermore published a series of pamphlets titled *Tracts for Rangoon,* clearly intended for English-speaking Christian residents in Burma, presumably colonial officials and British male patrons of the brothels whom the pamphlets sought to proselytize.[37] The cover of the second pamphlet, for example, featured this Biblical reference: "Upon her forehead is a name written: BABYLON the great, MOTHER of HARLOTS, and of the abominations of the earth—Rev., 17:5."[38] In the fifth pamphlet, entitled *Rangoon's Scarlet Sin; or, Lust Made Lawful,* Cowen likewise drew on Christian teachings to appeal to his audience: "Lust, when it hath conceived, bringeth forth Sin; and Sin, when it is full-grown, bringeth death—James, 1:15."[39] Cowen's *Tracts* and his public abolitionist campaign were aimed principally, if not exclusively, at British and other European men.

Cowen's report is interesting not only for the information it offers about government-regulated prostitution in colonial Burma but also for its discussion of the widespread practice of "temporary unions" entered into by European men. He concluded that a great amount of prostitution in Rangoon existed due not so much to the depravity of British regiments as to the colonial administration's encouragement of sexual relations between colonial officers and indigenous women. In a section titled "Condonement of European Vice," Cowen stated that the attitude of the administration towards European men who cohabited with Burmese women was one not merely of leniency but of "positive friendliness."[40] As evidence, he cited the government grants for illegitimate children of British men by Burmese mothers in the form of orphan stipends, boarder stipends, and apprentice stipends. He explained that the grants, while they represented "a merciful arrangement from the point of Burmese mothers who have been abandoned with their children, by Englishmen temporarily resident in a district," recklessly released the European father of the responsibility of fatherhood.[41] Colonial authorities saw things differently. They acknowledged their preference for cohabitation over marriage but insisted that irregular and temporary unions—which "Burmese women have always shown themselves very ready to contract"[42]—were, "according to the ideas prevalent among [Burmese] people, not looked upon as disreputable."[43] Crosthwaite even remembered the "temporary marriage" as "quite a proper marriage and honourable in the view of the Burmese woman."[44] This view continued well into the 1910s, as shown by a 1914 report by a committee responsible for reviewing a bill intended to afford greater protection to minor girls, principally Burmese, who were commonly enticed into Rangoon on false pretences and tricked into a life of prostitution.[45] The chief objection to the bill, according to the report, was that its definition of the words "illicit intercourse" would lead to extensive abuse due to the prevalent practice by foreign men of taking Burmese girls as mistresses. "It is of course well known," the report claims, "that many foreigners residing in Burma take Burmese girls as mistresses, paying money to the guardians."[46] The report attributes this widespread practice by foreigners to Burma's "loose marriage laws," which, according to the report, freely sanctioned relations between men and women of different race, ethnicity, caste, and religion. The colonial administrators highlighted the "loose marriage laws" in Burma as the cause of the "illicit intercourse." In fact, prostitution too had its roots in local tradition, according to the extensive *Shuttleworth Report,* written by the then district superintendent of police in response to Cowen's campaign. Based on an investigation in 1916, the report, which had become the defining administrative paper on prostitution in British colonial cities (Calcutta, Madras, Bombay, and Rangoon), argues that "one of the chief causes leading to prostitution in the East is the religious and social sanctions to polygamy and concubinage, common to all religions and races in the East."[47]

Were illicit and temporary unions actually looked upon as "proper" and "honourable"? Did Burmese marriage laws freely sanction such relations?

Melford Spiro, who has produced one of the few anthropological studies of cultural conceptions and norms of marriage in Burma, posits that, on the contrary, parental and social approval or disapproval of a marriage depended primarily on the ethnicity and religion of the spouse: "The Burmese are no less ethnocentric than other people . . . and village parents, at least, strongly oppose marriage to a non-Burman and especially a non-Buddhist."[48] Foreshadowing Spiro's argument, an observer noted in 1913 that a derogatory reference to the Mon people, "Talaing," was used to refer to the offspring of Mon women who had married Indians.[49] Nonetheless, historians of Burma have argued, at least with regard to precolonial and colonial Burma, that "the indigenous races have no prejudice against alliances with foreigners and their religion offers no impediment to such."[50] In his study of eighteenth-century Burma, Thant Myint-U even claims that "foreign men visiting the country were encouraged to take local wives or mistresses."[51]

One explanation for this reported encouragement "to take local wives or mistresses" in precolonial Burma relates to the long-existing use of marriage as a mechanism for acculturation (or Burmanization) and for the cultivation of allegiance. In their effort to expand Burman political and cultural influence outside the lowlands, Toungoo and Konbaung kings arranged marriages between Tai and Burman aristocrats.[52] Foreign settlers and sojourners likewise used marriage as a way to form alliances and to build political influence. Filipe de Brito, a Portuguese adventurer-mercenary-turned-"king" of Pegu (1602–1613), married one of his sons to the daughter of the prince of Martaban in an attempt to consolidate the Portuguese domain in Lower Burma.[53] Incidentally, it was de Brito's 400-odd Portuguese followers, including many Eurasian children, who ended up the target of mass assimilation when in 1613 the king of Ava reconquered Pegu. They were resettled to the interior of Burma, where they were given land and Burmese wives and became a corps of the royal army. A century later, more than two hundred French war captives were added to this community and assimilated once again through the provision of Burmese wives.[54]

Burma scholars also attribute the existence and acceptance of intermarriage to local Buddhist ideas and customs of marriage that present no barriers to unions across caste, racial, ethnic, or religious lines. Not only do the various indigenous *dhammasat* legal texts make no mention of interracial, interethnic, or interfaith marriage (as discussed in chapter 1), but they also make explicit provisions for marriage between a local woman and a nonlocal man: "A man coming from a distant place gives bridal presents to the parents of a girl and lives with her; if he wishes to return to his place of residence, he shall intimate the date of his return to her and also provide means for her maintenance; if otherwise, her mother is entitled to take her back."[55] In addition, the various laws detailing the rights and responsibilities of a wife whose husband fails to return from a journey or contracts a second marriage during his absence indicate that "abandonment" by a husband and dissolution of marriage upon abandonment were not uncommon. For example, if a husband "has gone trading or in search of knowledge," a wife might rightfully remarry after eight years. Or if a husband took another wife during his absence and failed to provide suitable provision for the maintenance of his wife and children, the former wife could remarry after three years.[56] The *dhammasat* recognized a woman's right to remarry under other circumstances as well: "The parents or guardians of a widow or divorcee shall not forbid her marrying a man of her choice. A woman who has once been married is emancipated from the control of parents or guardians, and is at liberty to marry again any man of her choice."[57] In short, there is little, if any, indication that a local woman would have been dishonored through her marriage—even temporary—to a settler or sojourner.

It is conceivable that these elements of the Burmese Buddhist legal and ethical conceptions and institutions facilitated marriages between local women and foreign itinerants and immigrants. It is also conceivable, however, that in the context of the Burmese Buddhist ethical and legal treatises, a "foreigner" would have had to be perceived as a Buddhist. That precolonial Burmese Buddhist ethical and legal texts do not comment upon marriage between a Buddhist woman and a non-Buddhist man has been interpreted to mean that Burmese Buddhist culture did not hinder interfaith marriage.[58] Yet this silence may also be interpreted to mean that such marriages could not be contracted, that marriage was something that occurred between Buddhists, and that interfaith marriage was in theory unthinkable. It may also signify the infrequency with which interfaith marriage was contracted. The fact is that we currently lack conclusive studies that would enable us to make secure claims about Burmese attitudes towards intermarriage prior to the colonial period. What we do know, however, is that intermarriage became a morally and culturally reprehensible practice in the twentieth century.

THE PROBLEM OF WHOM TO MARRY: NATIVE PERSPECTIVES

The spousal choice of Burmese women appeared on the agenda of various women's associations. The first public denunciation of intermarriage by women's associations took place on July 11, 1921, at a demonstration organized by the General Council of Burmese Associations to protest the imprisonment of U Ottama. Addressing those who were gathered at a park in downtown Rangoon for the protest, members of one Wunthanu Konmaryi Athin (Patriotic Women's Association) declared that Burmese women should not marry men of a religious faith other than Buddhism.[59] In Rangoon and in Mandalay, members of women's associations continued to speak publicly against mixed marriages, and in 1927 the Legislative Council debated a resolution to apply the laws of the *dhammasat* to marriages that involved Burmese women. As the proponents of the resolution explained, the problem underlying mixed marriages concerned a woman's loss of her Buddhist spousal rights, as represented in the legal texts, if she married a non-Buddhist. The loss of such rights, especially those related to divorce and inheritance, occurred through multiple and multilayered processes. Many court cases were consequences of a Burmese Buddhist woman discovering, after cohabiting with a foreign man "in such manners as would raise the presumption that they are man and wife by Burmese custom,"[60] that she was not legally his wife due to the personal laws to which the man was subject. The problem was described as follows in the Legislative Council:

[In] the time of . . . kings, Mindon and Thibaw, foreigners were at liberty to marry Burman women provided the marriages were governed by Dhammathat and not by personal laws of the foreigners. . . . [N]ow a marriage with a Hindu was not valid because a caste Hindu could not marry outside his caste; a marriage with a Moslem could not be legally effected unless the Burman Buddhist woman became a Moslem convert; even after such conversion, the Moslem husband retained the right to marry as many as four wives and he had only to pronounce the word Talak three times if he desired to divorce his Burman wife or any other wife.[61]

Though the Special Marriage Act of 1872 provided the forms and procedures for Buddhists and non-Buddhists to contract valid marriages, "such marriages took the families outside the pale of Burmese customary law."[62] Therefore women did not obtain the benefits of the status of a married woman under Burmese Buddhist law—for example, in the event of divorce, an equal share in the property acquired by a woman and her husband during the marriage, and joint custody of all the children, whom the husband must support through their years as minors.[63] Where nationalists and feminists once highlighted the "traditional" progressiveness of women in Burma to encourage women to challenge their status quo, the progressive rights and privileges of Burmese women in this context were highlighted, no longer to discuss their enhancement through modern institutions and expertise, but rather to speak of their loss under colonialism.

The critiques of marriages between Burmese women and foreign men also reflected the political climate at the time. Nalini Chakravarti has argued that as a result of "the oft-repeated policy of the Government of Burma to prepare the country for ultimate separation from India," by the 1920s "'separation' and 'self-government' had become synonymous for a large section of Burma politicians."[64] Many Burmese nationalist members of the Legislative Council pushed legislation that would secure the separation of Burma from India as quickly as possible. They did so, in part, through alarmist discussions of the "Indian menace," such as the "menace" posed by the Indo-Burmese marriage and the continued immigration of Indians to Burma. "Unless we are separated now," warned U Ba Pe, an ardent pro-separatist, "we are sure to be swamped."[65] That the discourse on the "Indian menace" was fueled less by anti-Indian sentiments than by the desire to attain self-government was discernible in the policies that pro-separatist politicians pursued. Chakravarti points out that Sir J. A. Maung Gyi supported rapid Burmanization of the civil services and yet "never recommended summary dismissal of Europeans and Indians from Burma services."[66] Similarly, U Pu, another staunch pro-separatist, was "highly respected and trusted by Indians for his moderate views."[67] Not all nationalist politicians supported alarmist representations of the "Indian menace" in their bid to secure and speed up the granting of self-government for their country, however. Those such as U Ottama were against the separation of Burma from India.[68] The "Indian menace" was promoted and revisited precisely because not all nationalist politicians were separatists; it remained central to local political discourse until 1937, when Burma was separated from India.[69]

Likewise, the condemnations of intermarriage in the 1930s were in all likelihood informed by the rhetoric of "us versus them"—that is, Burmese nationalists versus colonialists—used by the *thakin* of the Dobama Asiayone. In their slogans and publications, the *thakin* espoused a binary concept of *dobama* (our Burma) versus *thumya bama* (their Burma).[70] Their motto not only captures the rhetoric used by *thakin* but also conveys what they meant by *dobama*:

Burma is Our Country
Burmese is Our Literature
Burmese is Our Language
Love Our Country
Cherish Our Literature
Uphold Our Language[71]

Thumya bama, therefore, were perceived as Burmans who did not consider Burma to be their country or, if they did, lacked respect and devotion to their country, language, and literature. The term *thumya bama* had other implications, however. Take, for example, the following passage from a pamphlet distributed by the Dobama Asiayone in 1936:

> If there exist *dobamas,* there also exist *thumya bamas.*
> Be aware of them.
> *Thumya bamas* do not cherish our Buddhism, do not respect it,
> They go into the councils,
> They try to dominate monks whether directly or whether indirectly,
> They take advantage of the law, accept bribes.[72]

Used in such contexts, *thumya bama* could mean variously "Burma dominated by the Burmese of their (the British) side," "Burma ruled by the British together with Burmese collaborators," "the Burmese people of their (the British) side," or "the Burmese who collaborated with the colonial regime."[73] The term *thumya bama* reflected the self-identification of *thakin* as distinctly different from and opposed to not only the British but also, more importantly and more specifically, the *thumya bama*—that is, Anglo-Burman and other "mixed" Burmese people, the privileged echelon of Burmese society composed of members of the Indian Civil Service, and nationalists who favored dominion status over complete independence.[74] Within this framework in which nationalists appealed to the notion of "our Burmese" and "their Burmese" in order to integrate the country into a coherent community, the wives and mistresses of foreign men represented the quintessential *thumya bama.*

The print media of the period show that concerns over the questionable status and harmful effects of intermarriage were widespread, rather than confined to the elite political and legislative circles. A 1925 cartoon, for example, offers insight into the way contemporary Burmese people perceived mixed marriages and, in particular, Anglo-Burmese unions. Titled "On Being a Foreigner,"[75] the cartoon begins with a picture of a Burmese woman flatly rejecting what appears to be a marriage proposal from a European-looking man. She says, "You think you're worthy of me?" Her mother, however, entreats her daughter to accept the foreigner's proposal, which prompts the daughter to ask why. The mother, envisioning the foreigner with his servants, replies that marrying him will mean that the couple will get to be chauffeured in cars. The daughter evidently accepts the foreigner's proposal because, explains the caption next to the couple, "she is opportunistic." Later, just as she gives birth to the foreigner's child, a servant instructs her: "Go! Go! The wife from the home country is coming!" Presumably, the foreigner's wife in Britain is on her way to Burma to join her husband. The cartoon concludes with the Burmese "wife" in tears, accompanied by the caption: "Oh, the impermanent nature of life."[76]

While the cartoon, which is tinged with Buddhist teaching about impermanence, was clearly meant to be a sarcastic commentary on *tuiṅ khrā* (foreign) men, it also sheds light on how some members of the Burmese public understood relationships between a European man and a Burmese woman. The relationship appeared at first to be a mutually beneficial arrangement that gave the man access to sexual companionship and familial relations and provided the woman and her family with socioeconomic benefits. As Barbara Andaya suggests regarding forms of "temporary marriage" in precolonial Southeast Asia, a local woman not only acquired financial benefits but also enhanced her status and that of her family through marriage to a foreign man who was accorded economic importance as well as high social status.[77] The *bo* personified white prestige, and his car and servants symbolized the luxurious lifestyle of a *bo*. The "marriage," however, turned out to be a sham. The visible grief of the woman in the cartoon stemmed from her ignorance of the man's existing marital ties—a situation, according to the *dhammasat,* that would have brought disgrace on the "bride" and her family.[78] Such disgrace was also a consequence of the manner in which she was deserted. Whereas abandonment by a husband who failed to return from a journey was not uncommon in precolonial Burma, as explained above, the woman in the cartoon was not merely abandoned but thrown out and left with no provisions for herself and the child. Because Burmese marital practices were matrilocal and it was customary for the groom to move into the bride's house (with her parents), the husband, not the wife, would have been expected to leave. He would have been expected, additionally, to provide maintenance for his abandoned wife and child. The cartoon thus conjured a repudiation not only of the Burmese wife but also of local marriage and kinship norms and practices, portraying the Anglo-Burmese marriage as ultimately deceptive and destructive. In so doing, it echoed the concerns of legislators that they were seeing too many cases of foreign men "[luring] young and ignorant Burmese women into what seemed to be a marriage."[79]

The Indo-Burmese marriage was likewise represented as deceptive and exploitative in the Burmese press. For example, a 1939 magazine article entitled "Burmese Women Meet with Troubles" gave an account of a Burmese woman, Ma May Myit, who had married an Indian man about fourteen years earlier. According to the article, Ma May Myit was taken to India by her husband in November 1938. Upon her arrival, she found herself ill treated at the hands of her husband and his first wife before she was ultimately kicked out of the house. Ma May Myit then went to Calcutta, where she found Burmese residents who financed her passage back to Burma.[80]

The critics of both Anglo-Burmese and Indo-Burmese marriages alleged that they were harmful to Burmese women and undermined local marital traditions. Although the critics do not make explicit the implications of either type of intermarriage for Burmese men, the very exclusion of Burmese men from their criticisms reveals the dislocation that they must have experienced. Officialdom, wealth, and such modern accoutrements of power and prestige as a car and a chauffeur had become the prerogative of foreign men who immigrated to Burma under the auspices of the British colonial administration. Intimate relations with foreign men thus offered socioeconomic benefits that Burmese men could not provide. This disparity between Burmese and foreign men in socioeconomic power and status would have widened in the 1930s due to the Depression, a period during which increasing numbers of Burmese men and families became indebted. As the extensive literature on the 1930s crisis in Burma has documented, an unprecedented number of Burmese traders, peasants, and laborers—both men and women—lost their livelihood and were forced to look for new jobs.[81] One of the occupations to which such displaced women doubtless turned was prostitution and other forms of "irregular" and "temporary" relations that helped alleviate the adverse ramifications of the Depression. It is conceivable that the Depression therefore had the effect of making more Burmese women more easily sexually available to foreign men—especially if in the 1930s, as in the 1910s, the clients of brothels in Burma were predominantly British and Indian troops and sepoys—and strengthened the image of foreign men as exploiting Burmese women and alienating Burmese men. In 1930s Burma, it was not only socioeconomic power and prestige but also sexual prowess and productivity that were increasingly denied to many local men. In all likelihood, intermarriage, in addition to exacerbating the image of foreign men as parasitical, evoked an image of Burmese men as emasculated. Intermarriage was inimical to Burmese women as well as Burmese men and served to perpetuate a colonial social structure that disempowered Burmese men.

The differences between Anglo-Burmese and Indo-Burmese marriages need to be noted, however. The latter marriage was clearly interpreted as a more demeaning relationship. Although the British and the Indian husband alike kicked out the Burmese wife, only the Indian husband was represented as abusive (and only in the latter case was the Burmese wife subjected to maltreatment directly by the first wife). *Kala* men were thus characterized as more abusive than *bo* men. Newspaper articles published prior to and in the wake of the anti-Indian riots also reveal that Indo-Burmese marriage was perceived as harmful not only to the Burmese woman herself but to Burmese society at large. The 25 July 1938 issue of *Thuriya* featured an article accusing immigrants to Burma who professed other religions of "seducing Burmese Buddhist women to become their wives, causing dissension in order to create such communities as *Dobama Muslim* (We Burmese Muslim)."[82] In November of the same year, an article in the *10,000,000*, published under the heading "Burmese Women Who Took Indians," blamed Burmese wives of Indians for ruining Burma's "race and religion":

> You Burmese women who fail to safeguard your own race, after you have married an Indian[,] your daughter whom you have begotten by such a tie takes an Indian as her husband. As for your son, he becomes a half-caste and tries to get a pure Burmese woman. Not only you but your future generation also is those who are responsible for the ruination of the race.[83]

An Indo-Burmese marriage threatened, as the author of *The Problem of Mixed People* argued, a spiraling degeneration of Burmese society.[84] According to U Pu Galay, however, the problem was not the corruption of "pure" Burmese women. A two-page passage at the beginning of the book summed up the problem, as he saw it:

> It's worse to be *kabya* in mind than to be *kabya* in body; even if a person happens to be *kabya* in body, if he or she lives in Burma and will die in Burma, it would be fitting for him or her to think like a Burmese person. . . . [E]very person who lives in Burma and dies in Burma ought to share *ta sve:* [one blood], *ta cit* [one soul], with Burmese people; he or she should not stray from or get in the way of the struggle for Burma's independence.[85]

U Pu Galay concedes that "a person who is not mixed is truly rare"[86] and that all human beings are *kabya* in one way or another.[87] What he found troubling was that *kabya* people in Burma, in his opinion, did not share the views and perspective of Burmese people. They were not Burmese in blood or soul and thwarted Burma's struggle for freedom.

In actuality, there were plenty of patriotic *kabya* people in Burma, and many of them played influential roles in the *wunthanu* (patriotic) movement, most notably Abdul Razak, or U Razak, a minister of education and national planning who was assassinated in 1947 along with Aung San, then president of the Anti-Fascist People's Freedom League (AFPFL), the most popular political party in postwar Burma, and the de facto national leader. Born in Mandalay to an Indian father, who was a police inspector, and a Burmese Buddhist mother, U Razak was the only Muslim among his siblings. A student at Rangoon College, U Razak was among the leaders behind the first university boycott and the national education movement. He founded and became the headmaster of the central national high school in Mandalay in 1921. In 1945, U Razak became the chairman of the Mandalay branch of the

AFPFL and "won wide recognition for organizing Burma's Muslims under the AFPFL flag."[88] At the same time, he was known for his knowledge of Pali and Buddhism; in fact, the success of his national high school was credited to its curriculum, which "reinvigorat[ed] Burmese studies and promot[ed] Burmese culture, patriotism and nationalism," and to his efforts to ensure that "all Buddhist students attended their prayers and religious lessons."[89] Even the case of U Razak signals, however, that in the 1920s and 1930s, it had become incumbent upon *kabya* people to prove that they were *do bama*. U Razak demonstrated his patriotism not only through his involvement in the national education movement but also through his appreciation of Buddhism. *Kabya* people, like the wives and mistresses of foreign men, had become vulnerable to accusations of being *thumya bama*.

Moreover, if the Burmese public in the 1920s and the early 1930s regarded Anglo-Burmese marriage as a means to socioeconomic advancement, or marrying up, an Indo-Burmese marriage was characterized as marrying down. The 1925 cartoon "On Being a Foreigner" described above acknowledged the allure and benefits of the Anglo-Burmese marriage, which presented the woman and her family with not only socioeconomic advancement but also white prestige. In contrast, in representations of the Indo-Burmese marriage, it is unclear what socioeconomic incentives, if any, encouraged the marriage. An examination of a story entitled "A European's Mistress,"[90] published in 1934, further illustrates this point (figure 5.1). The title refers to the main character of the story, Ma May Thoun, whose mother, Daw Aw Hma, has arranged for her daughter to marry a *bo* named Bo Galay (Young European Lad). The story opens with the mother and the daughter in the kitchen, deep in conversation:

Daughter: Mother, the neighbors are going to sneer at me. Everyone's going to make a mockery out of me.
Mother: So what if they sneer at you? It's because they are envious of you. Once the marriage is finalized, they'll be the first to befriend you.
Daughter: They say all sorts of insulting things about *bo gadaw* . . . that they're very sly . . .
Mother: That's because they themselves haven't found a *bo* who is interested in them. Don't listen to such things.[91]

Daw Aw Hma instructs her daughter to not dwell on the neighbors' apparent scornfulness and to focus instead on the glorious life the marriage will bring her. She tells her daughter: "You just worry about being a good wife, May Thoun. A *bo* cherishes and takes great care of his wife and children. . . . [O]ne day, you will make your grand return to the village as a *bo gadaw* and show off in front of those who now scoff at you."[92]

In the ensuing conversation, the reader learns that while neither of them knows for certain the details of Bo Galay's life (such as his family background or occupation), they presume that he owns a business that handles extremely valuable goods and that he has secretaries working for him. When the daughter points out that she doesn't know how to cook European dishes, Daw Aw Hma tells her not to worry, because "a European has chauffeurs, butlers, servants and cooks," and reassures her daughter that she won't have to step into the kitchen.[93] But Ma May Thoun quickly finds her (and her mother's) dream of living a *bo* life shattered upon her marriage to Bo Galay, who, it turns out, is not really a *bo* but a European-looking Muslim *kala* by the name of Yusuf.[94]

Figure 5.1 "Bo gadaw" (A European's mistress), in *Youq shin lan hnyun*, 22 June 1934, 24.

The story, like the cartoon "On Being a Foreigner," cautions Burmese people who view Anglo-Burmese liaisons as socioeconomic leverage. But the author renders Daw Aw Hma and her daughter's visions of the life of a *bo gadaw* as ill conceived not because they err in their assumptions about the Anglo-Burmese marriage but because Bo Galay turns out to be *kala.* The story implies that a genuine *bo gadaw* is in fact all that Ma May Thoun and her mother had expected, thereby reinforcing the allure of the *bo gadaw.*

At the same time, the term *kala,* as it was disseminated in the Burmese media in the 1920s and 1930s, pigeonholed immigrants from the Indian subcontinent as uneducated, lower-class (or lower-caste) men and women, typically of skin color darker than that of Burmese people, when in fact many of those categorized as "Indian" in Burma were relatively prosperous, accounting for 55 percent of the municipal taxes paid in Rangoon.[95] A cigarette advertisement featured in *Thuriya* in 1937 illuminates how the Burmese print media portrayed Indians in Burma (figure 5.2). The Burmese men (the cigarette smokers) represent college students, one of whom has just returned from a trip upcountry during an academic break and is accompanied by a *kala* coolie, carrying his luggage.

Representations of *kala* women, while less prevalent, were similarly unflattering. In an article entitled "Muslim Women"[96] in a 1936 issue of

Figure 5.2 Advertisement for Polo Cigarette, in *Thuriya,* 22 January 1937.

Myanmar alin, the author contrasts Buddhist Burmese women with *kala* Muslim women in Burma. U Ka begins with a lengthy exposition on purdah, which he describes as "a Muslim custom of hiding women at home" for the sake of preventing them from tempting Muslim men to be lustful and immoral.[97] He then outlines the various ways that a Muslim woman is allegedly deprived of numerous privileges. He asserts that although she is virtually locked up at home to perform domestic duties, she must accompany men to nurse the injured when there is a war. "What is this belief," deplores U Ka, "that a Muslim woman should undertake a hajj when she is prohibited from entering a mosque?"[98] He adds that Muslim women in Burma are not able to read religious texts, newspapers, or anything written in English. U Ka contrasts the desolate account he has presented of the life of a Muslim woman with the uplifting portrayal of Buddhist women in Burma: "Young Buddhist women graduate with bachelor and master degrees. They become administrators, doctors, teachers, members of councils, and municipal representatives. They have not only established large stores and businesses but have even become editors for newspapers and magazines. Isn't that quite admirable?"[99]

The racist overtone of the attacks on the Indo-Burmese marriage and of the representation of Indians is unmistakable. The accusations of "the ruination" of the Burmese race made against Burmese women who married Indians and produced *kabya* children were imbued with biological racism and the eugenics discourse of the "degeneration" of the race. The portrayal of Indians in the Burmese popular press demonstrated a striking resemblance to the racist stereotype of Indian immigrants to Burma in British travel literature:

> The principal settlers from India are the Hindu Chetties from the Madras Presidence. They are a remarkable class of people, very wealthy, very keen at business, men of their word in all transactions, being fully alive to the value of keeping their credit by an unstained reputation in finance. . . . Yet with all this, they dress, eat, and live as if they had a very meagre income, and have the appearance of mere savages. The vast amount of naked skin they show is almost black in complexion, and they have almost no education beyond the bare necessities of finance.[100]

In Hart's description of Indians, as in popular images of *kala* in 1920s and 1930s Burma, race is not only biological but also culturally encoded and performed.[101] "Hindu Chetties" are compelled by their racial and cultural background to live and behave like the half-naked, barefooted, and brawny-but-uneducated *kala* coolie in the cigarette advertisement discussed above. In that advertisement, furthermore, the Indian coolie is juxtaposed with the educated (or soon to be educated) Burmese college students who, by wearing elaborate clothes and shoes and smoking cigarettes, display what Ann Stoler has termed "cultural competence."[102]

What we see in the criticisms of the Indo-Burmese marriage is a coexistence of biological racism with cultural racism invoking categories of class, manners and behavior, social customs, and religious belief and practices. White, middle-class, and English cultural sensibilities were deemed incompatible with colored, lower-class, and *kala* cultural sensibilities. Yet the race of the Burmese students in the advertisement does not preclude them from acquiring the culture—that is, the lifestyle, customs, and worldview—of the English. It is also interesting to note that precisely because race was mapped onto class, cultural racism seems to have fit within and operated upon prevailing ideas of class (even as they were modified by cultural racism), such as the importance of stringent observation of class divisions, the desirability of class endogamy, and, conversely, the undesirability of interclass marriage. Ironically, and as shown in chapter 3, Burmese intellectuals, monks, politicians, students, writers, and journalists were challenging at this very moment the colonial ideology of racial superiority—that the superior qualities of the British "race," such as "an inherent superiority in the British character, military prowess, religious beliefs and probity, and a general capacity to govern fairly and well,"[103] legitimized British colonialism. Burmese as well as Indians were excluded from British clubs and private meeting places; British men who married Burmese women, and their children, found themselves ostracized by the expatriate European community, which regarded intermarriage and miscegenation as a threat to the racial hierarchy and alleged supremacy of English culture that the colonial bureaucracy sought to cultivate.[104] Burmese critics of such segregationist practices shared with the British colonizers the idea that racially mixed people would inevitably degenerate, as well as anxieties about the cultural incompetence not only of half-caste children but also of women who engaged in interracial marriage.[105] They promoted cultural-cum-racial segregation between Burmese and non-Burmese people and the racial hierarchies between Burmese and Indians even as they contested the policing of racial boundaries by the British administration and the expatriate European community.

FORBIDDEN INTIMACIES

In Burma in the 1920s and 1930s, a woman's spousal choice was intimately tied to her political and "national" affiliations and served as an index for measuring her patriotism. As her intimacy with a foreign man and procreation of *kabya* children conjured the fear that the intermingling of Burmese people with foreigners reinforced political and economic colonization with cultural and biological imperialism, the body of a Burmese woman became the basis on which colonialism might be fueled or resisted. The figure of the Burmese wife/mistress who racially and culturally degraded her people by getting into bed with a foreign man provided an outlet for a critique of the impact of colonial rule on Burmese society. By discussing the negative impact of inter-marriage on Burmese women, men, and society, critics indirectly accused the British colonial state of disenfranchising and oppressing the indigenous population through its economic, legal, and immigration policies—the impact of which Burmese people felt particularly acutely during and in the aftermath of the 1930s economic depression. Women who "mixed" with for-eign men also functioned as sites for confronting questions of national affili-ation and who could be considered and counted as "Burmese" before a formal conception of Burmese national identity developed. The discourse on inter-marriage and miscegenation in Burma echoes colonial debates about métis children who were perceived as threats to the carefully constructed belief that "Europeans in the colonies made up an easily identifiable and discrete biological and social entity[,] a 'natural' community of common class inter-ests, racial attributes, political affinities and superior culture."[106] In similar fashion, *kabya* men and women undermined the fundamental premise on which the potency of Burmese nationalist movements came to rest: the exis-tence of a stable and "easily identifiable" community of *bama* people bounded by "one blood, one soul." To colonialists and nationalists alike, sex and sub-version were inextricably intertwined, and both sides of the colonial struggle deployed racialized senses of belonging and exclusion, which converged on the bodies of Burmese women.

Yet the public denunciations of intermarriage and miscegenation that developed in the 1920s and 1930s cannot be reduced to mere political rhet-oric or strategy manipulated by the anticolonial and nationalist elites. We need to take seriously the possibility that the attacks reflected and informed significant changes in patterns and understandings of intermarriage, and that marriage between a foreign man and a local woman challenged local mar-riage and kinship norms and practices. Similarly, we cannot underestimate the importance of the gendered conditions of colonial rule. As was noted ear-lier, the mass immigration of unattached men and the reduction in power and authority among Burmese men made marriage to foreign men more attrac-tive and more likely. The actual rise in intimate relations between foreign men and local women, combined with the frequent inability of Burmese men, unlike foreign men, to offer socioeconomic advancement to Burmese women through marriage, contributed to the already prevalent and indiscriminate image of foreign men as exploitative colonizers who were displacing indigenous men. We also need to take into consideration the impact of the worldwide Depression on changing perceptions of intermarriage, not only in terms of its entrenchment of anticolonialist sentiments but also with regard to the growing poverty and indebtedness of Burmese people and the increasing commoditization of women and of intimacy.

Finally, a historical analysis of intermarriage in Burma needs to take account of emergent cosmopolitan ideas of religion and race. The structure of precolonial Burmese society was dominated by class cleavage. Although class continued to serve as a key source of identity and social status during the colonial period, the British colonial administration used race and religion as primary categories of social division. The representations of Anglo-Burmese and Indo-Burmese marriage examined here demonstrate that this notion of cultural racism, which defined "culture" in limited, class-, religion-, and race-specific ways, had a particularly powerful impact on changing views of intermarriage in colonial Burma. Although both types of intermarriage were criticized, the former, which was associated with socioeconomic advancement, was clearly less objectionable than the latter, which was perceived as socioeconomic decline. Emergent notions of race thus converged with precolonial understandings of class divisions, evident in the disapproval of marriages contracted across disparate classes. Colonial economic, legal, and immigration policies and practices, the inseparability of sex and subversion in nationalist politics, the Depression, and the codification and coalescing of religion and race as categories of classification and bases of national affiliation all helped to produce a context in which intermarriage became a powerful symbol of disloyalty. At the same time, colonialism reinforced already existing indigenous understandings of intermarriage as unacceptable.

6

The Self-Indulgent *Khit hsan thu*

Culture, Nation, and Masculinity on Trial

Wives and mistresses of foreigners were not the only unpatriotic women to appear in colonial-period Burmese discourses. The *khit hsan thu* and other variants of the fashionable female (discussed in chapter 4) also became the target of censorious and often misogynistic representations of Burmese women in the media. These representations, in the form of books, editorials, commentaries, and cartoons that ranged from sarcastic to derogatory, displayed an intense contempt towards fashionable women and their sartorial habits and consumer practices. Take, for instance, the caricature of a *tet khit thami* that appeared in the March 1938 issue of *Thuriya* (figure 6.1). Flaunting all the external trappings of the *tet khit*—high heels, wristwatch, purse, a pet dog on a leash, a cigarette between her lips—the stylish *tet khit thami* exudes consumerism and materialism. She stands in sharp contrast to the older woman beside her, dressed in a simple blouse and wearing a pair of slippers. The intense reaction of the older woman, who stares in shock at the young woman and exclaims, "Huik" (Oh my!), evokes the latter's disregard for tradition. The young woman's aloof demeanor and obvious indifference conjure up the need to tame and discipline her, as does her designation as *thami* (girl or daughter), which renders her unattached and free floating.

The public castigation of the bodily practices of the *khit hsan thu* culminated in the late 1930s, when women who dressed in the *khit hsan* fashion were harassed by groups of *yahan byo* (young, fully ordained Buddhist monks).[1] A group of *yahan byo* gathered at the Mahāmuni Pagoda in Mandalay to set on fire bundles of *eingyi pa* (sheer blouses), and similar incidents of blouse

Figure 6.1 "Tet khit thami" (Modern girl), in *Thuriya,* March 1938.

burning led by *yahan byo* took place in cities near Mandalay—cities around which monastic life in Burma clustered. In addition to the blouse burnings, the British administration reported intense and physically violent incidents of *yahan byo* tearing off blouses from the backs of women with hooks and scissors.[2] The blouse burnings and the persecution of women wearing *eingyi pa* by the *yahan byo* are striking for a number of reasons. First, the choice by the *yahan byo* of the *eingyi pa* as the target of their campaign is curious, given that both violence and physical contact between a Buddhist monk and a woman are contrary to Buddhist monastic discipline outlined by the canonical Vinaya. Second, not only was there little apparent animosity between women and the *sangha* in Burma, but political monks such as U Ottama attracted a large female following. These women followers regularly participated in anticolonial demonstrations organized and led by monks, as was seen in chapter 3. Finally, what also stands out about the denunciation of the *khit hsan thu* is that whereas the espousal of *khit hsan* fashion by Burmese men went unremarked, similar behavior by a woman was construed as a flagrant violation of cultural norms and an insult to Burmese nationalist movements. The *khit hsan thu* alone was unethical and unpatriotic. She, like the wives and mistresses of European and Indian men, epitomized the *thumya bama.*

This chapter examines these criticisms and their motivations, and the social and political roles and meanings encoded in the bodily practices of *khit hsan thu*. Existing historical scholarship has attributed the critique of the dress and comportment of modern women, like the criticisms of intermarriage, to the anticolonial campaign of boycotting foreign goods, as well as to communalist hostilities and anticolonial sentiments that were aggravated by the economic crisis of the 1930s.[3] Admittedly, early nationalists in Burma associated foreign men and imported goods with colonialism and cast their protest against modern clothing as a symbolic rejection of British colonial rule. Anticolonial politics, however, fail to explain why women, not men, became the targets of public criticism. Although Burmese men appropriated and fashioned *khit hsan* habits no less actively than did Burmese women, discussions in the popular press linked the female gender to low-brow consumerism, materialism, and Westernization. The *khit hsan thu* alone, not the *khit hsan tha* (fashionable lad), was portrayed as a willing culprit of imperialist, capitalist, and Western modernity.

The literature on the politics of dress posits that men could wear Western dress because they represented nationalists in doing so, whereas women, as bearers and wearers of tradition, were required to wear national or ethnic dress. It is an argument that has certainly proved profitable in some studies of the politics of dress. In the case of colonial Indonesia, for example, Jean Gelman Taylor has contended that because the Western-style suit embodied the ability to enforce power, Indonesian men in suits "declared themselves to be heirs of the Dutch in their roles as rulers."[4] At the same time, their wives and fellow female politicians and officials in the traditional style of dress were rendered the "keepers of national essence"[5] and excluded from power and modernity. Yet if the case of Indonesia reinforces the argument made by scholarship on dress in South Asia—that there was "more at stake in women signifying the purity of their 'culture' than for men"[6]—Mina Roces has asserted in her study of twentieth-century Philippines that "women were not necessarily always the 'bearers of tradition' even in the gendering of costume."[7] In post-independence Philippines, as she shows, it was men clad in traditional attire who represented the nation. The case of colonial Burma similarly challenges "the binary division of men/modernity/political power/Western dress versus women/tradition/ no political power/national dress."[8] By and large, Burmese male politicians, not only nationalist men, dressed in traditional Burmese attire. Even those who were "Westernized," such as Dr. Ba Maw—a Burmese Christian barrister turned chief minister (1937–1939), who had a bachelor's degree from Cambridge and a doctorate from the University of Bordeaux and spoke Burmese with an English accent—chose *longyi* and Burmese slippers over trousers and shoes.[9]

The following pages show that although the problem of what to wear was central to serious political concerns in colonial Burma, neither the plea for traditionalism nor the intensifying nationalist appeal for women—as both signs and custodians of tradition—to safeguard essential Burmese cultural boundaries sufficiently explains the preoccupation with the bodily practices of the *khit hsan thu*. The discourse on the contentious feminine figure was a strategy not only of conceptualizing a Burmese national identity but also of reconstructing and negotiating manhood. Investment in particular feminine tropes reveals as much about the construction of masculinity as about that of femininity. For example, male literati in late imperial China deployed feminine tropes in their writings to reexamine their own gender identities and come to terms with perceived challenges to their manhood.[10] My examination of the culture and economy of sex and marriage in the preceding chapter suggests one way that the experience of manhood under colonial rule engendered a crisis within dominant masculinity. Here, I consider other challenges to the manliness of Burmese men and explore how the colonial politics of masculinity informed the assault on the *khit hsan thu*.

THE PROBLEM OF WHAT TO WEAR

Critiques of the dress and comportment of the *khit hsan thu* first surfaced in the late 1910s when *Thuriya* began publishing cartoons and articles that accused the women who wore the *eingyi pa* of betraying *wunthanu* (patriots).[11] The articles claimed that, in an era of *wunthanu,* the appropriate behavior for Burmese women was to thrust aside the sheer blouse and to wear clothing more befitting their lineage. In mocking the sheer blouse, the writers and cartoonists for *Thuriya* saw themselves as patriots who propagated the idea that women, like men, had responsibilities to the Burmese nation. *Thuriya's* censure of the sheer blouse was reinforced shortly thereafter by members of various women's associations who, as seen in chapter 3, condemned the wearing of imported clothing and advocated the wearing of *pinni* and *yaw longyi*. Dobama Asiayone joined the campaign against imported clothes and textiles in the early 1930s, explicitly listing clothing and shoes among the goods to be boycotted (also mentioned were cigarettes, umbrellas, furniture, and foreign cuisine).[12] By the mid-1930s, not only *Thuriya* but also numerous other widely circulating journals and magazines featured articles that discussed some aspect of the *khit hsan* fashion as a grave problem for Burmese society. Take, for example, the writings by Daw Amar (then writing as University Ma Amar). In an article entitled "Our Evil Influences,"[13] published in the 1936 New Year's Special Edition of *Myanmar alin,* Daw Amar indicted *khit hmi amyothami* (contemporary women) for their blind admiration and adoption of *bo hsan* (Westernized)[14] culture. Though Daw Amar was only twenty years of age and at the beginning of her career as a writer and journalist at the time the article was published, her left-leaning disposition was already apparent. She claimed that *khit hmi amyothami* were obsessed with fashion and with adorning themselves with whatever came from abroad. She added that *khit hmi amyothami* wanted to own cars, wear diamonds the size of an elephant, and spend their spare time living a "high life" of "tea parties," "dinner parties," and "card games" as though they were "the wives of British men."[15] Most disquieting for Daw Amar was her conviction that the desire of *khit hmi amyothami* for a trendy, *bo hsan* lifestyle prompted them—not only the young women but also their mothers—to choose their husbands (or sons-in-laws, in the case of the mothers) on the basis of a man's wealth. She thus equated the understanding of *toe tet yay* (progress) of young women with capitalism, consumerism, and Westernization, which she asserted had little to do with the greater good of the *bama amyo,* the Burmese people.

Like many Indian nationalists who condemned the destruction of "Indian tradition" for the sake of "meaningless imitation" of Western dress, Daw Amar accused her fellow Burmese youth of thinking that the mere trappings of modernity could amount to progress.[16] Her emphasis, however, was decidedly on the (mis)understanding of *toe tet yay,* not on the assault on tradition. To Daw Amar, the individualistic *khit hsan thu* who prized self-fulfillment and self-expression—through the acquisition of novel and *bo hsan* material and habits—over the collective good was symptomatic of a misguided view of *toe tet yay.* Her critique of the *khit hsan thu* had in common with widespread conservative critiques of modernity elsewhere in the world the fear that the ethos of the era privileged individual self-realization and promoted hedonistic impulses that opposed the requirements of a moral and ordered society.[17] This is not to suggest that other critics of the Westernized dress and habits of women, such as the caricature discussed earlier (see figure 6.1), were not concerned with the preservation of tradition. In that illustration, the juxtaposition of the old woman and the *tet khit thami,* and the former's indignation at the sight of the latter, were intended to signify the erosion of Burmese society and tradition at the hands of the fashion-crazed youth. At the same time, writers for a popular contemporary bilingual magazine, *Ngan hta lawka,* detected increased anxiety over the "revolutionary" thinking of the younger generation. In an article titled "The Age of Criticism in Burma," H.M. claimed that in Burma "there are people, steeped in conservatism and in tradition, who think of the past in terms of the golden [age] and who are shedding tears because of the revolutionary ideas of the young people born after the advent of the Kala [the British]."[18] The struggle between old-fashioned elders and "revolutionary" youth to privilege competing visions of the *khit kala* (present era) was one of the defining characteristics of new social formations in colonial Burma. The critique of the bodily practices of the *tet khit thami* may then be interpreted as an effort by the old guard to make traditional values and customs relevant to the project of modernity. Yet the generational element of the denunciation of the *tet khit thami* can be overemphasized, as many of the critics, like Amar, were themselves young men and women advocating change and even revolution. Amar's view of the capitalist and materialist lifestyle as antithetical to progress, particularly towards national independence, represented a view advocated by the *thakin*. Amar herself was a part of this student nationalist movement, which was strongly influenced by Marxism-Leninism, and one of the pioneering female student activists. These student activists, like Marxist and socialist intellectuals elsewhere, believed that consumerism "distract[ed] modern women from the more pressing issues of politics and class."[19]

Ultimately, however, neither conservatism nor the changing tides of ideological and political movements in the emergence of young Marxist-Leninist intellectuals and nationalists account for the gendered nature of the censure of the *khit hsan thu*. There was no shortage of Burmese men who were Westernized. Writing in 1908, U May Oung, an "England returned" barrister and the father of Daw Mya Sein (discussed in chapters 2 and 3), lamented that young Burmese men "were learning to drop Burmese ideals, to forget and even to despise the customs and habits of [their] ancestors, and to hanker after much that was bad and very little that was good in those alien races."[20] One of the earliest Burmese novels, *Rhve prañ cui:* (Ruler of a golden realm, 1914), by U Lat (1866–1921), provided the now classic caricature of the Burmese Anglophile in the character of Maung Thaung Pe, a young returnee from England and a newly minted barrister. Maung Thaung Pe shows no gratitude towards his father, U Ya Kyaw, who incurred a large debt to finance his son's education abroad. Instead, he upsets his father with his Westernized behavior; his form of greeting is a handshake,[21] and he refuses to sit on a mat on the floor because, in his Western trousers, he prefers to sit in a chair.[22] Yet it was the *khit hsan thu,* not the *khit hsan tha,* who became the subject of controversy. The one exception was the "modern monk," made famous through Thein Pe Myint's *Tet hpongyi* (The modern monk),[23] published in 1937. The book was a highly controversial novel about the immoral life of a corrupt Buddhist monk who indulges in lay activities ranging from sexual intercourse to the accumulation of personal wealth and goods. The author himself explained his satirical depiction of the *tet hpongyi* as a reflection on the destructive impact of British colonial rule on both the Buddhist clergy and the laity in Burma.[24]

The *tet hpongyi,* then, was a male counterpart to the *tet khit thami.* The public reception of the novel is revealing, however. The satirical depiction of the *tet hpongyi* created quite a sensation and garnered intense publicity at the time of its publication, not because of its popularity but because of the furious backlash that it prompted from the sangha, which led to the banning of the book by the government and a public apology from Thein Pe Myint.[25]

No less conspicuous than the absence of controversy over the *khit hsan tha* is the appearance of the irreverent and self-indulgent *khit hsan thu* in the popular press at a historical juncture when there appeared to be no lack of *myo chit* (patriotic) women. Burmese women in the 1920s and 1930s showed no signs of becoming unpatriotic. On the contrary, an increasing number of Burmese women were being mobilized by the *wunthanu* movement. For every nationalist organization founded, a women's branch appeared; women university students and factory workers participated actively in anticolonial protests. Why did images of the unwise and materialistic *khit hsan thu* who flouted tradition for the sake of Westernization appear at this very moment when patriotic women had become more visible? Was she a figment of the imagination, bearing no relation to actual women? Louise Edwards points out that the discourses about the "policing" of modern women in Republican China were "synecdochical discussions" about governing a modernizing population, engaged in by reformist male intellectuals who sought to reclaim their role as leading advisers for the nation. As such, "focusing on the detailed behavior of China's women obscures the deeper significance of the debate."[26] Similarly, Sarah Stevens argues that in interwar China, the new woman and the modern girl reflected conflicting emotions arising from ideas of modernity, progress, urbanization, "new" China, and a changing gender ideology.[27] Were discussions about the *khit hsan thu* likewise synecdochical? The choice of women over men as symbols of capitalist and consumerist modernity would have been logical given that in Burma, as in other Theravada Buddhist societies, women had long been associated with attachment to the realm of desire, and the influential role of women in the worldly sphere of commerce, profit seeking, and monetary affairs—the very attribute that gave women their autonomy and power—was deemed spiritually polluting.[28] The commercialization of the *khit hsan thu* in the popular press, especially in advertisements, would have also made the gendered trope readily available for deployment.

According to Journal Gyaw Ma Ma Lay, arguably the foremost defender of the fashionable woman, the frivolous and self-indulgent *khit hsan thu* was indeed a fabrication. Ma Ma Lay, whose given name was Ma Tin Hlaing, was a daughter of a manager of Dawson Bank, the only British-owned bank based in the country. From childhood, she had led, in her own words, "a modern lifestyle comparable to that of the British."[29] She attended the ABM school in

Hpyapon and then the Myoma National Girls' High School, but because of her mother's mental illness, she left school before completing the tenth grade. At home, she spent all of her time reading, not merely to entertain herself but "to study the craft of writing."[30] She transitioned from a reader to a writer in 1936 at the age of twenty when she submitted an article to *Myanmar alin* about a disagreement she had with a local women's association.[31] Apparently, fifteen members of the association sent Ma Ma Lay an anonymous letter chastising her for playing badminton with young men and threatening to write about her in the *Myanmar alin* if she persisted in her "shameless" and "unladylike behavior."[32] Although the submission was not published itself, it led to her first article, "To Have Brains with a Capital B"[33] which appeared in *Myanmar alin* under the pseudonym "Ya Way Hlaing." The article, not unlike her initial submission, was a rejoinder to a newspaper article by a Maung Tha Thin, which criticized young Burmese women who played badminton.[34] Just two years later, she married U Chit Maung, then editor of *Myanmar alin*. With her husband, Ma Ma Lay founded, edited, and published *Journal gyaw,* the most popular journal and one of only two widely circulating journals in Burma in the years immediately before the Second World War. U Chit Maung was only thirty-four years old when he passed away in 1946, leaving Ma Ma Lay a young widow with three children and *Journal gyaw* to look after. Were it not for his tragic death, her career as a writer and journalist might have been overshadowed by the husband-wife partnership. But she came into her own as she took charge of the weekly paper as its sole director, manager, and chief editor—an unconventional undertaking at a time when most, if not all, publishing houses and periodicals were owned and run by men. Her command of *Journal gyaw* at the young age of twenty-nine significantly contributed to the opinion of the public and the literary community that Ma Ma Lay was a talented woman of letters.[35]

By her own admission, Ma Ma Lay enjoyed wearing high-end clothes and shared with her sisters a keen interest in fashion; she made sure that she was groomed, coiffed, and made-up even if she was just staying home. U Chit Maung himself told her that when they first met, he was greatly surprised to see such a *khit hsan* woman. Ma Ma Lay was also a firm believer in the equality of the sexes, as might be expected from her debut article. She declared to U Chit Maung that she never thought of herself as an inferior being because of her gender and would not let others treat her as such. As for U Chit Maung, who confessed to having relatively low regard for the female sex in the past, he credited her with correcting his own sexist views.[36] It is hardly surprising, then, that she was at the forefront of the defense of *khit hsan thu* in the popular press. In the January 1940 issue of *Journal gyaw,* Ma Ma Lay wrote an article titled "The Deteriorating State of the Mentality of Men."[37] She began the article by referring to a letter she received from a *hti sayay ma galay* (young female clerical worker at a lottery shop),[38] who told Ma Ma Lay that she, like the majority of *hti sayay ma galay* in Yangon, was constantly taunted at her job by male customers who called her a *krak tū rve: ma* (female parrot). This particular form of insult had spread among the predominantly male clientele of lottery shops as a result of a cartoon, published in *Myanmar alin,* that alleged that a *hti sayay ma galay* must have committed sins in her past life to end up in the trade; although a human in appearance, she had the karma of a female parrot: a pretty and colorful creature on display who talks mindlessly and incessantly with strangers. The author of the letter asked, "Am I to blame for making a living this way?"[39]

Ma Ma Lay pointed out that the experience of the young woman was representative of a pervasive problem of male chauvinism:

> We Burmese women cannot move our hands or feet without them [Burmese men] telling us we are too "busy." If we stay at home, then we are "hiding," but if we go out then we're "jack of all trades." Our clothes are too sheer or too thick, too long or too short. We should neither shorten nor lengthen our eyebrows. . . . We live in an era when Burmese men deride everything we women do![40]

The motive behind such criticisms, Ma Ma Lay explained, was not to be found in the way young Burmese women carried themselves but in the inability of Burmese men to cope with women who not only worked outside the home but also possessed office jobs:

> For some Burmese men, happiness is when their women subsist only on their [men's] earnings. To be a woman, for such men, is to be a dependent. These men cannot stomach women holding office jobs, as men do, that require going to offices and sitting at desks. These men taunt such women as the *hti sayay ma galay* who wrote to me, because they cannot bear to acknowledge that women can perform as well as men in professional careers.[41]

Ma Ma Lay then proceeded to describe the working conditions of women in "Western countries":

> In the West, all women—young and old, single and married, daughters and mothers—exercise skills they have gained both inside and outside the home to earn their living. And they dress themselves stylishly and according to the fashion appropriate to their respective careers.[42]

Finally, she added that it was a well-known fact that adolescent Burmese women could not go out alone without getting harassed and jeered at by men. She asked, rhetorically, why this had become a common experience for Burmese women, so common that they had become used to it. Was it because the young women deserved to be harassed or because the men gave in to their base instincts? In her view, the problem lay not with the women but with the lustful beholders, the men who insisted on viewing women in public as objects of sexual desire. Although men were exhorting Burmese people to love their *amyo* (their own kind), they had disregarded their own principle and had failed to protect their *amyo*. In conclusion, she urged all young women workers to be resilient, ignore the ignoble behavior and mentality of their fellow men, and focus on succeeding in their careers.[43]

From the perspective of Ma Ma Lay, there was nothing shameful about the bodily practices of young Burmese women who dressed themselves "according to the fashion appropriate to their respective careers." Having a career demanded that a woman style herself appropriately for her profession. The attention paid to outward appearance was not a meaningless pursuit of a self-absorbed woman who cared only about appearances and aesthetics. It was neither offensive to "traditional" sensibilities, nor unpatriotic, nor sexually or otherwise provocative. What was offensive and unpatriotic was the mentality of sexist men who, despite their exhortation to love their *amyo,* harried their women. The reprehensible *khit hsan thu* was fictitious. Yet she was not entirely imaginary insofar as the censorious representations of the *khit hsan thu* represented a reaction to actual and dynamic social and cultural transformations with which she was associated, in particular the increasing visibility of women in the public sphere and their undertaking of formerly "manly" work such as clerical and office jobs. The ongoing debate about the *khit hsan thu,* her bodily practices, and sexism in postwar 1940s Burma reinforces these interpretations and illustrates that the deeper significance of the castigation of the *khit hsan thu* can be unpacked only in relation to actual Burmese women whose behavior challenged normative masculine and feminine identities in a highly public fashion.

"LET THERE BE CREST HAIR!" THE DEBATE OVER THE *KHIT HSAN THU* CONTINUES

In December 1941 the Imperial Japanese Army began its attack against the British colonial government in Burma. Within a few months the Japanese had sent the British fleeing to India to set up the government of Burma in exile in Simla. By March 1942 the last British forces had fled Rangoon, and most of the estimated nine hundred thousand Indians in Burma had begun their treacherous trek to India.[44] The Japanese occupation of Burma during the Second World War took place more smoothly and quickly than even the Japanese army had expected. The fall of the British was "swift and irreversible."[45] Nevertheless, the Japanese were ousted almost as swiftly as they had displaced the British. In 1945 the British reoccupied Burma with the help of the Allied Forces.

During the *Japan khit* (Japanese era),[46] as the period of Japanese occupation is known in Burma, the majority of newspapers and periodicals—with the exception of *Thuriya* and *Myanmar alin*—were disrupted.[47] Many were abandoned. With the end of the war in 1945, however, the press quickly came back to life. In 1946 alone, approximately twenty newspapers were started.[48] The discussion about the *khit hsan thu* also resumed in the press. In 1947 the magazine *Thway thauk* (Comrade monthly) featured a series of editorials and letters on the *khit hsan* fashion. The January issue focused specifically on the *amauk* (crest hair) and contained a column full of letters from readers, the first of which proclaimed that the *amauk* had no harmful effects on women's virtue. The author, who signed the letter as a *"khit hmi thu,"* argued that women who adorned the *amauk* spent no more money on hair products than did men on such recreational habits as cigarette smoking. She also pointed out that women with the *amauk* were just as dutiful to their husbands as the women without it and that the hairstyle did not make them one minute late for work.[49] Another letter from a "1946 woman" stated that if men were to give up the *bo ke* (English haircut) and revert to the tradition of keeping long hair and wearing it in a *sadohn* (chignon), women, too, would stop wearing the *amauk*. "Perhaps then," she noted, "men will realize that though women today wear modern clothing, they, unlike men, have not gotten rid of the traditional *sadohn*."[50] She added that women did not frivolously adopt modern clothes but did so purposively to better suit their changing work environment.

In the February 1947 issue, letters by men defending the *amauk* were published. Maung Ba Maung, for instance, wrote: "If you're going to criticize women for keeping the crest hair, you ought also to consider men's fashion. You say to women, 'Don't follow every single crazy American trend.' Why don't you please first do something about the men who pay exorbitant prices for secondhand shirts and trousers from America and walk about town flaunting their 'stylish' outfit???"[51] The letter by Maung Ba Maung was published alongside one from a Maung Maung Aye, who made a plea for men in Burma to stop mocking women over such petty things as facial powder, the *amauk,* and women's eyebrows and to get along with women for the good of the country.[52]

Editorials published in conjunction with these letters similarly discussed the current uproar in Burma over the fashion sensibilities of modern-day Burmese women, with some representing it as a dispute between men and women and others as an issue of gender discrimination. An article in *Thway thauk* in July 1947 highlighted the hypocrisy of men's censure of the *khit hsan thu*. Men, too, wore shoes and pants and spent no less money than women on imported goods, but they were not berated. Why, the author questioned, were women who wore the *eingyi pa* and put on lipstick accused of being "prostitutes"[53] when such women were by and large perfectly respectable? She emphasized the active role of women in Burma as income earners and stressed that fashion and patriotism were not mutually exclusive; in her opinion, it was possible to look good and be a *myo chit may* (female patriot) at the same time. The author also stressed the need for all Burmese people to "change with the times"[54] and appealed to Burmese men to stop assailing the young *khit hmi amyothami,* who were only changing with the times.[55] Also in July 1947, Ngwe U Daung wrote an article for *Shumawa* titled "Let There Be Crest Hair!"[56] in which he observed that "while it may be the 'law of nature' for men to criticize, to attempt to marginalize, and to oppress women, there are many reasons why men in the East have far outdone the sexist behavior of men in the West."[57] He drew attention to the fact that there was nothing new or unusual about controversial fashion trends. What was shocking was the obsessive and extreme reaction of Burmese men to the *khit hsan* fashion and the way women insisted on espousing it despite the castigation. He reckoned that, in due time, the *amauk* would become rather ordinary and women would come up with yet another *catuiṅ sac* (new style). "So," he concluded, "let women *amauk* to their hearts' content!"[58]

Ma Ma Lay also contributed to this discourse on the sexist current of the social and cultural milieu of 1940s Burma. Her article "Wife,"[59] published in January 1948, is of particular interest. In the first half of the article, Ma Ma Lay appeared to replicate the discourse on the separate spheres encountered in chapter 3: the conceptualization of men as breadwinners and women as housewives and mothers, and the association of men and women with the public and domestic spheres, respectively. The article began by asserting that women were the foundation of the domestic realm and that while men are away from home governing the world and engaging in large businesses and national and international politics, wives maintain and ensure the health, order, and safety of their homes.[60] Ma Ma Lay herself had aspired to be such a wife. Her self-portrayal as the devoted and selfless wife of a nationalist leader in *A Man Like Him* conveyed in no uncertain terms that the main duty of a wife was to support her husband and take care of their family.[61] However, the trajectory of the article then took a turn: "But men will not admit that they rely on their wives to uphold them, to nourish and to shelter them—that husband and wife are mutually dependent."[62] "In fact," Ma Ma Lay argued, "men think they can do as they like to their wives and keep them in whatever condition they please."[63] As in her article examined above, Ma Ma Lay blamed Burmese men who refused to recognize women as their equal and who chose to scorn women who strove to support Burmese men by excelling in both the domestic and the public realms. The article was not about the patriotic wife-and-mother who protected the integrity and future prosperity of the nation. In order for Burma to move forward, Ma Ma Lay proclaimed, men would have to recognize that the progress of their wives and women was as crucial as that of men: "Of the several important national concerns in Burma today, the most important is the group that holds the key to the welfare of the country: *meinma.*"[64]

These postwar writings on the battle between the sexes further complicate an understanding of why the *khit hsan thu* was relentlessly and consistently caricatured and castigated. As is so often the case with the "new woman" and the "modern girl," the *khit hsan thu* symbolized disruptions in existing gender roles and expectations. Whether pursuing higher education, writing along-side male writers and editors for the press, appropriating new hairstyles and clothes, or organizing workers' strikes, Burmese women actively explored the possibilities of the *khit kala*. In the guises of writer, student, professional, laborer, and politician, they served as prominent icons of progress and mod-ernization and challenged existing cultural norms and practices, particularly those pertaining to notions of femininity and masculinity. Fashion, as the epitome of change and mutability, embodied these developments. The pil-lorying of *khit hsan thu* in the media represented a reactionary response to the newfound social mobility and authority of educated, politicized, and working women in Burma. The behaviors of actual Burmese women were therefore fun-damental, not irrelevant, to the discourse on the *khit hsan thu.* She thrived in the press precisely because of the very real activism of Burmese women of vari-ous ages who called into question the contours of prevailing gender identities.

An article in the August 1938 issue of *Ngan hta lawka,* entitled "If Wives Should Receive Salaries!" exemplifies this point. The author, who questioned what would happen "if husbands were to give monthly salaries to their wives," claimed that "there would be less [women] robbing men of their jobs" and explained as follows: "As wives they would have less worry and more income for they could exploit their personal charms and blandishments with greater success than as clerks and typists in offices."[65] A prospective wife would hag-gle with her suitor over her salary, the author posited: "If she were just a plain woman with a high school qualification and very few other attainments, she would not demand much. Whereas, if she were a [university graduate] with honors in some subject like Pali, and knew how to play the [piano] and cook delicious dishes and had a Diana-like face with a stream-lined figure, then she would demand a very high salary."[66] Other wifely demands the author imagined were "an increment after a year's service" and a raise "with the coming-in of every newcomer into the family."[67] The author then concluded, "Such, in short, are few of the incidents which . . . are apt to create domestic strife and discord if husbands should, in a spirit of generosity and because of the strike of wives who will no longer hold their portfolios without salaries, grant salaries to their better halves!"[68] Here marriage functioned as a metaphor for relations between the sexes, and a "salaried" wife symbolized redefinitions of established gender norms and practices. The entrenchment of a capitalist economy had made capital the overriding consideration in the intimate sphere of domesticity (though men, who were thought to be generous, were less capitalistic than women, who were calculating and materialistic). Twentieth-century developments in women's education and employment had led men and women to compete against one another and made women more aware and assured of their own worth and abilities. Women were not afraid to use their feminine wiles and flaunt their assets, including their attractive figures. Self-realized and confident women robbed men of their jobs, salaries, and domestic bliss. Gender relations were thus presented as a zero-sum game: women's gains were men's losses, and the advancement of women translated into the disempowerment of men. Previous chapters have shown that not everyone in Burma perceived the achievements made by women as a loss incurred by men. Many women and men advocated for female education and employment as vital social reforms indispensable to national progress and independence. Yet others commented on the transgressive behavior of Burmese women as an indirect means of discussing what the authors portrayed as the emasculation of Burmese men.

We need not assume that masculinity had to be "in crisis" to be contemplated, for both masculinity and femininity are inherently unstable categories perpetually defined and redefined. Yet we find embedded in the discourse on modern-day women in colonial Burma clear signs of embattled masculinity. Among the causes of this embattled masculinity, as the fear of gender subversion conjured in "If Wives Should Receive Salaries!" indicates, were shifts in gender norms, practices, and relations, real as well as imaginary. Women in 1930s Burma took an increasingly active role in government administration, anticolonial protests, and nationalist organizations, all of which had largely been the sole purview of men. They actively used such developments as government-funded education, the popular print media, and women's political organizations and sought access to professional careers and government offices to represent themselves in public. They emerged alongside and in competition with their male counterparts as aspiring and leading decision makers in modern Burmese society. The self-assuredness and eagerness with which women embraced these opportunities—or at least were imagined to have done so—were powerfully represented by the *khit hsan thu,* who exerted control over her own body and defied criticisms of her decisions about how she spent her income or groomed herself. The emergence of educated, working, politicized, and independent-minded women was at the root of serious crises in masculinity in many societies the world over at the turn of the twentieth century. The expansion of female education, the rise of suffragettes and female political activism, and the sexually liberated and self-reliant "new woman" who undertook masculine work all served as threats to dominant masculinity and raised fears about the unruliness of the modern woman.[69] In this sense, the transformations in gender norms, practices, and relations in the late nineteenth and early twentieth centuries have to be conceptualized as borderless phenomena occurring simultaneously and globally. What was taking place in colonial Burma was characteristic of the *khit kala.*

Nevertheless, we can also identify a constellation of conditions that were distinct to British Burma. As noted earlier, historians of colonial Burma have been correct to point out that the influx of foreign men displaced the indigenous population from key socioeconomic niches.[70] Burmese men were not merely deprived of socioeconomic opportunities, for they were marginalized in more intimate ways. The growth of various forms of intimate relationships among native women and foreign men, discussed in the preceding chapter, diminished the prestige and virility of Burmese men. We must also consider the colonial politics of masculinity. While the imperial powers in the region—British, French, American, and Japanese—were propagating an understanding of the ideal man as hardy, courageous, disciplined, and martial, and promoting what Alfred McCoy has called "a cult of masculinity"[71] with an emphasis on military service as the rite of passage to manhood, many men in Burma were ideologically and institutionally denied these qualities of manliness.[72] The British viewed ethnic-minority Karens, Chins, and Kachins as belonging to the "martial races," a familiar category produced through the elaborate colonial and ethnographic literature on India.[73] However, the majority of Burmese men, particularly the ethnic-majority Burman, were perceived as "nonmartial," and Christian missionaries and colonial officers produced and perpetuated Orientalist images of Burmese men as not only lazy, henpecked, and lacking in ambition but also undisciplined and unwarriorlike.[74] Chief Commissioner Charles Crosthwaite, for example, characterized

Karens as courageous and hardy, Kachins as trustworthy and the strongest race in Burma, and Burman men as "hopelessly unfit."[75] His view of English men stood in sharp contrast:

> It is a fact of which we may all be proud that the average young English gentleman when thrown into conditions which demand from him courage, energy, and judgment, and the power of governing, answers to the call. Whether he comes from a good school or university, or from his regiment, from the sea or the ranch, whether he has come through the competitive system or has obtained his appointment by other means, he will in the majority of cases be found capable, and sometimes conspicuously able.[76]

The British were not unanimous in their opinions of the manliness of Burmese or Burman men. In his account of the Second Anglo-Burmese War, Colonel W. F. B. Laurie quoted testimonials from other British colonels that Burmese troops fought with "unusual strength and care" and demonstrated bravery and obstinacy they had "never witnessed in any troops."[77] He himself observed that Burmese men made "constitutionally brave" soldiers whose "persevering obstinacy" would not be easily overcome by troops "less perfectly disciplined than those of England."[78] Not long after the final annexation of Burma, however, differing views of Burmese manhood became dominant. Writing in 1898, British officer Harold Fielding Hall remarked that Burmese men had never developed "a cult of bravery" or regarded it as "the prime virtue of a man," a lack Hall attributed to Buddhist teachings that failed to praise "aggressive courage."[79] The Burman man, like the educated but effeminate "Bengali babu," was portrayed as cerebral rather than martial, suitable only for white-collar jobs.[80] Not surprisingly, the indigenous population were well represented in public administration, and Burmans dominated the posts in law and instruction; in 1931, Burmese people represented 63.4 percent of those in public administration, 56 percent of those in the teaching profession, and more than 70 percent of lawyers of all kinds in Burma.[81] Yet the colonial administration admitted fewer and fewer Burmese men into the administrative machinery as the Depression of the 1930s halted the expansion of government employment, even as Rangoon University continued to graduate a growing population of Burmese men equipped precisely with the skills of clerical workers.

Fictional Burmese literature produced during the colonial period expressed an awareness of these unflattering stereotypes and an urgency in recovering the manliness of Burmese men. For instance, the aforementioned caricature of the

Anglophile barrister Maung Thaung Pe by U Lat can be read as a critique not only of the Westernization of young Burmese men but also of their internalization of the Orientalist image of Burmese men. Also, that Burmese historical novels, which began to appear in the late 1910s, featured mighty kings and soldiers from Burma's past is unlikely to have been a coincidence. Of the two famous novels Ledi Pandita U Maung Gyi wrote, the first, *Nat Shin Naung* (1919), was about the soldier-poet-prince of Toungoo, Nat Shin Naung; the second, *Tabin Shwe Hti vatthu* (1924–1928), was a four-volume epic about two of the great warrior kings of Burma, Tabin Shwe Hti (r. 1531–1550) and his brother-in-law Bayin Naung (r. 1551–1581). These were followed in 1931 by U Thein Maung's *Rai mran mā* (Burmese heroes), a life story of King Alaung Hpaya (r. 1752–1760), revered as one of the greatest conquerors Burma ever saw and, in the words of the author, "one of the great heroes of Burma."[82] In 1932 the historical novelist Shwe Satkya made his debut with *Nā: khaṃ tau* (Royal herald), which gave an account of the recapturing of Pegu by King Anauk Pet Lun (r. 1606–1628) from Filipe de Brito. The following year, Dagon Khin Khin Lay published *Rhve cvan nyui* (Golden kite), about noble leaders of a gang of bandits who battle the British during their pacification campaign of 1886–1887. *Sū pun krī:* (A great rebel; 1936) and *Cac thvak sū* (A soldier going to the battlefront; 1939), by Maha Swe, told similar stories about the resistance put up by Burmese people against invaders de Brito and Tho Han Bwa, the Shan king of Ava who infamously killed 360 prominent monks.[83] These novels sought to restore interest and pride not only in the history of Burmese people but in Burmese men as well.[84] Yet at the same time that the historical figures of fierce and valiant Burmese warriors—and, in particular, Burman warriors—contested the image of Burmese men as nonmartial, they nevertheless confirmed that the "aggressive courage" of Burman men had been lost and needed recuperation in the *khit kala.*

In addition, in contrast to other colonies such as the Philippines where men enlisted in the colonial armies, Burmese men were categorically denied entry into the military. Mary Callahan has calculated that at the outbreak of the First World War, the number of indigenous members of the army and the military police in Burma was probably no more than three hundred, and there were 2.5 indigenous members of the armed forces for every 100,000 people in Burma.[85] The ban against the enrollment of Burmans into the army was lifted only in 1935. The ethnic composition of the armed forces in Burma in 1941 still showed a conspicuous disproportion: Burmans made up more than 75 percent of the entire population but only about 25 percent of the armed forces, while Indians, Karens, and Chins made up 32, 35, and 16 percent of the armed forces, respectively.[86] The *tat* (army) movement of the 1930s is best understood as a response to this exclusionary policy. In 1930 a former Legislative Council member for education (who in 1940 became the first indigenous defense councilor) established the first *tat,* called Ye Tat (Brave Army), in order to "organize and give youths basic military and physical training for the nationalist movement."[87] Dobama Asiayone followed with the Bama Letyone Tat (Burman Forearm Army) in 1935, as did the university students' union with the Thanmani Tat (Steel Army) in 1936. According to Callahan, every major nationalist or religious organization had established its own *tat* by the middle of the 1930s, all for the purpose of providing paramilitary training (though without any firearms).[88] The goal of these volunteer corps, who wore uniforms and marched through towns, was surely not only to show support for the *wunthanu* movements but also to publicly reject the image of Burmese men as nonmartial and unmanly.[89] The imperative to restore and demonstrate the manliness of Burmese men also sheds light on the enthusiasm with which thousands of ethnic-majority Burmans enlisted in the first national armies in Burma, of which the Burma Independence Army (BIA) was the first. Established in 1941 across the border in Thailand, the BIA troops consisted of Burmese men trained by the Japanese. The BIA followed Japanese forces into Burma in December 1941 and provided vital support to the Japanese army by collecting intelligence and supplies and sabotaging British operations during the invasion.[90] Within six months the BIA had enlisted twenty-three thousand mostly Burman men.[91] There was no shortage of volunteers for the Burma National Army (BNA), a second national army formed under the Japanese after the BIA was disbanded; BNA forces totaled roughly fifteen thousand troops and officers in 1943.[92] The Japanese occupation of Burma had thus given Burmese and Burman men an opportunity to prove that they were in fact a martial race. The British, however, set out to demobilize the BNA as soon as it had reoccupied Burma and to sideline Burman men in the postwar British Burma army, despite the assistance the BNA had provided the Allied Forces in their campaign against the Japanese.[93]

In other words, British colonial rule produced a set of conditions whereby the manliness of indigenous men was attacked from many fronts. Various transgressions of normative gender boundaries represented one of these fronts. The debate over the *khit hsan thu* in the media was a way for men (and women) to come to terms with the predicament of embattled masculinity. Other studies on the relationship between manhood and nationhood have revealed that efforts to enforce normative femininity often seek to compensate for and negotiate a crisis in masculinity.[94] Similarly, by excoriating the behavior of the *khit hsan thu,* Burmese men endeavored to assert moral authority over their own women and reassert their manliness. The discourse

on the *khit hsan thu* was about negotiations and redefinitions of both femininity and masculinity.

THE POLITICS OF FASHION AND MASCULINITY

The bodily practices of the *khit hsan thu* exemplified new social formations and hierarchies and stood for irreducibly plural motives and interests.
For female college students and graduates in 1920s and 1930s Burma, *khit
hsan* fashion served to distinguish them as members of the growing educated middle class who had career ambitions to be achieved through learning
and self-advancement. For women such as Ma Ma Lay, the attention young
women of the *khit kala* paid to makeup, grooming, and clothes signified
their conscious undertaking of new roles. Caring for the outward self was an
external manifestation of, not the inattention to, the cultivation of the inner
self. The bodily practices of a *khit hsan thu* symbolized her participation in a
khit kala characterized by mobility and self-realization.

Yet "if clothing is one form of 'text,'" as Mina Roces explains, "several
meanings can be attributed to it, often meanings different from the wearer's
agenda."[95] What some Burmese women intended as a conscious effort at
self-reconstruction, others perceived as mindless mimicking of the West
and its values and lifestyle that emphasized wealth, consumption, and self-
gratification. Amid a nationalist discourse undergirded by traditionalism,
on the one hand, and Marxism-Leninism, on the other, fashionable young
women were imagined as agents and symptoms of a new era entrapped in
colonialism, capitalism, consumerism, and hedonism. In the hands of those
who sought to illustrate to the Burmese public the pernicious effects of
colonial rule on the *dobama,* the *khit hsan thu* was made to personify desire,
pleasure, and the physical. She functioned as an object lesson on the folly of
desire for the colonial, the foreign, and the Western. Images of the *khit hsan
thu,* like those of the wives and mistresses of foreign men, served to edify a
singular notion of modernization and nationalism.

Last but not least, the *khit hsan thu* was a metaphor for displaced fears and
anxieties about the advancement of Burmese women and the emasculation of
Burmese men. The criticisms of the sartorial choices of Burmese women represented an attempt to circumscribe not only their political role—as wearers
and bearers, not leaders, of nationalism—but also their social and cultural
roles. If in Dutch Indonesia women in traditional dress were associated with
the colonial past and thus made to embody immobility and disempowerment, women in *khit hsan* fashion in British Burma personified mobility and
empowerment. To denounce the *khit hsan thu* was to denounce the mobility

and self-actualization of young women and to express the desire and need for control, stability, and discipline. These young women were to be disciplined and controlled, furthermore, *by Burmese men* whose manhood and virility had been tried seriously by the humiliating experiences of colonialism: defeat by the British, continued subjugation by a colonial administration that rendered Burman men unmanly, economic marginalization that was exacerbated in the 1930s by the Depression, and foreign men's increased access to the bodies of Burmese women. The censure and policing of the *khit hsan thu* was one of the ways that men and women in Burma attempted to remasculinize Burmese men.

This is not to suggest that critics who targeted young Burmese women in their nationalist campaigns were not actually motivated by nationalism and antiforeign sentiments. On the contrary, this chapter has suggested that the nationalist movement in Burma and efforts to remasculinize Burmese men were interrelated. While further research is necessary to determine whether the sense of castration among lay Burmese men can be legitimately extended to the sangha, I would argue that even the violent attack on Burmese women by scissor-wielding monks was not merely about the protection of the Burmese nation and tradition but simultaneously about the redemption of their manhood. Not all of the persistent concerns with changing gender identities and relations that animated popular discourses in colonial Burma were concerns about the nation, however. The controversy over the *khit hsan thu* was also about a *khit kala* that unsettled long-existing notions of femininity and masculinity.

Conclusion

In 1973, eighteen years after the publication of her celebrated *Mon ywe mahu* (Not out of hate), Ma Ma Lay published *Thway* (Blood).[1] This less well-known novel revisits the theme of the encounter between different cultures but takes a stance decidedly at odds with her earlier position on the possibility of cross-cultural understanding. In *Thway*, foreign culture is embodied by its Japanese heroine, Yumi, who arrives in Burma in 1967 to search for her younger half-brother, Maung Maung, whom she has never met. Her deceased father had married a Burmese woman by the name of Ma Htway Htway while he was stationed in Burma during the Second World War. They had a son who was only ten months old when Japan lost the war and Yumi's father was pulled out of the country along with his battalion. She manages to find Maung Maung but discovers that he was stigmatized as a child for his mixed parentage—called by various derogatory names such as *gyapan put kale:* (rotten little Jap) and *gyapan cut* (lousy Jap)—and as a result, has grown to detest Japanese people.[2] Throughout the novel, his unconcealed resentment towards Yumi intensifies, but she relentlessly tries to gain the trust and affection of her only flesh and blood.

The contrasts between *Thway* and *Mon ywe mahu* are immediate and striking. Unlike the anglicized U Saw Han of *Mon ywe mahu,* Yumi shows great respect for Burmese history and culture. She not only studied Burmese language for her undergraduate and graduate degrees but also demonstrates familiarity with modern Burmese poetry and revered Burmese historical figures such as King Anawratha, Kyanzittha, Alaungpaya, and Bayinnaung; she is passionate about Burmese painting, music, and performing arts; she gives up her *bo* dress, wears *longyi* and *eingyi,* and eats with her fingers, in the traditional way. She is the antithesis of U Saw Han, not because she has become Burmanized—Yumi does not disregard her Japanese heritage and conducts herself in the manner of a respectable Japanese woman when appropriate—but rather because she possesses knowledge and appreciation of Burmese culture.

In addition, in *Thway,* Ma Ma Lay went to great lengths to depict the relationship between Yumi's father, Major Yoshida, and Ma Htway Htway, and between Yumi and Thet Lwin—Maung Maung's adoptive brother—as genuine, caring, and based on mutual understanding, as though to compensate for the uncompromisingly negative view of the marriage between U Saw Han and Way Way that the author expressed in *Mon ywe mahu.* Major Yoshida was already a widower when he met Ma Htway Htway, not a married man with a Japanese wife waiting for him back home. He formally married her, after having asked her father, a *thu gyi* (hereditary headman), for her hand in marriage. He loved his son very much and would have returned to Burma to find him if not for his deteriorating health. That is to say, his relationship with Ma Htway Htway was neither deceitful nor exploitative. Ma Ma Lay described the relationship between Yumi and Thet Lwin in similarly positive ways. *Thway* is filled with extended conversations between the two, comparing Japanese and Burmese painting, music, cuisine, and Buddhism. Both parties immerse themselves in these cultural exchanges enthusiastically and without any prejudices. Significantly, they always see eye to eye, often noting the compatibility of Japanese and Burmese cultures. For example, the first time Thet Lwin lays eyes on paintings by Yumi, he compliments her for the harmonious incorporation of Japanese style in her rendition of tropical Burmese scenes.[3] Whereas in *Mon ywe mahu,* cultural mixing was deemed perilous and ultimately impossible, in *Thway* it not only is possible—Maung Maung is a testament to this possibility—but can also be "harmonious."

Mon ywe mahu and *Thway* are diametrically opposed in such distinctive and pronounced ways that the contrast cannot be a mere coincidence. So why the contrast? The facts of the Japanese occupation of Burma and Burmese narratives of the period do not support the view that Japanese colonizers and the *Japan khit* were perceived as less inimical or harmful than British colonizers and the *British khit.* The Japanese army, often with the cooperation of Burmese politicians, committed a multitude of atrocities during its brief occupation of Burma.[4] In the British war tribunals the number of people tried and found guilty for crimes committed in Burma (112) was second only to the number of those tried and found guilty in Singapore (404).[5] In fact, one of the Japanese battalions that committed the highest number of rape offenses in all Japanese-occupied territories was stationed in Burma.[6]

Among the most appalling policies and practices of the Japanese was the "Great Sweat Army."[7] This was a corps of laborers recruited for the construction of the Thailand-Burma Railway, also known as the Death Railway, which stretched four hundred kilometers from Bampong, Thailand, to Thanbyuzayat, Burma.[8] The approximately 60,000 prisoners of war employed in the construction of the railway were deemed insufficient by the Japanese army, so at the behest of the Japanese, the Ba Maw administration organized the Great Sweat Army, inaugurating it with an inspiring speech that it must play its historic role in Burma's struggle for independence and the welfare of future Burmese generations.[9] According to a Burmese man who volunteered for the army as a propagandist and whose task was to promote cooperation with the Japanese army among the laborers, 30,000 to 80,000 of the 177,000 laborers conscripted to work for the railway died.[10] The construction of the railway also entailed the establishment of the notorious "comfort stations" that brought together Korean "comfort women"—sexual slaves of the Japanese military—from other Japanese colonies and local women to serve the sexual needs of Japanese soldiers.[11] U Hla Pe, a former aide to Ba Maw and the director of press and publicity under the Ba Maw government, recorded in his memoir that women were recruited along with men for the construction of the railway, occasionally for labor, but mostly for "organized rape."[12]

Not surprisingly, Burmese narratives of the period have described the *Japan khit* as a tremendously brutal era.[13] Memoirs by political elites from the period—even those that have credited the Japanese with having delivered independence from colonial rule—have acknowledged the routine ill treatment of Burmese people by the Japanese military.[14] They also emphasize the betrayal of the Burmese by the Japanese. U Nu, for instance, wrote in his memoir: "Before the war so many Burmans were so ready to follow the seductive piping of the Japanese without realizing at all in what direction it was leading us. And it led us to the Japanese occupation and to the oppression that we suffered under Japanese rule."[15] This deception at the hands of the Japanese has come to be encapsulated in a short song that chastises a Burmese woman by the name of Sein Kyi, who is abandoned with child by a Japanese soldier:

Oh Sein Kyi . . . Sein Kyi
so reckless in her spousal choice
to Tokyo he has left, your Japanese master
left you, he has, rotund with child.[16]

In the song, Sein Kyi symbolizes the people of Burma who had been "seduced" by the Japanese. Not unlike the wives and mistresses of European and Indian men, Sein Kyi represents the dangers of consorting with and trusting foreigners. Although the postwar generations in Burma seem to know little about the *Japan khit,* many are familiar with this song. In *Thway,* in fact, Maung Maung is haunted by the song, which the children in his village regularly sang to humiliate him.

As these accounts of the Japanese colonizers suggest, the image of foreigners and their relations with Burmese people in *Thway* has less to do with the realities of the *Japan khit* than with a shift in the way Ma Ma Lay regarded the (in)compatibility of Burmese and foreign cultures. Perhaps because of her distance from the colonial period, she had altered her earlier position on the mixing of Burmese and other cultures, though precisely to what extent is uncertain. At the very least, *Thway* rejects a totalizing perspective on Burmese engagements with foreign people, ideas, and practices and gestures towards a more complex understanding of the relations between the Burmese and the foreign, even when the foreign is also imperialist. The emotional scars that Maung Maung carries bear witness to the damage done to individuals by historical narratives that categorically deny and devalue receptiveness to and appreciation of difference and the experiences and memories of reaching out across the colonizer-colonized and foreign-native divide.

In a similar vein, this book has sought to restore some of the complexities of colonialism and modernization in Burma. It has done so through a close analysis of gendered representations of the *khit kala* (present era) in Burma's burgeoning print culture that have allowed us to unpack what "modernity" meant and entailed for Burmese men and women. The educated young woman, or *yuwadi,* signified educational reforms, the growth of popular print literature, and the increased participation of women in the sphere of knowledge and cultural production. She was also a sign of the vital importance of self-cultivation and advancement, or *toe tet yay,* measured in terms of the status of women, to visions of the *khit kala.* The housewife-and-mother and the fashionable *khit hsan thu* were also icons of *toe tet yay,* self-improvement, and self-realization, but their means of fulfilling their potentialities and achieving progress was through the consumption of the latest scientific knowledge and commodities. These modern women exemplified how the rising consumer culture had shaped the tastes and desires of Burmese men and women and transformed what was expected of women in their role of wife and mother. Expectations of a wife and mother were also informed by the emergence of patriots, and the female patriot had the additional duty of nurturing and protecting a patriotic family. The increasing mobilization of women by nationalist and feminist movements also encouraged and obligated women to contribute to organized politics. Images of the *bo gadaw* and women who married Indian men and bore *kabya* children signified the entrenchment of racialized understandings of inclusion and exclusion and the consolidation of a Burmese national culture defined in limited, race-, class-, and religion-specific ways. In addition, the wives and mistresses of foreigners, along with the materialistic and self-indulgent fashionistas, personified an era of progress in which the self was privileged over the *amyo,* and Burmese people remained emasculated and subjugated by the inequalities, deceptions, and deprivations of the colonial period. In these last two forms, women of the *khit kala* embodied a modernity that failed to release Burma from the grips of colonialism—a "colonial modernity." They encapsulated a chauvinistic attitude that dismissed the contributions that Burmese men and women had made to local endeavors to advance and modernize their country precisely through associations with foreign and translocal people, ideas, and movements.

The feminine figuration of a colonial modernity is a familiar trope even today, and a leitmotif in representations of Aung San Suu Kyi by the Burmese government. As several scholars of contemporary Burmese politics have pointed out, the government has engaged in a campaign of character assassination against Aung San Suu Kyi since her emergence on the political scene in the late 1980s.[17] In their attempt to delegitimize Aung San Suu Kyi as the daughter of the Burmese national hero Aung San and to render her unpatriotic, the leaders and journalists of the government have avoided using her name, instead referring to her variously as "Mrs. Michael Aris," "the Veto Lady," "Mrs. Race Destructionist," "England returnee miss," "democracy princess," and, not surprisingly, *bo gadaw.*[18] Take, for instance, the following quote from the state-owned newspaper *Myanmar alin:*[19]

> According to Myanma customary law and Myanma Dhamma Rules, a bad and evil offspring shall not have the right to get inheritance from one's parents. The Bogadaw has lost her right to inherit her father's name "Aung San." According to English custom there is no reason to even call her Suu Kyi. She should be called Daw Michael Aris or Mrs. Michael Aris.
>
> In what bad and evil manner did the Bogadaw behave to lose the right of inheriting her father's name? The most simple answer is that in the plot to assassinate her father, it was the Englishmen who pulled the strings from behind the scene and provided assistance and it is because Suu Kyi had married an Englishman and given birth to two sons. . . . The fifth obligation of the children towards their parents is to safeguard [their] own race. As for Suu Kyi, who is the daughter of no ordinary person but a National Leader, instead of preserving the race of her parents, the Myanmar race which the father greatly loves, she destroyed it by mixing blood with an Englishman.[20]

Cartoons published in *Myanmar alin* during the 1990s similarly show that Aung San Suu Kyi's marriage to a *bo* has been a target of attacks by the Burmese government that seek not only to regenerate anticolonial resentment but also to denigrate her as morally compromised, untrustworthy, and "having more in common with the British than with the Burmese."[21] Likewise, the Burmese government has repeatedly castigated her as a "traitor puppet" of neocolonialists and an "axe handle," a euphemism for a tool of British and American neocolonialism used to "chop up" and destroy Burma.[22] Characterized as a minion of Western capitalist and neocolonial powers, Aung San Suu Kyi has become a specter of a modern yet colonial Burma.

It is no secret that the leaders of the postcolonial governments have used the purported threat that Western powers pose to the nation in order to justify their refusal to give up dictatorial rule. As in other postcolonial states in the region, the authoritarian regime in Burma has been inclined to reinvoke the trauma of colonialism to ratify the raison d'être of the state.[23] The female specter of colonial modernity, who conjures the loss of Burmese culture and nation to deceitful and exploitative foreigners, reenacts and revalidates the founding myth of the military regime as the only force capable of restoring and maintaining national sovereignty. What is less well known is that the gendered metaphor of the trauma of colonialism is not the product of the current Burmese government alone. It has formed a recurrent and crucial element of Burmese political discourse since at least the colonial period. Its efficacy derives precisely from older feminine figurations of the *thumya bama,* "their Burmese": the wives and mistresses of foreign men, the mothers of *kabya* children, the Westernized modern young women known as *tet khit thami,* and the self-indulgent, trendy *khit hsan thu* investigated in the preceding pages. What is even less readily acknowledged is that such representations of colonial modernity in Burma represented only one among many figurations of the *khit kala.*

As this study has revealed, negative depictions of the contemporary woman, or *khit hmi thu,* coexisted with positive as well as ambiguous portrayals that cannot be profitably assessed in isolation from one another or without taking into consideration the actual practices of modern Burmese women. The *khit hmi thu* expressed a yearning for change as well as stability, and for the foreign as well as the familiar. The images of the *khit hmi thu* as either progressive or degenerate, patriotic or unpatriotic, politicized or depoliticized, public or domestic, and educated or ignorant were selectively invoked to support the agenda of Burmese men and women who negotiated multiple salient models for modernization and envisioned alternatives to the either-or choice between *dobama* and *thumya bama.*

In other words, this gendered examination of colonialism and modernization prompts us to reckon squarely with the heterogeneity and irreducibility of the colonial encounter. It recognizes, on the one hand, the imprint of colonialism on Burmese modernity. Colonization affected the ways that Burmese men and women could, did, and desired to experience and imagine the *khit kala,* albeit in often unpredictable ways. I have emphasized, in particular, the differential impact of colonialism on men and women that contributed to making "Burmese women" a privileged idiom for discussing colonialism, modernization, and nationalism. The specific demands and circumstances of British colonial rule in Burma—the large influx of single men from England and British India, policies and practices by both the government and private businesses of employing migrant and immigrant men while indigenous and especially Burman men were sidelined, the official preference for "temporary unions" over marriage with native women, the establishment of coeducational institutions run by Christian missionaries often with the support of the British administration, the centrality of "the conditions of women" to the colonial civilizing mission, and colonial representations of strong and independent Burmese women and meek and unmanly Burmese men—affected colonized men and women differently. Any discussion of what modernity meant and entailed needs to consider the existence of colonialism and how it informed the distinctive ways in which Burmese men and women experienced, coped with, and made sense of the *khit kala.*

Yet, on the other hand, colonialism did not predetermine the shape of modernity in Burma. The historiography of colonial Burma to date has suggested that under the British, formidable forces of the outside world were unleashed upon Burma, but the world was not opened up to the Burmese. Shut out of the world beyond British Burma, excluded from processes of modernization, and socially atomized through a plural society that segregated and antagonized people of different race, religion, ethnicity, class, and occupation, the world and worldview of the Burmese in fact became more confined and parochial. This study has shown, however, that greater openness, mixture, and mobility existed in Burma's plural colonial society. Colonialism did not deter Burmese people from forming interracial, interethnic, and interfaith relationships or from taking advantage of increased access to and availability of a wide range of local and foreign texts, goods, skills, and technologies. Not only elites and intellectuals such as Ledi Pandita U Maung Gyi, Dagon Khin Khin Lay, Daw Mya Sein, Daw Amar, and Ma Ma Lay but also ordinary men and women experimented with newly available ideas, techniques, and commodities; as writers advocating the education and employment of women, as critics of *khit hmi* culture that valued novelty and self-fulfillment, as students and factory workers engaged in boycotts and nonviolent protests, as members of women's organizations speaking at public rallies and demanding parliamentary representation, as company owners advertising their businesses in newspapers, as readers of magazines submitting letters and essays to be published, and as consumers of a wide array of products, from soaps, cosmetics, toiletries, and fashionable clothing to condensed milk and contraceptives. The thoughts and actions of these people direct attention to the role that Burmese people played as cultural brokers and agents of change and modernization and illustrate that analyses emphasizing the influence of colonial discourse and institutions on the genesis of the modern can be taken only so far. They also demonstrate that local forms and practices developed in complex relationships with broader cosmopolitan discourses and movements concerning social reforms, feminism, anticolonialism, modernization, capitalism, consumerism, and scientific progress. The *khit hmi thu* in this book redirects our attention to these translocal and cross-cultural linkages.

These intricacies attest to the indispensability of multivocal, if dissonant, reformulations of colonialism and modernization. They illuminate the multiple interpretations, choices, and actions of colonized women and men who managed to carve out new possibilities for themselves and remain open to the outside world. These individuals penetrated and renegotiated cultural, political, racial, religious, and gender boundaries even as others within and without their communities sought to reify and enforce them. They struggled in creative and critical ways with the uncertainties, anxieties, and promise of what they took to be modern. The stories of the women of the *khit kala* examined in this book exemplify the conflicts and contradictions that characterized this dynamic process of being and becoming modern in colonial Burma.

Notes

INTRODUCTION

1 Chatterjee 1993; Barlow 1994; Ankum 1997; Göle 1996; Sato 2003.

2 Burmese: *khet kāla*.

3 Burmese: *khet mhī sū; ya khu khet amyui: sa mī:; khet chan sū; khet sac amyui: sa mī:; tak khet sa mī:*.

4 Burmese: *tui: tak re:*.

5 McClintock 1995, 5.

6 Furnivall 1956, 1991; Adas 1974; Mendelson 1975; Maung Maung 1980; Aung-Thwin 2003; I. Brown 2005; R. H. Taylor 2008.

7 Andaya 2006, 3.

8 Ibid.

9 Thakin Thein Pe Myint 1950; Nu 1954; Hla Pe 1961; Htin Aung 1965; Than Daing 1967; Ba Maw 1968; Burma Socialist Programme Party 1975.

10 Thant Myint-U 2001.

11 Mendelson 1975.

12 Furnivall 1956, 1991; Adas 1974; R. H. Taylor 2008.

13 Adas 1974; I. Brown 2005.

14 Furnivall 1956. For more on Furnivall, see Pham 2005.

15 Furnivall 1956, 157.

16 Burmese: *aok kya nok kya*. Furnivall 1957, j.

17 Adas 1974; Htin Aung 1967; Maung Maung 1980; R. H. Taylor 2008.

18 Koop 1960, 18–19.

19 C. Bayly 2003.

20 Maxim 1992, 5.

21 Furnivall 1957, xvii.

22 Adas 1974, 123.

23 Ibid., 107.

24 The works among recent literature on modernity are too numerous to name. For some examples, see Barlow 1997; Burton 1999; Mitchell 2000; Eisenstadt 2000; Gaonkar 2001; Chakrabarty 2002; Dube 2002; and Kaviraj 2005. For a useful review of some of this recent scholarship, see chapter 5 ("Modernity") in Cooper 2005.

25 Silverberg 1991, 244.
26 Silverberg 1991; Sato 2003.
27 Bingham 2004; Stevens 2003.
28 L. Edwards 2000, 117.
29 Barlow et al. 2005, 246.
30 "Self-sufficiency" or "indigenous goods" movement.
31 Pollock 2002, 15.
32 Ong 1998; Strassler 2008.
33 Lewis 2009, 1393. Also see Frost 2002; and Chua 2007.
34 P. Edwards 2004.
35 Strassler 2008.
36 Chakrabarty 2000.
37 Pollock 2002, 48.
38 For discussions on the debate over the names "Burma" and "Myanmar," see Houtman 1997; Callahan 2003, xvi; and Lintner 2003.
39 Honorific for older men; a rough equivalent of "Mr."
40 Honorific for older women; a rough equivalent of "Ms."
41 Honorific for younger women; a rough equivalent of "Ms."
42 Honorific for younger men; a rough equivalent of "Mr."
43 See http://www.dclammerts.com/transliteration.

CHAPTER 1: THE COLONIAL SETTING

1 Thant Myint-U 2001, 18; Leider 2008.
2 Thant Myint-U 2001, 20.
3 Leider 2008.
4 Furnivall 1956, 25.
5 Thant Myint-U 2001, 23.
6 Until 1862 the four provinces fell under the administration of different governors. Arakan was transferred to the government of Bengal, whereas Tenasserim remained under the governor-general of India until 1834, when the judicial and revenue branches of the administration were made over to Bengal. Martaban was allotted as a province to the commissioner of Tenasserim, while Pegu was assigned its own and separate commissioner, directly responsible to the governor-general (Furnivall 1956, 29, 39).
7 For a detailed discussion of state reforms in Burma during the second half of the nineteenth century that were undertaken in response to rapidly changing local and global conditions, see "The Grand Reforms of King Mindon," in Thant Myint-U 2001, 105–129.
8 Adas 1974, 4, 7–10.
9 Thant Myint-U 2001, 188.
10 Nisbet 1901, 79.
11 Ibid., 93–97.
12 Ibid., 220–222.

13 Burmese: *sū krī:; rvā sū krī:*. The term *thu gyi* refers generally to a hereditary headman of rural areas, but it appears to have been used as the standard term for a headman of a village (Trager and Koenig 1979, 40–41; Htun Yee 2006, 153–154).

14 Crosthwaite 1912, 81.

15 Burmese: *mrui.*.

16 Burmese: *mrui. sū krī:*.

17 Trager and Koenig 1979, 38–41; Htun Yee 2006, 164; Mya Sein 1973, 31–44.

18 Donnison 1953, 31–32. For more on the Village Regulation Act, see Mya Sein 1973 and Crosthwaite 1912.

19 Callahan 2003, 21–44.

20 Furnivall 1956, 23–61; R. H. Taylor 2008, 75. The territory beyond "Burma Proper" was called the "scheduled," "excluded," or "frontier" areas and consisted of the Shan states and the Chin and Kachin Hills region, where Shans, Kachins, Chins, and Karens together made up more than 95 percent of the population (Frontier Areas Committee of Enquiry 1947). In this system of territorial organization, direct rule by British colonial officials was implemented in Burma Proper, whereas populations of the "frontiers" were given a large degree of local autonomy. The Shan states, for instance, were ruled by *sawbwa* (*cau bhvā:*, from the Shan term *saohpa*), Shan hereditary chiefs, as this system was understood to be "at once cheap, effective, and better suited to the Shan people than any more elaborate system modeled after the districts in charge of British officers" (Nisbet 1901, 232).

21 Minute by Lord Dufferin dated 17 February 1886, quoted in Crosthwaite 1912, 11.

22 Furnivall 1956, 36.

23 Ibid., 77.

24 Nisbet 1901, 239.

25 Furnivall 1956, 49.

26 Ibid.

27 Callahan 2003, 25.

28 Nisbet 1901, 214.

29 Crosthwaite 1912, 100.

30 R. H. Taylor 2008, 75.

31 During the Japanese invasion of Burma, the British and Indian elements of the administration withdrew to India, and a government of Burma in exile, with a nucleus of a civil administration, was set up at Simla. The government of Burma resumed charge in October 1945 and remained in power until 4 January 1948, when British rule formally ended and Burma became an independent republic.

32 Lieberman 1978, 456–457.

33 Laichen 2000; Mya Than 1997; Sangermano 1995, 189. The term *tayoke* (Burmese: *ta rup* or *ta rut*) is commonly understood to have derived from the word "Turk" and referred originally to the Mongols, whose expeditionary forces to Burma would have consisted of Turkish tribes (Luce 1959, 69–70). However,

eminent scholar of Burmese language and literature Hpo Lat disputes this theory in his discussion of the etymology of the word. He proposes instead that *tayoke* is a combination of two Burmese words: *ta,* which means tremendous, and *rut rak* or *rup rak,* which means disturbance, interference, or intrusion. *Tayoke* thus means "those who cause great disturbance and interference" or "the great intruders" (Hpo Lat 1962, 263–271).

34 Frasch 2002, 65.

35 Subrahmanyam 2002, 111.

36 Charney 1998, 210.

37 Eaton 2002, 227.

38 Sangermano 1995, 217; P. Edwards 2004, 302.

39 Symes 1800, 214–215.

40 In 1867 there were only three rice mills in the region. By 1872 the number had increased to twenty-six.

41 Baxter 1941, 122; Furnivall 1956, 119; R. H. Taylor 2008, 147. According to Andrus, there were as many as 450,000 immigrants and 360,000 emigrants in one year at one point (1948, 34). However, it appears that the number of immigrants to and emigrants from *all* ports in Burma, not just Rangoon, never exceeded 428,300 and 399,200, respectively (Baxter 1941, 121). The average number of immigrants and emigrants to and from all ports in Burma between 1920 and 1930 was between 387,000 and 323,000 annually (Baxter 1941, 121).

42 Maxim 1992, 60; Burma Government 1928a, 4.

43 The word *bo* (Burmese: *buil*) was originally associated with the military ranking of a general. By the twentieth century, however, *bo* meant "European." Because over ninety percent of the total number of Europeans in Burma in the 1920s and 1930s were British subjects, that is, English, Irish, Scotch, or Welsh (India 1933a, 232; Koop 1960, 17), *bo* was used commonly as an equivalent of "British" or "Anglo" during the colonial period.

44 The word *kala* (Burmese: *kulā:*) can also mean "foreigners," including the British and more generally "Europeans." But in the twentieth century, the word began to refer almost exclusively to "Indians," and the word *bo* appeared instead as the common word used to denote "European."

45 This is the spelling used in the colonial records for "Telugu."

46 Burma Government 1928a, 3–12.

47 India 1933a, 136; Chen 1966; Charney 1999.

48 P. Edwards 2004, 302; Mya Than 1997, 117.

49 India 1923, 90–91; 1933a, 60–63.

50 India 1902, 6, 183–207; 1923, 55; 1933a, 54.

51 India 1923, 74.

52 India 1933a, 52.

53 Ibid., 230–232; Koop 1960, 22.

54 Maung Maung 1980, 60–63.

55 Hart 1897, 254.

56 Chief Justice Rutledge, quoted in Maung Maung 1980, 63.

57 Adas 1974, 196–198; Burma Government 1938b.
58 Riot Inquiry Committee 1939b.
59 Furnivall 1956, 117.
60 Burmese: *amyui:*.
61 The word *amyo* is often translated into English as "race" or "kin," but it can refer variously to race, breed, lineage, family, rank, caste, kind, sort, and species. In the twentieth century, *amyo* also took on the meaning of "nation" (Stewart and Dunn 1969, 282).
62 Gaung 1909.
63 Jardine 1934, 17–18.
64 Richardson 1896, 334–336.
65 Burmese: *amin. tau.*
66 There is widespread belief, even today, that the British gave preferential treatment to the ethnic minorities in Burma as a strategy of divide and rule. The administration's deliberate recruitment of soldiers among ethnic minorities—a policy discussed in chapter 6—is an example that is frequently cited to support this view (M. Smith 1999, 44–48; Gravers 2007).
67 Stoler 1989a, 1989b.
68 Dirks 2001; S. Bayly 1999.
69 Cohn 1987, 242.
70 Anderson 1991, 166.
71 Lieberman 1978, 458.
72 Hla Aung 1968, 67–88.
73 Adas 1974, 110–111, 123.
74 Ibid., 75–76.
75 Dhammasami 2004, 5.
76 Ibid., 11.
77 Taw Sein Ko 1913, 224. For more on Taw Sein Ko, see ibid., 143–145, and P. Edwards 2004.
78 Kaung 1963, 34–35.
79 Kaung 1930.
80 Kaung 1931, 4–5.
81 Ibid., 6–8.
82 Kaung 1963, 105; India 1923, 188; 1933, 171.
83 P. Edwards 2003, 40.
84 P. Edwards 2003; Womack 2008.
85 Saunder and Purser 1914.
86 Ibid., 62, 65–66.
87 Lwyn 1994, 66.
88 Burma Government 1917, 23.
89 Saunder and Purser 1914, 66.
90 Furnivall 1956, 55.
91 India 1922, 119.
92 Kaung 1931, 6–8.

93 Kaung 1963, 73, 79–80.
94 Ibid., 81.
95 J. G. Scott 1911, 164.
96 Burma Government 1917, 24.
97 Ibid., 8–9, 13, 56–58.
98 India 1922, 120.
99 Thant Tut 1980, 153.
100 Kaung 1963, 79.
101 Dhammasami 2004, 5.
102 Burma Government 1917, 22.
103 Burma Government 1928b, 28.
104 Aye Kyaw 1993, 14.
105 Taw Sein Ko 1913, 227.
106 Furnivall 1956, 130.
107 Burma Government 1931, 10.
108 Ibid., 5.
109 Ibid.
110 Taw Sein Ko 1913, 225.
111 Ibid., 228.
112 Kaung 1963, 43.
113 Aye Kyaw 1993, 12.
114 Furnivall 1957, xv.
115 For instance, textbooks on the history of Burma "written in the context of the imperial idea" were assigned, the national anthem was replaced with "The Prayer for the King-Emperor," and only British citizens or British descendants were appointed as college professors, lecturers, and principals of Anglo-vernacular schools (Aye Kyaw 1993, 15–16).
116 University Boycotters' Union 1922, 171–172.
117 Braun 2008, 180.
118 Malalgoda 1976; Braun 2008, 224.
119 Braun 2008, 225.
120 Burma Government 1923, 79–80.
121 India 1923, 188; 1933a, 171.
122 Kaung 1963, 76.
123 The quote, taken from a 14 September 1919 issue of *Burma Critic,* is cited in Saunder and Purser 1914, 90.
124 Khin Myo Chit 1976, 194–195; Po Ka 1914.
125 Khin Myo Chit 1976, 196.
126 Ba Than 1978, 21–22. Ba Than mentions that according to E. A. Blundell, the commissioner of Tenasserim from 1833 to 1843, the first Burmese-language newspaper (with an unknown title) was published in 1836 in Moulmein on a weekly basis (ibid., 21).
127 Cited in ibid., 2.

128 Ibid., 2–8; Womack 2003.

129 Ba Than 1978, 9, 13.

130 Charney 2006, 182–183, 195; Braun 2008, 141–143.

131 Frost 2002, 940.

132 By the turn of the century, Burma had developed a highly specialized single-product export economy focused on rice, which made the country rely heavily on the import of manufactured goods, and India had emerged as the primary source of paper, among many other commodities.

133 India 1923, 172–177.

134 The *Burmah Gazette* was renamed the *Burma News* in 1872.

135 Ba Than 1978, 24.

136 Ibid., 41–44, 49.

137 Tin Kha 1990, 147–150.

138 India 1923, 189.

139 Burma Government 1939b.

140 Burma Government 1946.

141 Roff 1972, 1. Roff notes that in addition to the 173 mostly Malay-language periodicals, 15 periodicals in Arabic and 9 in the Malay language were published by Christian missionaries in Singapore (1972, 1).

142 Marr 1981, 46–47.

143 Tekkatho Tin Gyi 1992, 155–177, 203–239.

144 Riot Inquiry Committee 1939a, 27.

145 Anderson 1991.

146 Burma 1939b.

147 Tin Htway 1972; Aung San Suu Kyi 1987.

148 Burma Government 1946.

149 Habermas 1989.

150 Anderson 1991.

151 Ba Than 1978, 45.

152 Saya Lun and his writings are discussed in chapter 2.

153 The nationalist boycott of foreign goods is discussed in detail in chapters 3 and 5.

154 Mendelson 1975, 197.

CHAPTER 2: WOMEN ON THE RISE

1 Coedès 1968; Reid 1988.

2 Reynolds 1995.

3 Atkinson and Errington 1990; Andaya 2000, 6; Ong and Peletz 1995; Tran 2008; Van Esterik 1996.

4 Ikeya 2006.

5 H. F. Hall 1995, 173.

6 R. G. Brown 1995, 216.

7 Saunder and Purser 1914, 63.

8 Ibid.
9 Nisbet 1901, 176–189; Sangermano 1966.
10 H. F. Hall 1995, 171–172.
11 Ibid., 189.
12 R. G. Brown 1995, 217.
13 British Commonwealth League 1933.
14 International Alliance 1933.
15 Mi Mi Khaing 1984, 26.
16 J. G. Scott 1911, 77.
17 Khin Myint 1937, 542.
18 Rodd 1991; Bingham 2004.
19 Said 1978; Mani 1998; Chakrabarty 2000.
20 L. Edwards 2000, 126.
21 Hallisey 1995.
22 Gascoigne 1896, 43.
23 Butler 1930.
24 Quoted in Chousalkar 1990, 214.
25 Ibid.
26 Nijhawan 2010.
27 *Stri Darpan,* February 1920, 80, quoted in Nijhawan 2010.
28 Ibid., 77.
29 Nijhawan 2010.
30 Ibid.
31 Quoted in Mi Mi Khaing 1984, 156. The purpose of the roundtable was to "deliberate upon the outlines of a Constitution for a Burma separated from India" (Burma Government 1932, iii).
32 L. Edwards 2000, 127.
33 Atkinson and Errington 1990; Spiro 1997; Kawanami 2000.
34 Mendelson 1975; Mi Mi Khaing 1984; Kawanami 2000.
35 Dharmasena 1991; Bartholomeusz 1994; Wilson 1996; Blackstone 1998.
36 Khin Myo Chit 1974, 8, 12.
37 Mi Mi Khaing 1984, 16.
38 Though village headmanships as well as chieftainships in the Shan hill states have been known to descend in the female line, hereditary lineages of female headmanship were rare. Richard James Carlson, who has examined in some detail the evidence for female hereditary lineage in his MA thesis on women, gender, and nationalist politics in Burma, concludes that by the eighteenth century at least "such lines were, with one recorded exception, non-existent above the village level and outside of the Pagan area" (1991, 15).
39 Andaya 2006, 166, 169.
40 The daughter of King Razadarit (1385–1423), Queen Shin Saw Pu held the throne, based in Pegu, from 1453 to 1472. Incidentally, the throne passed to Shin Saw Pu upon her father's death because, owing to palace massacres undertaken

to purge any rivals to the throne, no male descendant of Razadarit was left alive (Harvey 1967, 117). She was the only female ruler of a major state in Burma.

41 Reid 1988.
42 Mendelson 1975; Hansen 2006.
43 Dhammasami 2004.
44 Burmese: *sīla rhaṅ.*
45 Kawanami n.d.
46 Pe Maung Tin 1956, 288–292; Nan Hnin Yu Yu 1995, 24.
47 Hla Pe 1968, 135; Kawanami n.d.
48 However, that the prevailing practice of Theravada Buddhism in contemporary Burma excluded women from being ordained as monks and from joining the sangha does not diminish the active participation of women in, and their immense contributions to, the operation of the monastic Buddhist community in Burma as laywomen and nuns.
49 Kawanami n.d.
50 Andaya 2006, 54.
51 Charney 2006, 54–57.
52 Ibid., 53.
53 India 1893, 217–218; 1902, 79.
54 Arnold 1916, 7.
55 *Pwe* (or *pvai*) means variously public function, communal event, mass celebration, festival, fair, public entertainment, or a show open to all.
56 Arnold 1916, 6–7.
57 Ibid., 5.
58 Barmé 2002, 135.
59 Marr 1981, 206.
60 Burma Government 1923, 18, 54.
61 Saw Moun Nyin 1976, 78; Mi Mi Khaing 1984, 154.
62 Burma Government 1929, xix.
63 Barmé 2002, 135.
64 India 1921, 106–110; Burma Government 1923, 13, 104.
65 Burma Government 1923, 20–21.
66 Saw Moun Nyin 1976, 70–81, 88–95, 221–238.
67 India 1923, 246–255; 1933a, 145.
68 Her father, U May Oung, was a well-known barrister and Indian Civil Service officer who served as home member on the Legislative Council, one of the highest government positions open to Burmese people in colonial Burma, from 1924 until his death in 1926.
69 India 1933a, 145.
70 Burma Secretary 1932b.
71 The proposal to amend the law of disqualification on grounds of sex is outlined as follows in the act: "A person shall not be disqualified by sex or marriage from the exercise of any public function, or from being appointed to or holding

any civil or judicial office or post, or from entering or assuming or carrying on any civil profession or vocation, or for admission to any incorporated society (whether incorporated by Royal Charter or otherwise), and a person shall not be exempted by sex or marriage from the liability to serve as a juror" (India 1919b).

72 Exchequer 1919.

73 Civil Service Commissioners 1919, 1.

74 Ibid., 3.

75 Ibid., 4.

76 In a letter to the chief secretary of Burma, the commissioner of Mandalay Division suggested that the government needed to consider not only the increasing demand from educated Burmese women for appointment in government offices but also the increasingly favorable view of clerks in his office towards the employment of women in clerical posts (Mandalay Division 1931).

77 The prefixing of the title of newspapers and periodicals to the names of editors and columnists is a practice that remains common to this day. The practice appears to have sprung from the absence of surnames in Burma. In order to distinguish famous or public figures, who often possess matching names, an identifier of some sort is prefixed to their names. All eminent monks (*sayadaw,* usually translated as "abbots"), for instance, were distinguished by the name of the town, village, or monastery in which they resided.

78 It was U Razak (discussed in chapter 5), the headmaster of the high school in Mandalay that Daw Amar was attending, who began the translation of Collis' book. After translating a few chapters, however, he passed on to Daw Amar the task of translating the entire book (Bo Bo Lansin, e-mail message to the author, 6 May 2010).

79 Saw Moun Nyin 1976, 286–294; Kyan 1978, 306–308.

80 Saw Moun Nyin 1976, 261.

81 Literally the "eater of a *myo,*" *myo sa* (Burmese: *mrui. cā:*) referred to an aristocrat and appanage holder, usually a member of the royal family.

82 Ba Thaung 2002, 386–387.

83 Khin Khin Lay 1961, 44–45.

84 India 1933a, 170.

85 Khin Maung Htun 1975, 221. As with other contemporary periodicals in Burma, *Dagon*'s publication was interrupted by the Second World War.

86 Allott 1986, 6.

87 Hotta 1987. He took on the name "Thakin Kodaw Hmaing" in the mid-1930s when he joined the Dobama Asiayone movement (discussed in chapter 3) and became a patron of its younger, *thakin* nationalists.

88 Tin Htway 1972, 24–25; Aung San Suu Kyi 1987, 71.

89 Burmese: *yuvatī cakkhu.* The word *yuvatī* is the feminine counterpart of the Pali noun *yuvan* (youth).

90 U Maung Gyi received the prefix "Ledi Pandita" as a monk in Ledi Sayadaw's monastery. U Maung Gyi may also have been behind *Dagon*'s publication of

biographies of such famous historical Burmese women as Queen Shin Saw Pu (1453–1472) and Queen Supayalat (1859–1925) in the mid-1920s. For more information on U Maung Gyi and Ledi Sayadaw, see Hla Pain 1967; Paragu 1995; and Braun 2008.

91 Pali: *lokiya*, "worldly"; "belonging to the world."

92 Sape Beikman 1964; Ba Thaung 2002, 328–331.

93 Carroll 2007, 189.

94 Reyes 2008, 22–26.

95 Khin Khin Lay 1961, 53–54.

96 Khin Toke 1926.

97 I have been unable to find Khin Swe's letter to which Khin Toke refers, and thus I am unable to identify with certainty the transgression under discussion. However, numerous historians of the sangha in Burma point out that rivalries between monks and between monks and laymen plagued the sangha from roughly 1924 until 1927 (Sarkisyanz 1965, 132–133; Mendelson 1975, 205).

98 Maung Maung 1980, 58–59.

99 Khin Toke 1926, 202.

100 Burmese: *khet kāla amyui: sa mī: kale:.*

101 Burmese: *atat chan:.*

102 Khin Toke 1926, 205.

103 Ibid., 206.

104 Ibid., 216.

105 Burmese: *paññā.*

106 Tun Shein 1919.

107 In his study, Braun examines Ledi Sayadaw's "life-long campaign for the education of the laity through preaching, social organizing, and the production of books and pamphlets" (2008, 32) and illustrates that Ledi Sayadaw promoted a practice of self-cultivation and reflection based on textual study and meditation "as a means to make sense of the modern world—its scientific knowledge, its technology, its societal challenges—from a Buddhist perspective" (ibid., 406).

108 Ibid., 261–264, 404.

109 Khin Swe 1929, 351.

110 Chatterjee 1993, 128; Stevens 2003, 83; Sato 2003, 14.

111 Sape Beikman 1964, 251.

112 Burma Socialist Programme Party 1975, 70–73. The demonstration is discussed in detail in chapter 4.

113 Khin Swe 1927, 240.

114 See Carlson 1991, 86–101, for an informative discussion of the arguments made for and against the legislative resolution by the council members.

115 Burmese: *o jā.*

116 Khin Swe 1927, 240, 242. The dominance of Queen Supayalat over King Thibaw is noted in virtually every historical study of the Konbaung period, and she has often been blamed for the demise of the last Burmese dynasty. Daw

Mya Sein, for instance, referred to Queen Supayalat and her mother as "the two women who have had to take so much blame for the misrule of the last king of Burma and the subsequent British annexation of Upper Burma" (1972, 291).

117 For a brief description of the *Lomasakassapa jātaka*, see Malalasekera 1960, s.v.

118 Khin Swe 1927, 244.

119 Burmese: *Balaṃ cando balaṃ suriyo || Balaṃ samaṇa brahmaṇa || Balaṃ velā samuddassa || Balā ti balam itthiyo ||* (ibid.).

120 Ibid., 240–241.

121 Khin Khin Lay 1961, 47–48.

122 Burmese: *therī bhāsā pran.*

123 Burmese: *bhāsā pran.*

124 Okell 1967; Pruitt 1994; McDaniel 2003, 2008.

125 McDaniel 2003, 7–8.

126 Khin Khin Lay 1961, 55.

127 Burmese: *yuvatī kre: mhum.*

128 Burmese: *Samuddā varaṇā bhūmi || pākārā varaṇaṃ gharaṃ || narindā varaṇā desā || cariyā varaṇa thiyo ||.* This "Yuwadi kye hmoun" column was published in two parts (*Deedok gyanay,* 8 and 14 November 1925).

129 For a brief description of the *Magghadeva* or *Makhadeva jātaka*, see Malalasekera 1960, s.v.

130 Win Myint 1972, 9–11.

131 McDaniel 2003, 16.

132 Ibid.

133 Khin Maung Htun 1974, 60–62; Kyan 1978, 283, 290.

134 Tin Tin 1940, 5.

135 The women editors and writer-journalists of these featured columns reappear in subsequent chapters.

136 Burmese: *tarup praññ n* khet kāla amyui: sa mī: myā: khoṅ: choṅ ne prī.*

137 Kyan 1978, 293–294.

138 L. Edwards 2000, 117.

139 L. Edwards and Roces 2004.

140 Chatterjee 1993, 128.

141 Chatterjee 1993; L. Edwards 2000; Barmé 2002.

142 *Rangoon Times*, 3 February 1927.

143 India 1930.

144 Taw Sein Ko 1913, 239.

145 Ibid.

146 Roces 2004, 29.

147 Kartini 1992.

148 Than Htut and Thaw Kaung 2005, 74. Tabin Shwe Hti (1515–1551) and Nat Shin Naung (1578–1613) both reigned as king of Burma, the former from 1531 until 1550 and the latter for merely one year, from 1609 until 1610.

149 Barlow 1994; Chatterjee 1993; L. Edwards 2000.
150 Göle 1997.

CHAPTER 3: BETWEEN PATRIOTISM AND FEMINISM

1 While the word *amyothami* (Burmese: *amyui: sa mī:*) was used in *yuwadi* columns, it was usually qualified as *amyui: sa mī: kale:*, or "young woman."
2 Burmese: "Amyui: smī: tui. e* tui: tak re:."
3 Burmese: "Amyui: smī: lam: pra."
4 Burmese: "Aim rhaṅ ma myā: atvak." Kyan 1978, 284.
5 The identity of the "women" authors of the "Women's Advancement" articles in *Toe tet yay,* Khin May and Mya Galay, remains a mystery. The celebrated nationalist author and journalist Khin Mya—better known by her pen name "Khin Myo Chit," meaning "a woman who loves [*chit*] her kin [*amyo*]"—wrote for the magazine, but not until 1937, several years after the articles by Khin May and Mya Galay first appeared. It is possible that she wrote even earlier for the magazine using the names "Khin May" and "Mya Galay," especially given the patriotic content of the articles written by these women authors. It is also possible, however, that male writers such as Thakin Kodaw Hmaing, P. Monin, Dagon Nat Shin, and U Po Kya, who were known contributors to *Toe tet yay,* authored the articles pseudonymously (Khin Maung Htun 1975, 223; Ngwe U Daung 1978, 93). For more on Khin Myo Chit, see Saw Moun Nyin 1976, 273–278.
6 Burmese: "Mī dve: mettā."
7 Burmese: "Sati thā: kra nau mut chui: thī tve."
8 Bingham 2004, 84–85.
9 Khin May 1933a.
10 Khin May 1933b.
11 Burmese: "Amyui: smī: myā: cit e* yañ kye: mhu lui lā: ap kroṅ:."
12 Burmese: *ya khu khet.*
13 Mya Galay 1934a, 21.
14 Ibid., 59.
15 The article was first published in Burmese in *Myanmar alin* 2, no. 2, and then translated by Myint Tin into English and published in *Ngan hta lawka* 26, no. 188 (September 1940).
16 Burmese: *tuiṅ: praññ.*
17 Burmese: *mīn: ma.*
18 Stewart and Dunn 1969, 283.
19 Ibid., 282.
20 Mya Galay 1934a, 21.
21 Mya Galay 1934b, 70.
22 Ibid., 72.
23 Khin May 1933b, 113.

24 *Wunthanu* (Burmese: *vaṃsānu*) is derived from the Pali words *vaṃsa* and *anurakkhita,* meaning "lineage" and "protected," respectively, or a "protected lineage."

25 Kandiyoti 1991; Chatterjee 1993.

26 Anderson 1996, 291.

27 Brenner 1999, 32.

28 Burmese: *myui: khyac may.*

29 Ye Hlaing 1935.

30 Burmese: "Mran mā. prassanā akhyui. ."

31 Htun Shein 1936, 67.

32 Malalgoda 1976.

33 Mendelson 1975, 196–235; Maung Maung 1980, 13.

34 R. H. Taylor 2008, 183.

35 University Boycotters' Union 1922, 15–17.

36 Ibid., 183–184; Burma Government 1923, 18.

37 The immediate purpose of the NCE, founded in 1906, was the establishment of "national schools" to provide a refuge for students and teachers who had been dismissed from schools because of their involvement in Gandhi's *swadeshi* (indigenous goods) movement. The larger goal of the schools was to create a nationalist education that merged scientific knowledge with knowledge of the country and its literature, history, and philosophy. The initiative of the NCE had led to the establishment of the Bengal National College and School, and the Bengal Technical Institute in 1906, and by 1908 forty national schools with three thousand students had been set up in Bengal; however, only six national schools were still operating in 1917 (Basu 1974, 197–198).

38 Aye Kyaw 1993, 35.

39 Mendelson 1975, 196–235; Maung Maung 1980, 14, 19.

40 Aye Kyaw 1993, 36. What distinguished the national schools from the public schools was not so much the curricula or even the language of instruction (since vernacular schools all taught in Burmese) but the rules regulating student conduct. Students were allowed to read any newspapers, for example, whereas in public schools they were not permitted to read any, and they were not required to wear European-type shoes. Instead of observing British Empire Day, the King's Birthday, and Saturday and Sunday as holidays, national schools designated as holidays the Buddhist pre-Sabbath and Sabbath days and the anniversary of the day on which the students had boycotted their university (ibid., 36–37).

41 R. H. Taylor 2008, 180. A decade later the number of national schools recognized by the government had increased to fifty-five, but enrollment had decreased to approximately 7,000 (Aye Kyaw 1993, 39). The national college, founded in 1921 in Rangoon with eleven faculty members—five Indian, six Burmese—and twenty-three students, likewise suffered from poor funding and closed two years later. Its closure and shortage of funds were also due to the government's refusal to recognize degrees from the national college.

42 Burmese: *vaṃsānu asaṅ:*.

43 R. H. Taylor 2008, 193.

44 Maung Maung 1980, 52–54.

45 J. C. Scott 1976; Herbert 1982; Aung-Thwin 2003.

46 The two student leaders, who later came to be known as Thakin Nu and Thakin Aung San, spearheaded the Anti-Fascist People's Freedom League (AFPFL), which emerged from the Second World War and the Japanese occupation of Burma at the forefront of the nationalist and pro-independence movement in Burma. The British government recognized the AFPFL as the most popular political party in postwar Burma and eventually entered into negotiations with the party, namely Aung San, to draft a constitution for an independent Burma. The assassination of Aung San on 19 July 1947 placed Thakin Nu, the vice president of AFPFL, in a position to become the first democratically elected prime minister of Burma. See Maung Maung 1962; Butwell 1969; R. H. Taylor 1984; and Khin Yi 1988a.

47 They objected in particular to the following: the compulsory attendance in Judson College at Bible, social ethics, and assembly classes; the cost of tuition, board and lodging, and examination fees; and the prohibition of students not enrolled in Rangoon University from appearing for university examinations. The boycotters also demanded that the Students' Union be given the right to make representations on behalf of individuals or groups of students to the constituent colleges or to the university (Enquiry Sub-Committee 1936).

48 During the colonial period, the Shwedagon functioned as a primary site from which Burmese people contested colonial rule. That anticolonial and anti-Indian protests by the Burmese, if held in Rangoon, always began or ended at the Shwedagon is an interesting fact that historians have yet to explore in their analyses of the relationship between Buddhism and nationalism in Burma. See Sarkisyanz 1965; and Mendelson 1975, 173–235.

49 Enquiry Sub-Committee 1936, 3; Stephenson 1936, 3; Burma Socialist Programme Party 1975, 97–101.

50 Dobama Asiayone (Burmese: *tui. bamā acaññ: aruṃ:*) has also been translated as "We Burman Association." *Do* means either "our" or "we," and *bama* can be used as a designation for the Burman ethnic majority. *Bama* also refers, however, to all the people in Burma, irrespective of their ethnicity.

51 Burmese: *sakhaṅ*.

52 In addition, the Thakin Party made leftist literature available locally through the Nagani (Red Dragon) Book Club, which it established in 1937. Modeled after the Victor Gollancz Left Book Club in London and run by U Nu and other *thakin*, the club was established for the purpose of publishing Marxist and Marxist-derived books and articles in the Burmese language that conveyed the essence of contemporary international literature, history, economics, politics, and science at an affordable price (Zoellner 2006, 21).

53 R. H. Taylor 2008, 205.

54 Burmese: *are: tau puṃ*. There have been a number of eras in Burmese chronology, the current era having commenced in 639 CE. The Burmese calendar is lunisolar, and a Burmese year contains 12 months and 354 days in an ordinary year, and 13 months and 384 or 385 days in a leap year, which occurs every second or third year (Clancey 1906).

55 Khin Yi 1988a; Maung Maung 1980, 177; R. H. Taylor 2008, 214–215.

56 R. H. Taylor 2008, 195.

57 Burmese: *nuiṅ ṅaṃ re:*.

58 Burmese: *Amyui: sa mī: kumārī asaṅ:;* Pali: *kumārī,* "young woman," "maiden." As Richard Carlson has pointed out, "there is considerable confusion in the literature over the Burmese name of this society" (1991, 48). The name I use comes from a book on the political movements of women in Burma by the Burma Socialist Programme Party (1975). Other versions of the name include *Mran mā min: ma myā: asaṅ:* and *Mran mā kumārī asaṅ:*.

59 Burmese: *vaṃsānu kumārī asaṅ:*.

60 Maung Maung dates the formation of the YWBA earlier, to 1918 (Maung Maung 1988, 13). However, other sources date its establishment to 1919 and after the founding of the Burmese Women's Association, which is generally recognized as the first women's association (Burma Socialist Programme Party 1975).

61 Burmese: *paṅ nī*.

62 The concern with the loss by a Burmese woman of her Buddhist spousal rights upon marriage to a non-Buddhist is discussed in detail in chapter 5.

63 Burma Socialist Programme Party 1975, 27–32; Naing Naing Maw 1999, 21–24, 70–71.

64 Burmese: *sakhaṅ ma.*

65 Unfortunately, I have been unable to find in-depth studies of these women workers and their role in the eleven-month workers' strike. For details of the strike, see Burma Socialist Programme Party 1975, 101–123; and Maung Maung 1980, 171–194.

66 Reprinted in *Guardian* (Dobama Asiayone 1959).

67 For brief biographies of leading members of various women's associations in colonial Burma, see Saw Moun Nyin 1976, 22–68.

68 Thein Pe Myint rose to fame in 1937 upon publication of *Tak bhun: krī:* (The modern monk), a highly controversial novel (discussed in chapter 6). He was one of the founding members of the Burma Communist Party and remained active in politics throughout the 1930s and the next several decades. For more information on Thein Pe Myint in English, see Robert Taylor's introduction to his English translation of *Wartime Traveler,* by Thein Pe Myint (R. H. Taylor 1984).

69 Thein Pe Myint 1998, 34.

70 Thein Pe Myint 1974, 244–290; Minamida 1980, 19.

71 Thein Pe Myint 1970; Minamida 1980, 20.

72 Sinha 2000.

73 L. Edwards and Roces 2004, 10.

74 Burma Socialist Programme Party 1975, 30.

75 Ibid., 41.

76 Burmese: *Min: ma myā: ma krok pā nhaṅ.* || *Atvaṅ: van ruṃ sui. min: ma myā: ma vaṅ ra hu amin. thut thā: sañ ñ* || *Coṅ. krañ ñ. kra pā* || *Mran mā amyui: sa mī: myā: nui: krā: kra pā* || *British Parliament tvaṅ min: ma myā: amat phrac ne prī* (ibid., 71).

77 Mya Sein 1958, 123; 1998, 190.

78 International Alliance 1927.

79 Rupp 1997, 43.

80 *National Council of Women in Burma* 1927; Rupp 1997, 15. Daw Mya Sein (1972, 296) stated that the demonstration had been sponsored by the NCWB, though I have yet to come across another source that confirms this attribution.

81 Tusan 2003, 623.

82 Hydari 1928; Jayawardena 1995. The Theosophical Society had had branches in Burma since the mid-1880s and attracted Burmese supporters at least until the early 1890s (Turner 2009).

83 Weber 2008, 90.

84 Sinha, Guy, and Woollacott 1999.

85 I thank Shobna Nijhawan for bringing this to my attention and for sharing her work.

86 *Stri Darpan* 1917, as quoted in Nijhawan 2010.

87 Nijhawan 2010.

88 Burton 1994.

89 Ibid.; Fay 2008.

90 Carlson 1991, 107. Little is known about the Burmese Women's National Council (*Mran mā amyui: sa mī: ne rhaṅ nay kauṅ cī*), except that it contested writings on Burmese women in foreign newspapers that the council deemed harmful to Burmese women (Sape Beikman 1966, 59; Aye Aye Mu 1981, 75).

91 The NCWB investigated the labor conditions of women and children in Rangoon and its vicinities in 1929 and submitted a report to the Royal Commission on Labour in India. The report found that most of the women laborers in and near Rangoon were Burmese and Indian, though a small percentage were Chinese, Anglo-Burmese, and Anglo-Indian (National Council of Women in Burma 1929). This is the only such documentation that I have come across. While the government made an inquiry into the standard of living of the working class in Rangoon at around the same time, the brief paragraph on "employment of women and children" merely states that "there are not many women and children employed in factories in Rangoon" (Burma Government 1928a, 89).

92 Jayawardena 1995.

93 Sinha 2000.

94 Pearson 2004, 197–199.

95 Burton 1994, 169, 175.

96 Mi Mi Khaing 1984, 26.

97 Mya Sein 1998, 189.

98 Khin Myo Chit 1976, 193.
99 Jayawardena 1986; Ray 1995.

CHAPTER 4: MODERN WOMAN AS CONSUMER

1   Burmese: *aim rhaṅ ma.*
2   "Technologies of the self" are what Michel Foucault describes as procedures or techniques that "permit individuals to effect by their own means, or with the help of others, a certain number of operations on their own bodies and souls, thoughts, conduct, and way of being, so as to transform themselves in order to attain a certain state of happiness, purity, wisdom, perfection, or immortality" (Foucault 1994, 225).
3   Silverberg 1991; Hake 1997; Barlow et al. 2005.
4   Tarlo 1996.
5   C. Bayly 1986; Cohn 1996; Tarlo 1996; Trivedi 2003.
6   Nordholt 1997b; Roces 2005.
7   On the "no footwear" campaign, see Mendelson 1975, 197; and Khin Maung Nyunt 2004.
8   Sato 2003, 155.
9   Appadurai and Breckenridge 1995, 4.
10 J. G. Taylor 1997, 112.
11 Silverberg 1991, 244.
12 Silverberg 1991; L. Edwards 2000.
13 Burmese: *buil ke.*
14 Shwe Khaing Thar 1951, 81–84.
15 Burmese: *aṅkyī.*
16 Burmese: *aṅkyī pā.* The term literally means "sheer blouse."
17 Burmese: *rhaṅ mī: aṅkyī.*
18 Burmese: *jā baulī.*
19 Burmese: *cham thuṃ:.*
20 Burmese: *a mok.*
21 Hake 1997; Barlow et al. 2005.
22 Pali: *kaññā,* "young (unmarried) woman," "maiden."
23 Burmese: *Aṅkyī—aṅkyī pā: ray nhaṅ. | myak thā: myak thā: khyui | kulā: lui lui | bamā lui lui | kyvan ma lak kui chvai | cut prai le kun po. | kyvan ma jā baulī* (Shwe Khaing Thar 1951, 86).
24 Tarlo 1996, 49.
25 Nordholt 1997a, 2.
26 Andrus 1948, 171–180; Aye Hlaing 1964, 5–41; I. Brown 2005, 87.
27 The hybridization of apparel was not a novel practice per se, nor was it unique to Burma. For instance, Maurizio Peleggi has pointed out that the refashioning of the appearance of the Siamese royalty in the latter decades of the nineteenth century followed an established pattern of hybrid clothing that signified their

royal status and "connection to a foreign civilization that was instrumental to the definition of their own identity and yet distinct" (2002, 60). In all likelihood, the modern hybrid outfit in Burma similarly mirrored the established custom among Burmese elites of fusing exotic fabrics (mainly from India during the precolonial era) and indigenous clothing to create a distinctive style symbolic of their cosmopolitanism.

28 India 1928, 639–650.

29 Ibid., 521–540.

30 The film was based on the best-selling English novel *East Lynne,* by Ellen Wood, which was also a hit in London and New York theaters when it was adapted for the stage.

31 In the movie title and the hairdo term, *BA* refers to a bachelor of arts degree.

32 Saw Moun Nyin 1976, 433.

33 Mya Galay 1934b, 71.

34 In fact, the 1931 census shows that occupations related to the textile and apparel businesses were held predominantly by the local population. Industry-wise, Burmese and other indigenous peoples held 54 and 38 percent of the occupations, respectively. While Indians born outside Burma constituted a larger proportion of those employed in commerce (33 percent), they still lagged behind the Burmese, who represented 41 percent of the occupation ("other indigenous Burmese" people were the third-largest constituent, at 12 percent). Industry and trade combined, and without incorporating the number of occupations held by Indo-Burmans or Indians born inside Burma, almost 90 percent of the textile and apparel businesses were operated by the indigenous population (India 1933b, 105–111, 190–193).

35 Andrus 1948, 171.

36 Thein Pe Myint 1998, 175.

37 Bo Min 1927, cited in Shwe Khaing Thar 1951, 77.

38 Alwis 1999.

39 Ibid., 183.

40 Ibid.

41 Ibid., 181.

42 Shwe Khaing Thar 1951, 86.

43 Mya Galay 1934b, 31.

44 Burmese: "Nok thap ma pro to. bhū:."

45 Stivens 1998, 63.

46 India 1933a, 79.

47 Scholarship on sexuality in twentieth-century Germany—the source of contraceptives and other sex-related products sold in colonial Burma—has shown that birth control was widely available before the 1960s, when the oral female contraceptive, or "the pill," first became available. Edward Ross Dickinson notes that the Weimer state supported the dissemination of contraceptives and contraceptive knowledge through the public health insurance system as a means

of "securing the reproductive health of the country" and combating abortion (Dickinson 2007, 230). Even in the Third Reich when "objects intended for indecent purposes" (i.e., birth control and sex toys) were outlawed, condoms, classified as prophylactics against venereal disease, were sold in vending machines (Waite 1998; Timm 2002; Heineman 2002). Similarly, Andrea Tone (1996) has shown that a profitable and growing birth control industry had developed in the United States by the early 1930s, despite long-standing legal restrictions. In addition to condoms, various female contraceptives such as vaginal jellies, douche powders and liquids, suppositories, and foaming tablets were sold under the legal euphemism "feminine hygiene" (ibid., 486). Tone points out that "pharmaceutical firms, rubber manufacturers, mail-order houses, and fly-by-night peddlers launched a successful campaign to persuade women and men to eschew natural methods in favor of commercial devices whose efficacy could be 'scientifically proven.'" By 1938 the contraceptive industry had annual sales exceeding $250 million and was declared one of the most prosperous new businesses of the decade by *Fortune Magazine* (ibid., 485).

48 *Youq shin lan hnyun,* 15 June 1934, 38.
49 Bernstein 1991, 7.
50 Manderson 1996, 201.
51 Bashford 2004, 112.
52 Smart 1913.
53 Burma Government 1921, 5.
54 Po Ka 1914, 73.
55 Burma Government 1921, 5.
56 Smart 1913, 1.
57 *Youq shin lan hnyun,* 15 June 1934, 38.
58 P. Edwards 2003, 34.
59 Khin Myint 1937, 542.
60 Nyi Nyi 1938.
61 Ein Shin Ma 1934, 33.

CHAPTER 5: MIXING RELIGION AND RACE

1 The word *kabya* (Burmese: *ka brā:*), in its most basic meaning, refers to people of mixed ancestry. The etymology of the word, however, is uncertain. Some argue that *kabya* is a derivative of the word *kaq pa,* which refers to a person who has taken up residence, temporarily or permanently, in a locality that is not his native place. *Kaq pa* also means "parasite." Others claim that *kabya* derived from the word *kwe bya,* which means "to be divided" or "to become various," a word especially applicable to living beings (Pu Galay 1939, 7; *Judson's Burmese-English Dictionary* 1953, 174, 250; *Mran mā–aṅgalip abhidhān* 1998, 4, 22).
2 Koop 1960.
3 Riot Inquiry Committee 1939b, 28.

4 Pu Galay 1939.
5 Burmese: *buil ka tau.*
6 See Khin Myo Chit's explanation of the phrase in Khin Myo Chit 1946. Interestingly, *Judson's Burmese-English Dictionary* (1953, 715) provides the former denotation of the phrase, while the *Mran mā–aṅgalip abhidhān* (Myanmar-English dictionary) published by the Burmese Ministry of Education (1998, 315) does not. See also Harada and Ono 1979, 309.
7 Burmese: *kulā: lū myui: nhaṅ. lak thap so mran mā amyui: sa mī:.*
8 Citing Mikael Gravers, J. A. Berlie (2008, 6–7) suggests that only those who converted to Islam were referred to as *kala,* though my research has shown that this was not necessarily the case.
9 Riot Inquiry Committee 1939a, 13.
10 India 1933b, xxxix.
11 Burma Government 1938a.
12 The term *zerbadee* (Burmese: *jer bhā dī*), which entered the British census for the first time in 1891, refers to a Muslim Burmese person, though during the colonial period it usually denoted a man or a woman with a Muslim father and a Buddhist mother (Yegar 1972, 33). The origin of the term is unclear, but according to Berlie (2008, 7), it derives from an old Persian name, "Zavier."
13 India 1933a, 211. It's unclear precisely how much less prevalent the "Burmese-Hindu marriage" was. After all, Indian Hindu men in Burma outnumbered Indian Muslim men by 153,875 in 1931, and over 75 percent of the Indian Hindu population in the country was male (ibid., 294–297). The administration appears to have concluded, based on the increase in the number of *zerbadee* in Burma from 94,316 in 1921 to 122,705 in 1931 that the "Burmese-Muslim marriage" had become frequent. The comparatively small increase in the population of Indian Buddhists—from 7,155 in 1921 to 12,600 in 1931—and the fact that practically all Hindus were Indians support the administration's observation that the "Burmese-Hindu marriage" was less frequent than the "Burmese-Muslim marriage." However, as the 1931 census notes, the significant growth in the *zerbadee* population was "partly due to the growth of racial consciousness, partly to better enumeration (it is probable that some of the Burmese Mahomedans recorded in 1921 were actually Zerbadis) and partly to the intermarriage of Indian Muslims with Burmese women" (ibid., 231).
14 I conducted this search through the India Office Family History Search (IOFHS) website, which offers searches of a database containing various biographical sources taken from military and marine service files, published resources, and baptism, marriage, and burial entries, among other sources. Ecclesiastical records for Europeans and Eurasian Christians in British India and Burma constitute the main source of the database, though records of registrar marriages—as opposed to church marriages—are also included. Unfortunately, the IOFHS database represents less than 10 percent of the holdings within the India Office Records.

15 In addition to the names, ages, occupations, and names of the bride and groom, the marriage records provide the names of their fathers, but never those of their mothers. Unless birth, baptism, or burial records are available, there is often no way to determine with certainty if a bride with a Christian first name—such as Anne Ma Ngwe Nu, daughter of Maung Ba Tin, who married Thomas Alexus Barry on 28 March 1936 at St. John's Church in Rangoon—was a Eurasian or a Christian Burmese. The case of Anne Ma Ngwe Nu is a typical example of official records of marriages in colonial Burma. Given the small number of registered marriages between Burmese men and European or Eurasian women, it is likely, though not definite, that Anne Ma Ngwe Nu had a Burmese mother.

16 Hamilton 1903.

17 Crosthwaite 1903.

18 India 1903a.

19 Pham 2005, 325; Vickers 2004, 3.

20 Crosthwaite 1903.

21 Twomey 1903.

22 India 1903a.

23 Ming 1983; Stoler 1989a, 1989b.

24 India 1903a.

25 Hamilton 1903.

26 India 1903a.

27 D. G. E. Hall 1980, 582, 584.

28 Ibid., 582.

29 Levine 2003, 92.

30 Vicinus 1973, 95–96.

31 Wright 1914, 2.

32 Rice 1915.

33 Ibid.

34 Ibid.

35 Cowen 1916, 3.

36 Ibid., 2–3, 6–7.

37 These pamphlets, two of which were considered libelous and banned by the government, range from seven to nine pages each and discuss in general and polemical terms what Cowen covered in his report to the AMSH.

38 Cowen 1914a.

39 Cowen 1914b.

40 Cowen 1916, 10.

41 Ibid.

42 India 1903a.

43 Hamilton 1903.

44 Crosthwaite 1903.

45 Burma Secretary 1905, 21–23.

46 India 1914.
47 Shuttleworth 1916, 24.
48 Spiro 1977, 155.
49 Cooper 1913, 2.
50 Maung Maung 1980, 61.
51 Thant Myint-U 2001, 244.
52 Lieberman 2003, 208.
53 Socarras 1966, 18.
54 Koop 1960, 17–18.
55 Gaung 1909, 76.
56 Richardson 1896, 141.
57 Gaung 1909, 89.
58 Maung Maung 1963.
59 Pu Galay 1939, 128.
60 Maung Maung 1980, 71.
61 Chakravarti 1971, 125.
62 Maung Maung 1980, 70.
63 Ibid., 61–72. Accordingly, the Buddhist Marriage and Divorce Bill, drafted in 1927, decreed that Burmese customary law be applied to marriages involving Buddhist women who belonged to any of the indigenous races of Burma, thus making Burmese customary law "territorial and not personal" (ibid., 70). It stipulated that if the couple cohabited without marriage being solemnized and recorded by the registrar or the village headman, then the woman or her parents, guardians, or siblings could inform the village registrar of it, at which time both parties were to be summoned and urged to legalize the union. If the man refused to legalize the union, a suit for breach of promise to marry or for seduction could be brought against him. If the union was legalized, Burmese customary law applied to all matters related to divorce, inheritance, succession, and ownership of properties. In addition, any child born before legalization of the union gained "legitimate" status.
64 Chakravarti 1971, 115.
65 Ibid., 134.
66 Ibid., xxi.
67 Ibid.
68 Ibid., 142.
69 The resolution providing for separation was passed in 1935 but did not come into effect until 1937.
70 Burmese: *sū myā: bamā.* An alternative and perhaps more common term for "their Burmese" was *sū tau bamā.*
71 Burmese: *bamā praññ sañň—tui. praññ || bamā cā sañň—tui. cā || bamā ca kā: sañň—tui. ca kā: || tui. praññ khyac pā || tui. cā kui khyī: mhraṅ. pā || tui. ca kā: kui le: cā: pā ||* (Khin Yi 1988b, 1). The translation of the slogan is also from Daw Khin Yi's *The Dobama Movement in Burma* (Khin Yi 1988a, 5).

72 This is Nemoto's translation (2000) of a passage from Komin Kochin Ahpwe, *Kuiy. maṅ: kuiy. khyaṅ: tañ ñ toṅ mhū cā cu amhat 1* [Collection of writings on the establishment of the Komin Kochin Organization 1] (Rangoon: Komin Kochin Ahpwe, 1936). I have used *thumya bama* rather than the synonymous *sū tau bamā* (Nemoto's *thudo-bama*) to stay faithful to the Burmese text.

73 Nemoto 2000, 1.

74 Ibid., 2–4.

75 Burmese: "tuiṅ khrā phrac ṭīkā."

76 The caption refers to the Buddhist law of impermanence that states that there is no permanent entity underlying human life.

77 Andaya 1998.

78 Gaung 1909, 83.

79 Maung Maung 1980, 61.

80 "Burmese Women Meet with Troubles," *Toe tet yay,* 29 April 1939, cited in Burma 1940.

81 Adas 1974; I. Brown 2005.

82 The passage from the letter, written and published in Burmese in the 25 July 1938 issue of *Thuriya,* was quoted in English translation in Riot Inquiry Committee 1939a, 11.

83 "Burmese Women Who Took Indians," *10,000,000,* 27 November 1938, cited in Burma Government 1940.

84 Pu Galay 1939, 8.

85 Burmese: *lū ka prā: thak cit ka prā: ka chui: sañ ñ || lū ka prā: paṅ prac sau lañ ñ: | bamā prañ ñ tvaṅ ne r* | bamā prañ ñ tvaṅ se mañ ñ. sū mhan ka | bamā cit thā: thuik sañ ñ || . . . mran mā prañ ñ tvaṅ ne r* mran mā prañ ñ tvaṅ se mañ ñ. sū tuiṅ || mran mā tuiṅ: raṅ: sā: myā: nhaṅ. ta sve: ta cit thañ ñ: rhi saṅ. sañ ñ || bamā. lvat lap re: tuik pvai tvaṅ ta bhak ta lam: alup kui ma lup ||* (ibid., 11–12).

86 Burmese: "ka prā: ma hut sū aṅ ma tan rhā: sañ ñ."

87 Pu Galay 1939, 11.

88 Yeni 2007.

89 Ibid.

90 Burmese: "Buil ka tau."

91 "Bo gadaw" (A European's mistress), in *Youq shin lan hnyun,* 22 June 1934, 24.

92 Ibid.

93 Ibid., 25.

94 Ibid., 26–27.

95 Berlie 2008, 38.

96 Burmese: "Muslim amyui: sa mī: myā:."

97 Ka 1936, 49.

98 Ibid., 51.

99 Burmese: *Buddhabhāsā amyui: sa mī: kale: tve || bhī ae | am ae aoṅ || vat lum | van thok | charā van | charā ma tve lup kra | maṅ: tuiṅ paṅ vaṅ kra | mrū nī cī pāy mhā choṅ rvak kra || tuik chuiṅ krī: tve phvaṅ. kra rum ma ka bhū: | sa taṅ: cā | maggajaṅ: mhā aydītā myā: tauṅ lup kun kra prī || bhay lok myā: ā: kya ca rā koṅ: sa lai ||* (ibid., 52).

100 Hart 1897, 255.
101 Ghosh 2006, 11.
102 Stoler 1992.
103 Hawes 1996, 58.
104 McPhedran 2002; P. Edwards 2002.
105 Stoler 1992.
106 Stoler 1989a, 635.

CHAPTER 6: THE SELF-INDULGENT *KHIT HSAN THU*

1 Burmese: *rahan: pyui.*
2 Riot Inquiry Committee 1939a, 186–187.
3 Adas 1974; Singh 1980; Furnivall 1991; Gravers 1999.
4 J. G. Taylor 1997, 113.
5 Ibid.
6 Alwis 1999, 181.
7 Roces 2005, 355.
8 Ibid.
9 For a brief biography of Dr. Ba Maw, see *Who's Who in Burma* 1962, 101–102.
10 Huang 2006.
11 Shwe Khaing Thar 1951, 86.
12 Khin Yi 1988b, 70.
13 Burmese: "Tui. payoga."
14 Burmese: *huil chan sañ.*
15 Amar 1936, 9.
16 Cohn 1996; Tarlo 1996, 11, 24.
17 Gaonkar 2001, 2–13.
18 H.M. 1936, 566.
19 Sato 2003, 56.
20 U May Oung, quoted in Aung San Suu Kyi 1990, 47.
21 The most proper and respectful way for a child to greet his or her parents is to *shikho* (Burmese: rhui khui:): to perform a prostrating bow while kneeling on the floor, touching the forehead to the ground. People make obeisance in this manner not only to their parents but also to their teachers, elders, and the Buddha.
22 Tekkatho Win Mun 1981, 250–251; Aung San Suu Kyi 1987, 69–70. For a history of the development of Burmese novels, see Tekkatho Win Mun 1981.
23 Burmese: *tak bhun: krī:.*
24 Mendelson 1975, 214–221.
25 D. E. Smith 1965, 208.
26 L. Edwards 2000, 115.
27 Stevens 2003.
28 Kirsch 1985; Andaya 2002. It has to be said that although the female sex, more than the male counterpart, is associated with attachment to desire within

Theravada Buddhism, qualities such as chastity, self-sacrifice, and suffering, epitomized by the devoted female followers of the Buddha, donors, and renunciants who figure in Buddhist literature, are at the same time identified as feminine virtues.

29 Ma Lay 1995, 20.

30 Ibid., 24. For biographical accounts of Ma Ma Lay, see her *Thu lo lu* (A man like him), recently translated into English by Ma Thanegi, and the introductions to the English translations of her novels *Thway* (Blood) and *Mon ywe mahu* (Not out of hate), by Than Than Win and Anna Allott, respectively (Ma Lay 1995, 2008; Than Than Win 2004; Allott 1991).

31 Ma Lay 1995, 14.

32 This information comes from the translator's introduction to the English translation of *Thu lo lu* (Ma Lay 2008, 18). Ma Ma Lay does not explain the content of the article in the original version, and the translator, Ma Thanegi, does not indicate from where she obtained the information.

33 Burmese: "Nasat ññan amraṅ rhi kra ran."

34 Saw Moun Nyin 1976, 280; Ma Lay 1995, 34; 2008, 24.

35 Khin Maung Htun 1974, 93–94.

36 Ma Lay 1995, 20, 97, 116, 133.

37 Burmese: "Yokyā: thve. rai. atve: akhau hā aok kya lha khye. ka lā:."

38 Burmese: *thī cā re: ma ka le:.*

39 Ma Lay 1940, 15.

40 Ibid.

41 Ibid.

42 Ibid.

43 Ibid., 18.

44 Only about five hundred thousand of these men, women, and children survived the arduous journey to reach India (Chakravarti 1971, 170).

45 Callahan 2003, 46. As astonishing as the sweeping arrival of the Japanese army in 1942 might have been, it was not entirely unexpected. A survey of prewar newspapers in Burma indicates that Burmese people were informed of the developments leading to World War II such as the Russo-Japanese War, the Sino-Japanese War, and the interest of the Japanese army in the Burma Road. In fact, one of the reasons for the ease and speed with which the Japanese were able to occupy Burma was the collaboration between Burmese politicians and the Japanese that had begun in earnest in 1939 (ibid., 47). When the Japanese invaded Burma at the end of 1941, they did so with the "Thirty Comrades"—thirty *thakin*— who had been trained by the Japanese military outside of Burma and included Aung San and Ne Win (who took power in the military coup of 1962 and remained the country's socialist dictator until 1988). Thus, when the Japanese army landed in Burma in 1942, it had the backing of Burmese nationalists who were of the opinion that help from outside was the only viable means to decolonization. The Thirty Comrades, however, went on to found the Anti-Fascist People's Freedom League, which fought to rid Burma of the Japanese.

46 Burmese: *Japan khet.*
47 There were fewer than ten papers in print in wartime Burma (Ba Than 1978, 68).
48 Tekkatho Htin Gyi 1992, 336–340.
49 Khit Hmi Thu 1947, 6.
50 46-Khu Nhac Amyothami 1947, 6.
51 Ba Maung 1947, 29.
52 Maung Maung Aye 1947, 29.
53 Burmese: *praññ. tan chā.*
54 Burmese: *khet aluik proṅ: lai.*
55 Hlaing Wut Yee 1947, 34, 36.
56 Burmese: "Mok sā mok."
57 Ngwe U Daung 1947, 11.
58 Ibid.
59 Burmese: "Mīn ma."
60 Ma Lay 1948, 39.
61 For a concise analysis of the relationship and marriage between Ma Ma Lay and U Chit Maung, see Khin Mar Mar Kyi 2002, 29–33. I am grateful to Craig Reynolds for bringing this thesis to my attention.
62 Ma Lay 1948, 39.
63 Ibid.
64 Ibid., 40.
65 Auzam 1938, 308.
66 Ibid.
67 Ibid.
68 Ibid.
69 Sinha 1995; Ankum 1997; Reyes 2008.
70 Furnivall 1957; Adas 1974; Maung Maung 1980.
71 McCoy 2000.
72 On the topic of colonial masculinity, see Mrinalini Sinha's now classic study, *Colonial Masculinity: The 'Manly Englishman' and the 'Effeminate Bengali' in the Late Nineteenth Century* (1995).
73 Ibid.; Sadan 2007, 48–51.
74 Shway Yoe 1989, 53, 65, 497.
75 Crosthwaite 1912, 65, 131.
76 Ibid., 117.
77 Laurie 1885, 21.
78 Ibid., 29.
79 H. F. Hall 1995, 76.
80 See Sinha's work (1995) on the Bengali babu, a popular stereotype of the effeminate Indian native that was constructed in opposition to the manly British imperialist.
81 R. H. Taylor 2008, 137–138.
82 Paragu 1981, 94.
83 Lieberman 2003, 135.

84 For summaries of these novels and information on their authors, see Paragu 1981.
85 Callahan 2003, 34.
86 Ibid., 29–42.
87 Ibid., 37.
88 Ibid., 36.
89 In February and May 1938, these armies conducted 105 and 201 parades, respectively. For more information on the formation of *tat* during the colonial period, see Callahan 2003, 36–40.
90 Ibid., 48.
91 Guyot 1966, 47.
92 Callahan 2003, 60.
93 Ibid., 87–113.
94 Chatterjee 1993; Sarkar 2001; Huang 2006.
95 Roces 2005, 369.

CONCLUSION

1 A film based on the novel was produced by a Japanese director in 2003, and in 2004 the novel was translated into English (Ma Lay 2004).
2 Ma Lay 1973, 94–95.
3 Ibid., 275–276.
4 The Thirty Comrades and other *thakin* continued to work with the Japanese during the *Japan khit*. The Japanese also courted the older generation of Burmese politicians such as Ba Maw and former colonial servants of the British government "who ultimately dominated all geographical and functional levels of the occupation-era civil service" (Callahan 2003, 55).
5 These crimes included forced labor, interrogation and torture, the massacre of civilians, rape, and looting, pillaging, and scorching of villages (Chaen 1989, 252–259.).
6 Yoshimi 2000, 78–80.
7 Burmese: *khyve: tap krī.*
8 As one former prisoner of war who worked on the construction of the railway explained, the Japanese expected that the railway, by joining the rail systems of Burma and Thailand, would provide "a quicker and safer route than the sea lanes to support their armies in Burma" (E. R. Hall 1981, 1).
9 Maung Maung 1989, 72.
10 Lin Yone Thit Lwin 1968, 10. In order to facilitate the construction of the railway, the Japanese army carried out "enlightening propaganda operations" that would rapidly improve the "Burmese cooperative spirit toward the Japanese military forces" (Trager 1971, 236).
11 The Burmese government, unlike those of the Philippines or Indonesia, has so far taken no interest in espousing the issue of Burmese comfort women, and no comprehensive study of Burmese comfort women has been published.

Most personal accounts attesting to the sexual exploitation of women by the Japanese army are confessions by Japanese ex-soldiers or testimonies given by non-Burmese ex–comfort women (Nishino 1993; Hicks 1995; Yoshimi 2000). However, the interviews with Japanese ex-soldiers as well as several studies on comfort women have revealed that Burmese women were indeed forced into sexual slavery. George Hicks, for instance, notes that a Korean comfort woman who served at the comfort stations in Burma distinguished her workplaces as "anthropological museums" because a good deal of use was made of local women. He estimates that there were 10 Korean women to 4 Burmese to 0.8 Japanese (Hicks 1995, 94–95).

12 Hla Pe 1961, 19.

13 For examples, see Khin Myo Chit 1945; Thakin Thein Pe Myint 1950; and Thein Pe Myint 1943.

14 Ba Maw 1968.

15 Nu 1954, ix.

16 Burmese: *Cin Kraññ nau . . . Cin Kraññ laṅ yū pak cak sañ*ñ || *mā ca tā krī: tui kyui pran buik tac luṃ: nai. kyan* ||.

17 Skidmore 2004, 131–137; 2005.

18 Houtman 1999, 29.

19 *Myanmar alin* was nationalized in 1969.

20 Po Yaygyan 1997, quoted in ibid., 28.

21 Houtman 1999, 28. For examples of these cartoons, see the reprints in the Fall 1998 issue of *Burma Debate* (vol. 5, no. 4).

22 Houtman 1999, 28.

23 Heng and Devan 1995, 196.

Glossary of Frequently Used Burmese Terms

amauk crest hair; refers to curly bangs piled high on the forehead
amein daw the royal orders
amyo race, kin, breed, lineage, family, rank, caste, kind, sort, and species
amyothami female person; woman; wife; additionally means "a member of a nation or ethnic group" and "fellow countrywoman"
auk kya, nauk kya fall below, fall behind
bo European
bo gadaw wife or mistress of a European man
bo hsan Westernized
bo ke English haircut
British khit era of the British
dhammakathika group of political monks who played a key role in the formation of *wunthanu athin*
dhammasat legal and ethical treatises that outlined appropriate Buddhist social practices and methods of dispute settlement
dobama "our Burma"; "our Burmese"; "our Burman"
Dobama Asiayone "Our Burmese Association"; "Our Burma Association"; "Our Burman Association"
ein shin ma housewife
eingyi blouse
eingyi pa extremely sheer muslin blouse
hpongyi monk
hti sayay ma galay young female clerical worker at a lottery shop
Japan khit "Japanese era"; the period of the Japanese occupation during the Second World War (1942–1945)
kabya people of mixed ancestry
kala Indian; foreign; foreigner
khit hmi up-to-date
khit hmi amyothami contemporary woman
khit hmi thu contemporary woman; up-to-date woman
khit hsan fashionable; trendy
khit hsan tha fashionable lad

khit hsan thu fashionable woman; trendy woman

khit kala present era; present times

khit thit new era

khit thit amyothami woman of the new era

konmaryi young woman; maiden

lady-kanya young (unmarried) woman; maiden

lady-khin high heels

longyi saronglike ankle-length skirt

meinma female person; woman; wife

myo town; city; district consisting of a main town, a market, and surrounding
villages and smaller towns

myo chit may woman who loves her kind or people; female patriot

myo thu gyi hereditary headman of a town

nain ngan yay politics; affairs of the country or state

nat spirit

nissaya word-by-word translation of a Pali text often followed by more elaborate
vernacular glosses by the translator

pinni light brown, homespun cotton

pinnya knowledge

sadohn customary chignon

sāsana teachings of the Buddha

sawbwa Shan hereditary chief (Shan *saohpa*)

sayadaw elder abbot

shinmyi eingyi chemise blouse made of silk or satin

taing pyi country or nation

tayoke Chinese

tet hpongyi modern monk

tet khit era of advancement

tet khit thami girl/daughter of the era of advancement

thakin literally "master"; the term employed by members of the Dobama Asiayone
to refer to themselves as a symbol of the idea that the Burmese people, not the
British, were the rightful masters of Burma and as an expression of their goal to
transform Burma into a classless society of only masters

thami daughter

thila shin Buddhist nun; "keeper of the precepts"

thu gyi hereditary headman of rural areas, usually of a village or a town

thumya bama "their Burma"; "their Burmese"; "their Burman"

tika commentary

toe tet yay progress; advancement

wunthanu patriot; protector of national interests

wunthanu athin village-level "patriotic association"

ya khu khit amyothami present-day woman

ya khu khit meinma present-day woman

yahan (or *yahan byo*) young, fully ordained Buddhist monk

yuwadi young woman; the word *yuvati* is the feminine counterpart of the Pali noun *yuvan,* "youth"

"Yuwadi kye hmoun" "Young Ladies' Mirror"

"Yuwadi sekku" "Young Ladies' Eyes"

ywa thu gyi hereditary headman of a village

zar bawli corsetlike lace bodice

Bibliography

ARCHIVES

India Office Records and Private Papers, British Library, London (IOR)
Myanmar National Archives, Yangon (NAD)
Universities Central Library, Yangon University, Myanmar
Universities Historical Research Centre, Yangon University, Myanmar

PUBLISHED AND UNPUBLISHED SOURCES

46-Khu Nhac Amyothami. 1947. "Buil ke pāy rań amok pran phrut may" [If you lose the English haircut, we'll lose the crest hair]. *Thway thauk,* no. 14 (January): 6.

Adas, Michael. 1974. *The Burma Delta: Economic Development and Social Change on an Asian Rice Frontier, 1852–1941.* Madison: University of Wisconsin Press.

Allott, Anna J. 1986. "Thahkin Ko-daw Hmaing." In *Far Eastern Literatures in the 20th Century: A Guide,* ed. Leonard S. Klein, 5–6. New York: Ungar.

———. 1991. Introduction to *Not Out of Hate: A Novel of Burma by Ma Ma Lay,* trans. Margaret Aung-Thwin, xiii–xxviii. Athens: Center for International Studies, Ohio University.

Alwis, Malathi de. 1999. "'Respectability,' 'Modernity' and the Policing of 'Culture' in Colonial Ceylon." In *Gender, Sexuality and Colonial Modernities,* ed. Antoinette Burton, 177–192. London and New York: Routledge.

Amar. 1936. "Tui. payoga" [Our evil influences]. *Myanmar alin,* New Year's special edition (April): 9.

Andaya, Barbara Watson. 1998. "From Temporary Wife to Prostitute: Sexuality and Economic Change in Early Modern Southeast Asia." *Journal of Women's History* 9, no. 4 (Winter): 11–34.

———. 2000. "Gender and the Historiography of Southeast Asia." In *Other Pasts: Women, Gender and History in Early Modern Southeast Asia*, ed. Barbara Watson Andaya, 1–26. Honolulu: University of Hawai'i Press.

———. 2002. "Localising the Universal: Women, Motherhood and the Appeal of Early Theravada Buddhism." *Journal of Southeast Asian Studies* 33, no. 1: 1–30.

———. 2006. *The Flaming Womb: Repositioning Women in Early Modern Southeast Asia.* Honolulu: University of Hawai'i Press.

Anderson, Benedict. 1991. *Imagined Communities: Reflections on the Origin and Spread of Nationalism.* Rev. ed. London and New York: Verso.

———. 1996. "Bullshit S/He Said: The Happy, Modern, Sexy, Indonesian Married Woman as Transsexual." In *Fantasizing the Feminine in Indonesia,* ed. Laurie J. Sears, 270–294. Durham, NC, and London: Duke University Press.

Andrus, J. Russell. 1948. *Burmese Economic Life.* Stanford, CA: Stanford University Press.

Ankum, Katharina von, ed. 1997. *Women in the Metropolis: Gender and Modernity in Weimar Culture.* Berkeley and Los Angeles: University of California Press.

Appadurai, Arjun, and Carol A. Breckenridge. 1995. "Public Modernity in India." In *Consuming Modernity: Public Culture in a South Asian World,* ed. Carol A. Breckenridge, 1–20. Minneapolis and London: University of Minnesota Press.

Arnold, G. F. 1916. "Letter from the Deputy Commissioner of Bassein to the Secretary to the Government of Burma (Rangoon)." In file 6E-19, "Education-Best Methods of Extending and Improving Female Education in Burma," 1/15 (E) 4033, NAD.

Atkinson, Jane Monnig, and Shelly Errington, eds. 1990. *Power and Difference: Gender in Island Southeast Asia.* Stanford, CA: Stanford University Press.

Aung San Suu Kyi. 1987. "Socio-political Currents in Burmese Literature, 1910–1940." In *Burma and Japan: Basic Studies on Their Cultural and Social Structure,* 65–83. Tokyo: Burma Research Group.

———. 1990. *Burma and India: Some Aspects of Intellectual Life under Colonialism.* New Delhi: Indian Institute of Advanced Study in association with Allied Publishers.

Aung-Thwin, Maitrii. 2003. "Genealogy of a Rebellion Narrative: Law, Ethnology and Culture in Colonial Burma." *Journal of Southeast Asian Studies* 34, no. 3: 393–419.

Auzam, Albert Ainley. 1938. "If Wives Should Receive Salaries!" *Ngan hta lawka* 24, no. 163: 308.

Aye Aye Mu. 1981. "Mran mā. lvat lap re: krui: pam mhu tvaṅ pā vaṅ so amyui: sa mī: myā: e* kaṇḍa (1919–1948)" [Burmese women's role in the independence movement (1919–1948)]. MA thesis, Yangon University.

Aye Hlaing. 1964. *A Study of Economic Development of Burma, 1870–1940.* Rangoon: Department of Economics, University of Rangoon.

Aye Kyaw. 1993. *The Voice of Young Burma.* Ithaca, NY: Southeast Asia Program, Cornell University.

Ba Maung, Maung. 1947. "Amok prassanā" [The crest hair problem]. *Thway thauk,* no. 15 (February): 29.

Ba Maw. 1968. *Breakthrough in Burma: Memoirs of a Revolution, 1939–1946.* New Haven, CT: Yale University Press.

Ba Than, UPI. 1978. "Mran mā nuiṅ ṅam cā nay jaṅ: samuiṅ:" [The history of journalism in Burma]. In *Cā nay jaṅ samuiṅ: cā tam: myā:* [Essays on the history of journalism], 1–75. Yangon: Sape beikman.

Ba Thaung, Bo Hmu. 2002. *Cā chui tau myā: atthuppatti* [Biography of literary figures]. Yangon: Ya pyi.

Barlow, Tani E. 1994. "Theorizing woman: Funü, Guojia, Jiating." In *Body, Subject, and Power in China,* ed. Angela Zito and Tani E. Barlow, 253–289. Chicago: University of Chicago Press.

———, ed. 1997. *Formations of Colonial Modernity in East Asia.* Durham, NC, and London: Duke University Press.

Barlow, Tani E., Madeleine Yue Dong, Uta G. Poiger, Priti Ramamurthy, Lynn M. Thomas, and Alys Eve Weinbaum. 2005. "The Modern Girl around the World: A Research Agenda and Preliminary Findings." In *Gender and History* 17, no. 2: 245–294.

Barmé, Scott. 2002. *Woman, Man, Bangkok: Love, Sex, and Popular Culture in Thailand.* Lanham, MD: Rowman and Littlefield.

Bartholomeusz, Tessa J. 1994. *Women under the Bo Tree: Buddhist Nuns in Sri Lanka.* Cambridge and New York: Cambridge University Press.

Bashford, Alison. 2004. "Medicine, Gender, and Empire." In *Gender and Empire,* ed. Philippa Levine, 112–134. Oxford: Oxford University Press.

Basu, Aparna. 1974. *The Growth of Education and Political Development in India, 1898–1920.* Delhi: Oxford University Press.

Baxter, James. 1941. *Report on Indian Immigration.* Rangoon: Office of the Superintendent, Government Printing and Stationery.

Bayly, Christopher. 1986. "The Origins of Swadeshi (Home Industry): Cloth and Indian Society, 1700–1930." In *The Social Life of Things: Commodities in Cultural Perspective,* ed. Arjun Appadurai, 285–322. Cambridge: Cambridge University Press.

———. 2003. *Rangoon (Yangon) 1939–49: The Death of a Colonial Metropolis.* Centre of South Asian Studies Occasional Paper no. 3. Cambridge, UK.

Bayly, Susan. 1999. *Caste, Society and Politics in India from the Eighteenth Century to the Modern Age.* Cambridge: Cambridge University Press.

Berlie, J. A. 2008. *The Burmanization of Myanmar's Muslims.* Bangkok: White Lotus Press.

Bernstein, Gail Lee, ed. 1991. *Recreating Japanese Women, 1600–1945.* Berkeley and Los Angeles: University of California Press.

Bingham, Adrian. 2004. *Gender, Modernity, and the Popular Press in Interwar Britain.* Oxford: Clarendon Press.

Blackburn, Anne M. 2001. *Buddhist Learning and Textual Practice in Eighteenth-Century Lankan Monastic Culture.* Princeton, NJ: Princeton University Press.

Blackstone, Kathryn R. 1998. *Women in the Footsteps of the Buddha: Struggle for Liberation in the Therigatha.* Richmond, Surrey: Curzon.

Braun, Eric Christopher. 2008. "Ledi Sayadaw, Abhidhamma, and the Development of the Modern Insight Meditation Movement in Burma." PhD diss., Harvard University.

Brenner, Suzanne. 1999. "On the Public Intimacy of the New Order: Images of Women in the Popular Indonesian Print Media." *Indonesia* 67 (April): 13–37.

British Commonwealth League. 1925. "Letter to the Secretary of State for India." In file 1913, "Suffrage and Equal Citizenship of Women," L/PJ/6/1878, IOR.

———. 1933. "Letter to the Secretary of State for India, India Office." In file L/P&J(B)512, "Status of Women under New Constitution," M/1/81, IOR.

Brown, Ian. 2005. *A Colonial Economy in Crisis: Burma's Rice Cultivators and the World Depression of the 1930s.* London: RoutledgeCurzon.

Brown, R. Grant. 1995. "Burmese Women" (1911). In *Shades of Gold and Green: Anecdotes of Colonial Burma (1886–1948),* comp. N. Greenwood. New Delhi and Madras: Asian Educational Services.

Burma, Government of. 1917. *Fifth Quinquennial Report on Public Instruction in Burma, for the Years 1912–13 to 1916–17.* Rangoon: Office of the Superintendent, Government Printing and Stationery.

———. 1921. *Report on the Sanitary Administration of Burma for the Year 1920.* Rangoon: Office of the Superintendent, Government Printing and Stationery.

———. 1923. *Sixth Quinquennial Report on Public Instruction in Burma for the Years 1917–18 to 1921–22.* Rangoon: Office of the Superintendent, Government Printing and Stationery.

———. 1928a. *Report of an Enquiry into the Standard and Cost of Living of the Working Classes in Rangoon.* Rangoon: Labor Statistics Bureau.

———. 1928b. *Seventh Quinquennial Report on Public Instruction in Burma, for the Years 1922–23 to 1926–27.* Rangoon: Office of the Superintendent, Government Printing and Stationery.

———. 1929. *Annual Report on Public Instruction in Burma for the Year 1927–28.* Rangoon: Office of the Superintendent, Government Printing and Stationery.

———. 1931. *Report of the Committee to Consider and Report upon Buddhist Religious Instruction for Buddhist Pupils in Vernacular Lay Schools under Buddhist Management, 1928–29.* Rangoon: Office of the Superintendent, Government Printing and Stationery.

———. 1932. *Burma Round Table Conference Proceedings, 27th November, 1931–12th January 1932.* Rangoon: Office of the Superintendent, Government Printing and Stationery.

———. 1936. "Extracts from Fortnightly Report for the Second Half of February, 1936." In file P&J(B)1508, "Rangoon University Strike, 21 March–22 July 1936," M/1/147, IOR.

———. 1938a. "Extract from the *Times,* 29 November 1938." In file B3932/38(i), "Burma Riots: Situation Reports," M/3/513, IOR.

———. 1938b. "Minute Paper, Burma Office." In file B3932/38(i), "Burma Riots: Situation Reports," M/3/513, IOR.

———. 1939a. Buddhist Women's Special Marriage and Succession Act (Burma Act XXIV). In file 2A-22, "Buddhist Women's Special Marriage and Succession Act," 1/1 (B) 877, NAD.

————. 1939b. "Note on the Press in Burma." In file 408, "Burmese Press, 1938–47," L/I/1/622, IOR.

————. 1940. "Burma Press Abstracts." L/R/5/207, IOR.

————. 1946. "Confidential Memo: Burmese Daily Newspapers." In file 408, "Burmese Press, 1938–47," L/I/1/622, IOR.

Burma, Secretary to the Government of. 1905. "Letter to the Inspector General of Police, Burma," 2 October. In file 1L-3, "Legislation Relating to Protection of Minor Girl," 1/15 (D) 471, NAD.

————. 1932a. "General Department Letter to All Commissioners of Divisions (except Mandalay) and Heads of Departments." In file 1/15 (D) 2916, NAD.

————. 1932b. "Question Regarding the Appointment of Women to Clerical Posts under Government." In 1/15 (D) 2916, NAD.

Burma Socialist Programme Party. 1975. *Mran mā nuiṅ ṅaṃ amyui: sa mī: myā: e* nuiṅ ṅaṃ re: lhup rhā: mhu* [The political movements of women in Myanmar]. Yangon: Sape beikman.

Burton, Antoinette. 1994. *Burdens of History: British Feminists, Indian Women, and Imperial Culture, 1865–1915.* Chapel Hill and London: University of North Carolina Press.

————, ed. 1999. *Gender, Sexuality and Colonial Modernities.* London and New York: Routledge.

Butler, Sir Harcourt. 1930. "Burma and the Burmans." *Times of India* (18 February).

Butwell, Richard. 1969. *U Nu of Burma.* Stanford, CA: Stanford University Press.

Cady, John Frank. 1958. *A History of Modern Burma.* Ithaca, NY: Cornell University Press.

Callahan, Mary P. 2003. *Making Enemies: War and State Building in Burma.* Ithaca, NY, and London: Cornell University Press.

Carlson, Richard James. 1991. "Women, Gender, and Politics in Burma's Nationalist Movement, 1900–1931." MA thesis, Cornell University.

Carroll, Lorrayne. 2007. *Rhetorical Drag: Gender Impersonation, Captivity, and the Writing of History.* Kent, OH: Kent State University Press.

Chaen, Yoshio. 1989. *BC-kyū senpan eigun saiban shiryō* 2 [Documents on British military tribunals of class B and class C war crimes, vol. 2]. Tokyo: Fuji shuppan.

Chakrabarty, Dipesh. 2000. *Provincializing Europe: Postcolonial Thought and Historical Difference.* Princeton, NJ: Princeton University Press.

————. 2002. *Habitations of Modernity: Essays in the Wake of Subaltern Studies.* Chicago and London: University of Chicago Press.

Chakravarti, Nalini Ranjan. 1971. *The Indian Minority in Burma: The Rise and Decline of an Immigrant Community.* With a foreword by Hugh Tinker. London and New York: Oxford University Press.

Charney, Michael W. 1998. "Crisis and Reformation in a Maritime Kingdom of Southeast Asia: Forces of Instability and Political Disintegration in Western Burma (Arakan), 1603–1701." *Journal of the Economic and Social History of the Orient* 41, no. 2 (May): 185–219.

————. 1999. "Problematics and Paradigms in Historicizing the Overseas Chinese in the Nineteenth- and Twentieth-Century Straits and Burma." *Journal of the South Seas Society* 54 (December): 93–106.

————. 2006. *Powerful Learning: Buddhist Literati and the Throne in Burma's Last Dynasty, 1752–1885.* Ann Arbor: Centers for South and Southeast Asian Studies, University of Michigan.

Chatterjee, Partha. 1993. *The Nation and Its Fragments: Colonial and Postcolonial Histories.* Princeton, NJ: Princeton University Press.

Chen, Yi-Sein. 1966. "The Chinese in Rangoon during the 18th and 19th Centuries." In *Artibus Asiae Supplementum* 23, *Essays Offered to G. H. Luce by His Colleagues and Friends in Honour of His Seventy-Fifth Birthday,* vol. 1, *Papers on Asian History, Religion, Languages, Literature, Music Folklore, and Anthropology,* 107–111.

Chousalkar, Ashok. 1990. *Indian Idea of Political Resistance: Aurobindo, Tilak, Gandhi and Ambedkar.* Delhi: Ajanta Publications.

Chua, Ai Lin. 2007. "Modernity, Popular Culture and Urban Life: Anglophone Asians in Colonial Singapore, 1920–1940." PhD diss., University of Cambridge.

Civil Service Commissioners and Treasury. 1919. "Memorandum on the Bill to Remove Certain Restraints and Disabilities Imposed upon Women." In file 8115, "Sex Disqualification (Removal) Act," L/PJ/6/1642, IOR.

Clancey, J. C. 1906. "The Burmese Calendar." *Journal of the Royal Meteorological Society,* no. 366 (January): 54–59.

Coedès, Georges. 1968. *The Indianized States of Southeast Asia.* Ed. Walter Vella; trans. Susan Browning. Honolulu: East West Center, University of Hawai'i Press.

Cohn, Bernard S. 1987. *An Anthropologist among the Historians and Other Essays.* Oxford: Oxford University Press.

————. 1996. "Cloth, Clothes, and Colonialism: India in the Nineteenth Century." In *Colonialism and Its Forms of Knowledge,* 106–162. Princeton, NJ: Princeton University Press.

Cooper, Frederick. 2005. *Colonialism in Question: Theory, Knowledge, and History.* Berkeley: University of California Press.

Cooper, W. G. 1913. "The Origin of the Talaings." *Journal of the Burma Research Society* 3, no. 1: 1–11.

Cowen, John. 1914a. *Tracts for Rangoon: 29th Street by Day & Night.* Vol. 2. Rangoon: YMCA.

————. 1914b. *Tracts for Rangoon: Rangoon's Scarlet Sin or, Lust Made Lawful.* Vol. 5. Rangoon: YMCA.

————. 1916. "Public Prostitution in Rangoon: Report to the Association for Moral and Social Hygiene on Brothel-Keeping, Prostitution, Segregation and Immoral Conditions in Rangoon and Other Towns and Stations in Burma," 9 June. In file 2987/16, "Rangoon Brothels/Prostitution in Rangoon," L/PJ/6/1448, IOR.

Crosthwaite, Charles. 1903. "Letter to Sir Charles Lyall," 17 March. In file 517, "Marriages between European Officers in Burma and Burmese Women," L/PJ/6/629, IOR.

———. 1912. *The Pacification of Burma.* London: Edward Arnold.

Davin, A. 1992. "Imperialism and Motherhood." In *Tensions of Empire: Colonial Cultures in a Bourgeois World,* ed. Frederick Cooper and Ann L. Stoler, 87–151. Los Angeles and Berkeley: University of California Press.

Dhammasami, Khammai. 2004. "Between Idealism and Pragmatism: A Study of Monastic Education in Burma and Thailand from the Seventeenth Century to the Present." PhD diss., Oxford University.

Dharmasena, Thera. 1991. *Jewels of the Doctrine: Stories of the Saddharma Ratnavaliya.* Albany: State University of New York Press.

Dickinson, Edward Ross. 2007. "Policing Sex in Germany, 1882–1982: A Preliminary Statistical Analysis." *Journal of the History of Sexuality* 16, no. 2 (May): 204–250.

Dirks, Nicholas. 2001. *Castes of Mind: Colonialism and the Making of Modern India.* Princeton, NJ: Princeton University Press.

Dobama Asiayone. 1959. "The Dobama Manifesto." *Guardian* 6, no. 1 (January): 21–26.

Donnison, F. S. V. 1953. *Public Administration in Burma: A Study of the Development during the British Connexion.* London and New York: Royal Institute of International Affairs, in cooperation with the Institute of Pacific Relations.

Dube, Saurabh. 2002. "Introduction: Colonialism, Modernity, Colonial Modernities." In "Critical Conjunctions: Foundations of Colony and Formations of Modernity," ed. Saurabh Dube, Ishita Banerjee Dube, and Edgardo Lander, special issue, *Nepantla: Views from South* 3, no. 2: 197–219.

Eaton, Richard. 2002. "Locating Arakan in Time, Space, and Historical Scholarship." In Gommans and Leider 2002, 225–232.

Edwards, Louise. 2000. "Policing the Modern Woman in Republican China." *Modern China* 26, no. 2: 115–147.

Edwards, Louise, and Mina Roces, eds. 2004. *Women's Suffrage in Asia: Gender, Nationalism and Democracy.* London and New York: RoutledgeCurzon.

Edwards, Penny. 2002. "Half-Cast: Staging Race in British Burma." *Postcolonial Studies* 5, no. 3: 279–295.

———. 2003. "On Home Ground: Settling Land and Domesticating Difference in the 'Non-Settler' Colonies of Burma and Cambodia." *Journal of Colonialism and Colonial History* 4, no. 3 (Winter).

———. 2004. "Relocating the Interlocutor: Taw Sein Ko (1864–1930) and the Itinerancy of Knowledge in British Burma." *Southeast Asia Research* 12, no. 3: 277–335.

Ein Shin Ma. 1934. "Amyui: sa mī: lam: pra" [Women's guide]. *Youq shin lan hnyun* 1, no. 17 (19 January): 33–35.

Eisenstadt, S. N. 2000. "Multiple Modernities." *Daedalus* 129, no. 1: 1–29.

Enquiry Sub-Committee. 1936. "Report of the Enquiry Sub-Committee Appointed by His Excellency the Chancellor." In file P&J(B)1508, "Rangoon University Strike, 21 March–22 July 1936," M/1/147, IOR.

Epstein, Maram. 2007. "Bound by Convention: Women's Writing and the Feminine Voice in Eighteenth-Century China." *Tulsa Studies in Women's Literature* 26, no. 1 (Spring): 97–105.

Exchequer, Chancellor of the. 1919. "Secret Letter to the War Cabinet on the Women's Emancipation Bill." In file 8115, "Sex Disqualification (Removal) Act," L/PJ/6/1642, IOR.

Fay, Mary Ann. 2008. "Introduction: Early Twentieth-Century Middle Eastern Feminisms, Nationalisms, and Transnationalisms." *Journal of Middle East Women's Studies* 4, no. 1 (Winter): 1–5.

Foucault, Michel. 1994. *Ethics: Subjectivity and Truth.* Ed. Paul Rabinow; trans. Robert Hurley et al. Vol. 1 of *The Essential Works of Michel Foucault, 1954–1984.* New York: New Press.

Frasch, Tilman. 2002. "Coastal Peripheries during the Pagan Period." In Gommans and Leider 2002, 59–78.

Frontier Areas Committee of Enquiry. 1947. *Report of the Frontier Areas Committee of Enquiry.* Rangoon: Office of the Superintendent, Government Printing and Stationery.

Frost, Mark. 2002. "'Wider Opportunities': Religious Revival, Nationalist Awakening and the Global Dimension in Colombo, 1870–1920." *Modern Asian Studies* 36, no. 4: 937–967.

Furnivall, J. S. 1956. *Colonial Policy and Practice: A Comparative Study of Burma and Netherlands India.* New York: New York University Press.

———. 1957. *An Introduction to the Political Economy of Burma.* 3rd ed. Rangoon: Peoples' Literature Committee and House.

———. 1991. *The Fashioning of Leviathan: The Beginnings of British Rule in Burma.* Canberra: Economic History of Southeast Asia Project and Thai-Yunnan Project.

Gaonkar, Dilip Parameshwar. 2001. *Alternative Modernities.* Durham, NC, and London: Duke University Press.

Gascoigne, Gwendolen. 1896. *Among Pagodas and Fair Ladies: An Account of a Tour through Burma.* London: A. D. Innes and Co.

Gaung, U. 1909. *Translation of "A Digest of the Burmese Buddhist Law Concerning Inheritance and Marriage; Being a Collection of Texts from Thirty-Six Dhammathats."* Rangoon: Office of the Superintendent, Government Printing and Stationery.

Ghosh, Durba. 2006. *Sex and the Family in Colonial India: The Making of Empire.* Cambridge: Cambridge University Press.

Göle, Nilüfer. 1996. *The Forbidden Modern: Civilization and Veiling.* Ann Arbor: University of Michigan Press.

———. 1997. "The Gendered Nature of the Public Sphere." *Public Culture* 10, no. 1: 61–91.

Gommans, Jos, and Jacques Leider, eds. 2002. *The Maritime of Burma: Exploring Political, Cultural and Commercial Interaction in the Indian Ocean World, 1200–1800.* Leiden: Koninklijke Nederlandse Akademie van Wetenschappen.

Gopal, Ram. 1956. *Lokamanya Tilak: A Biography.* Bombay: Asia Publishing House.

Gravers, Mikael. 1999. *Nationalism as Political Paranoia in Burma: An Essay on the Historical Practice of Power.* 2nd ed. Richmond, Surrey: Curzon.

———. 2007. "Introduction: Ethnicity against State—State against Ethnic Diversity?" In *Exploring Ethnic Diversity in Burma,* ed. Mikael Gravers, 1–33. Copenhagen: NIAS Press.

Guyot, Dorothy. 1966. "The Political Impact of the Japanese Occupation of Burma." PhD diss., Yale University.

H.M. 1936. "The Age of Criticism in Burma." *Ngan hta lawka* 21, no. 132: 566.

Habermas, Jurgen. 1989. *The Structural Transformation of the Public Sphere: An Inquiry into a Category of Bourgeois Society.* Studies in Contemporary German Social Thought. Cambridge, MA: MIT Press.

Hake, Sabine. 1997. "In the Mirror of Fashion." In Ankum 1997, 185–201.

Hall, D. G. E. 1950. *Burma.* London and New York: Hutchinson's University Library.

———. 1980. "Obituary: Gordon Hannington Luce." *Bulletin of the School of Oriental and African Studies* 43, no. 3: 581–588.

Hall, E. R. 1981. *The Burma-Thailand Railway of Death.* Armadale, Victoria, Australia: Graphic Books.

Hall, Harold Fielding. 1995. *The Soul of a People.* Bangkok: White Orchid Press. Originally published in 1898.

Hallisey, Charles. 1995. "The Road Not Taken." In *Curators of the Buddha: The Study of Buddhism under Colonialism,* ed. Donald Lopez Jr., 31–61. Chicago and London: University of Chicago Press.

Hamilton, George. 1903. "Letter to His Excellency the Right Honourable the Governor General of India in Council," 10 April. In file 517, "Marriages between European Officers in Burma and Burmese Women," L/PJ/6/629, IOR.

Hansen, Anne. 2006. *How to Behave: Buddhism and Modernity in Colonial Cambodia, 1860–1930.* Honolulu: University of Hawai'i Press.

Harada, Masaharu, and Toru Ono. 1979. *Birumago jiten* [Burmese-Japanese dictionary]. Osaka: Nihon Biruma bunka kyoukai.

Hart, Alice Marion Rowlands. 1897. *Picturesque Burma, Past and Present.* London: J. M. Dent and Co.

Harvey, G. E. 1967. *History of Burma: From the Earliest Times to 10 March 1824; The Beginning of the English Conquest.* London: Cass.

Hawes, C. J. 1996. *Poor Relations: The Making of a Eurasian Community in British India, 1773–1833.* New York and London: Routledge.

Heineman, Elizabeth. 2002. "Sexuality and Nazism: The Doubly Unspeakable?" *Journal of the History of Sexuality* 11, nos. 1–2 (January–April): 22–66.

Heng, Geraldine, and Janadas Devan. 1995. "State Fatherhood: The Politics of Nationalism, Sexuality, and Race in Singapore." In Ong and Peletz 1995, 195–215.

Herbert, Patricia M. 1982. *The Hsaya San Rebellion (1930–1932) Reappraised.* London: Department of Oriental Manuscripts and Printed Books, British Library.

Hershfield, Joanne. 2008. *Imagining la Chica Moderna: Women, Nation, and Visual Culture in Mexico, 1917–1936.* Durham, NC: Duke University Press.

Hicks, George. 1995. *The Comfort Women.* St Leonards, New South Wales, Australia: Allen and Unwin.

Hla Aung. 1968. "The Effect of Anglo-Indian Legislation on Burmese Customary Law." In *Family Law and Customary Law in Asia: A Contemporary Legal Perspective,* ed. David C. Buxbaum, 67–88. N.p.: Kluwer Law International.

Hla Pain. 1967. *Lay tī ganthavaṅ kyau mya samuiṅ* [History of famous people of Ledi monastery]. Mandalay: Thukhawadi poun hneik taik.

Hla Pe. 1961. *U Hla Pe's Narrative of the Japanese Occupation of Burma.* Recorded by U Khin. Vol. 14. Ithaca, NY: Southeast Asia Program Publications, Cornell University.

———. 1968. "The Rise of Popular Literature in Burma." *Journal of Burma Research Society* 51, no. 2: 123–144.

Hlaing Wut Yee, Sagaing. 1947. "Yokyā: thve—yokyā: thve" [Men, men]. *Thway thauk,* no. 20 (July): 34, 36.

Hotta, Keiko. 1987. "Some Aspects of Modernization in 'Story of Maung Hmaing, the Roselle Seller.'" In *Burma and Japan: Basic Studies on Their Cultural and Social Structure,* 102–116. Tokyo: Burma Research Group.

Houtman, Gustaaf. 1997. "Burma or Myanmar? The Cucumber and the Circle." *International Institute of Asian Studies Newsletter,* no. 12 (Spring): 20–21.

———. 1999. *Mental Culture in Burmese Crisis Politics: Aung San Suu Kyi and the National League for Democracy.* Study of Languages and Cultures of Asia and Africa Monograph Series, no. 33. Tokyo University of Foreign Studies, Institute for the Study of Languages and Cultures of Asia and Africa.

Hpo Lat. 1962. *Mran mā ca kā: aphvaṅ. kyam:* [Explanation of the Burmese language]. Vol. 1. Yangon: Paññā nanda.

Htin Aung. 1965. *The Stricken Peacock: Anglo-Burmese Relations, 1752–1948.* The Hague, Netherlands: Martinus Nijhoff.

———. 1967. *A History of Burma.* New York: Columbia University Press.

Htun Shein. 1936. "Mran mā. prassanā akhyui." [Some of Burma's problems]. *Myanmar alin,* New Year's special edition (April): 65–67.

Htun Yee. 2006. *Collection of Hpyat-sa (Legal Cases and Court Decisions of Myanmar in the Kon-baung Period).* Vol. 1, part 2. Yangon: Myanmar Affairs Bureau, Literature Bank.

Huang, Martin W. 2006. *Negotiating Masculinities in Late Imperial China.* Honolulu: University of Hawai'i Press.

Hydari, Nawab A. 1928. *The General Report of the Fifty-Second Anniversary and Convention of the Theosophical Society Held at Adyar, December 23rd to 29th, 1927.* Adyar, Madras, India: Theosophical Publishing House.

Ikeya, Chie. 2006. "Gender, History and Modernity: Representing Women in Twentieth-Century Colonial Burma." PhD diss., Cornell University.

India, Government of. 1893. *Census of India, 1891: General Report.* London: Eyre and Spottiswoode.

———. 1902. *Census of India, 1901.* Vol. 12, part 2. Rangoon: Office of the Superintendent, Government Printing and Stationery.

———. 1903a. "Confidential Memorandum Regarding Marriage between European Officials and Burmese Ladies." In file 517, "Marriages between European Officers in Burma and Burmese Women," L/PJ/6/629, IOR.

———. 1903b. "Letter to the Right Honourable Lord George Francis Hamilton, G.C.S.I., His Majesty's Secretary of State for India," 26 February. In file 517, "Marriages between European Officers in Burma and Burmese Women," L/PJ/6/629, IOR.

———. 1914. "Report of the Select Committee of the Imperial Legislative Council, 18 March 1914." In file 6L/8, "Bill to Make Further Provisions for the Protection of Women and Girls and Other Purposes," 1/15 (E) 12310, NAD.

———. 1919a. "Extract from the Minutes of a Meeting of the Committee of Home Affairs, Held on 16 May 1919." In file 8115, "Sex Disqualification (Removal) Act," L/PJ/6/1642, IOR.

———. 1919b. Sex Disqualification (Removal) Act. Available in file 8115, "Sex Disqualification (Removal) Act," L/PJ/6/1642, IOR.

———. 1920a. "Extract from the Abstract of the Proceedings of Council Relating to the University of Rangoon Bill." In file 2052, L/PJ/6/1662, IOR.

———. 1920b. University of Rangoon Act. Available in file 2052, "University of Rangoon Act," L/PJ/6/1662, IOR.

———. 1921. *Cost of Living, Rangoon.* Calcutta, India: Government Printing Press.

———. 1922. *Statistical Abstract Relating to British India from 1910–1911 to 1919–1920.* London: His Majesty's Stationery Office.

———. 1923. *Census of India, 1921.* Vol. 10, *Burma.* Rangoon: Office of the Superintendent, Government Printing and Stationery.

———. 1927. "Buddhist Marriage and Divorce Bill, Protest Against." In file 2398, L/PJ/6/1944, IOR.

———. 1928. *Indian Cinematograph Committee, 1927–28: Evidence.* Vol. 3. Calcutta: Government of India, Central Publications Branch.

———. 1930. "India: Enfranchisement of Women." *Times Educational Supplement.* Clipping in file 25/3, "Indian States: Enfranchisement of Women," L/I/1/171, IOR.

———. 1933a. *Census of India, 1931: Part One, Report.* Vol. 11, *Burma.* Rangoon: Office of the Superintendent, Government Printing and Stationery.

———. 1933b. *Census of India, 1931: Part Two, Tables.* Vol. 11, *Burma.* Rangoon: Office of the Superintendent, Government Printing and Stationery.

———. 1939. "Letter from the India Office to A. H. Joyce, Information Office, Burma Office." In file 408, "Burmese Press, 1938–47," L/I/1/622, IOR.

International Alliance of Women for Suffrage and Equal Citizenship. 1927. "Letter to the Under-secretary of State, India Office." In file "Status of Women under New Constitution," L/P&J(B) 512, IOR.

———. 1933. "Letter to the Secretary of State for India, India Office." In file 1913, "Suffrage and Equal Citizenship of Women," L/PJ/6/1878, IOR.

Jardine, John, trans. 1934. *King Wagaru's Manu Dhammasattham: Text, Translation and Notes*. Rangoon: Office of the Superintendent, Government Printing and Stationery.

Jayawardena, Kumari. 1986. *Feminism and Nationalism in the Third World*. London and Totowa, NJ: Zed Books.

———. 1995. *The White Woman's Other Burden: Western Women and South Asia during British Colonial Rule*. London and New York: Routledge.

Judson's Burmese-English Dictionary. 1914. Rangoon: Baptist Board of Publications.

Ka, U. 1936. "Muslim amyui: sa mī: myā:" [Muslim women]. *Myanmar alin*, New Year's special edition (April): 49–52.

Kandiyoti, Deniz. 1991. "Identity and Its Discontents: Women and the Nation." *Millennium: Journal of International Studies* 20, no. 3: 429–443.

Kartini, R. A. 1992. "Give the Javanese Education!" In *Letters from Kartini: An Indonesian Feminist, 1900–1904*, trans. Joost Coté, 529–547. Clayton, Victoria, Australia: Monash University.

Kaung, U. 1930. "The Beginnings of Christian Missionary Education in Burma, 1600–1824." *Journal of Burma Research Society* 20, no. 2: 59–75.

———. 1931. "1824–1853: Roman Catholic and American Baptist Mission Schools." *Journal of Burma Research Society* 21, no. 1: 2–13.

———. 1963. "A Survey of the History of Education in Burma before the British Conquest and After." *Journal of Burma Research Society* 46, no. 2 (December): 1–129.

Kaviraj, Sudipta. 2005. "An Outline of a Revisionist Theory of Modernity." *European Journal of Sociology* 46, no. 3: 497–526.

Kawanami, Hiroko. 2000. "Patterns of Renunciation: The Changing World of Burmese Nuns." In *Women's Buddhism, Buddhism's Women: Tradition, Revision, Renewal*, ed. E. B. Findly, 159–171. Boston: Wisdom Publications.

———. N.d. "Worldly Renunciation: The World of Burmese Buddhist Nuns." Unpublished manuscript.

Keyes, Charles F. 1984. "Mother or Mistress but Never a Monk: Buddhist Notions of Female Gender in Rural Thailand." *American Ethnologist* 11, no. 2: 223–241.

Khin Khin Lay, Dagon. 1961. *Nhac poṅ: 60* [60 years: An autobiography]. Yangon: Yuwadi.

Khin Mar Mar Kyi. 2002. "Gender, Colonisation and Nationalism: Selected Novels of a Burmese Feminist Writer; Gyanekyaw Ma Ma Lay." MA thesis, Australian National University.

Khin Maung Htun. 1974. *Mran mā gyānay samuiṅ: (1919–1941)* [A history of Burmese journals, 1919–1941]. Yangon: U Chit Aung.

———. 1975. "Mran mā maggajaṅ:" [Burmese magazines]. In *Mran mā mhu (1920–1970)* [Burmese affairs, 1920–1970], 1:216–258. Yangon: Tekkathomya poun hneik taik.

Khin Maung Nyunt. 2004. "The 'Shoe Question.'" In *Selected Writings of Dr. Khin Maung Nyunt*, 89–103. Yangon: Myanmar Historical Commission.

Khin May. 1933a. "Amyui: smī: tui. e* tui: tak re:" [Women's advancement]. *Toe tet yay* 1 (October): 29–30, 71–73.

————. 1933b. "Amyui: smī: tui. e* tui: tak re:" [Women's advancement]. *Toe tet yay* 2 (November): 38, 113–116.

————. 1933c. "Amyui: smī: tui. e* tui: tak re:" [Women's advancement]. *Toe tet yay* 3 (December): 23–24, 80.

Khin Myint. 1937. "Englishmen as Seen by Burmese Women." *Ngan hta lawka* (January): 542.

Khin Myo Chit. 1945. *Three Years under the Japs*. With a foreword by Deedok U Ba Choe. Rangoon: Khin Myo Chit.

————. 1946. "Maṅgalā naṃ nak cā" [Good morning]. *Zawana* 1, no. 6 (April): 34–36.

————. 1974. "Women in Buddhism." *Guardian* 21, no. 8: 8–12.

————. 1976. *Colorful Burma: Her Infinite Variety; A Collection of Stories and Essays*. Rangoon: KMCT Sazin.

Khin Swe. 1927. "Yuvatī cakkhu" [Young ladies' eyes]. *Dagon* (March): 240–253.

————. 1929. "Yuvatī cakkhu" [Young ladies' eyes]. *Dagon* (September): 351–361.

Khin Toke. 1926. "Yuvatī cakkhu" [Young ladies' eyes]. *Dagon* (December): 202–216.

Khin Yi. 1988a. *The Dobama Movement in Burma, 1930–1938*. Ithaca, NY: Southeast Asia Program, Cornell University.

————. 1988b. *The Dobama Movement in Burma: Appendix*. Ithaca, NY: Southeast Asia Program, Cornell University.

Khit Hmi Thu. 1947. "Amok kroṅ. akyui: ma yut pā" [The crest hair does not lessen one's virtue]. *Thway thauk*, no. 14 (January): 6.

Kirichenko, Alexey. 2004. "Social Changes, New Identities and Political Activism in Colonial Burma and India (c. 1880–1948)." Paper presented at the 18th European Conference of Modern South Asian Studies, Lund University, Sweden, 6–9 June.

Kirsch, Thomas A. 1985. "Text and Context: Buddhist Sex Roles/Culture of Gender Revisited." *American Ethnologist* 12, no. 2: 302–320.

Koop, John Clement. 1960. *The Eurasian Population in Burma*. New Haven, CT: Yale University, Southeast Asia Studies.

Kyan. 1978. "Amyui: sa mī: myā: nhaṅ. cā nay jaṅ: loka" [Women and the world of journalism]. In *Cā nay jaṅ: samuiṅ: cā tam: myā:* [Essays on the history of journalism], 279–312. Yangon: Sape beikman.

Laichen, Sun. 2000. "Ming-Southeast Asian Overland Interactions, 1368–1644." PhD diss., University of Michigan.

Laurie, W. F. B. 1882. *Ashé Pyee, the Superior Country; or, The Great Attractions of Burma to British Enterprise and Commerce*. London: W. H. Allen and Co.

————. 1885. *Our Burmese Wars and Relations with Burma: Being an Abstract of Military and Political Operations, 1824–25–26, and 1852–1853*. 2nd ed. London: W. H. Allen and Co.

Leider, Jacques P. 2008. "Arakan (1785–1885): From Burmese Subjection to British Exploitation." Paper presented at the 20th Conference of the International Association of Historians of Asia, Delhi, 14–17 November.

Levine, Philippa. 2003. *Prostitution, Race and Politics: Policing Venereal Disease in the British Empire.* New York and London: Routledge.

Lewis, Su Lin. 2009. "Cosmopolitanism and the Modern Girl: A Cross-Cultural Discourse in 1930s Penang." *Modern Asian Studies* 43, no. 6 (November): 937–967, 1385–1419.

Lieberman, Victor. 1978. "Ethnic Politics in Eighteenth-Century Burma." *Modern Asian Studies* 12, no. 3: 455–482.

———. 2003. *Strange Parallels: Southeast Asia in Global Context, c. 800–1830.* Vol. 1, *Integration on the Mainland.* New York: Cambridge University Press.

Lin Yone Thit Lwin. 1968. *Yui: dayā: mran mā mī: rathā: lan: kuiy tve. khyve: tap mhat tam:* [Thailand-Burma railway: Memoirs of a conscript]. Yangon.

Lintner, Bertil. 2003. "Burma/Myanmar." In *Ethnicity in Asia,* ed. Colin Mackerras, 174–193. New York: RoutledgeCurzon.

Loos, Tamara. 2006. *Subject Siam: Family, Law, and Colonial Modernity in Thailand.* Ithaca, NY: Cornell University.

Luce, G. H. 1959. "Note on the Peoples of Burma in the 12th–13th Century A.D." *Journal of the Burma Research Society* 42, no. 1 (June): 52–74.

Lwyn, Tinzar. 1994. "Stories of Gender and Ethnicity: Discourses of Colonialism and Resistance in Burma." *Australian Journal of Anthropology* 5, nos. 1–2: 60–85.

Ma Lay, Ma. 1940. "Yokyā: thve. rai. atve: akhau hā aok kya lha khye. ka lā:" [The deteriorating state of male mentality]. *Journal gyaw* (January): 15, 18.

———. 1948. "Min: ma" [Wife]. *Nainggan thit you soun* [A new nation's illustrated magazine] (January): 39–40.

———. 1955. *Mun: r* ma hū* [Not out of hate]. Yangon: Shumawa.

———. 1973. *Thway* [Blood]. Yangon: Seidana sape.

———. 1995. *Thu lo lu* [A man like him]. Vols. 1 and 2. Repr., Yangon: Sape.

———. 2004. *Blood Bond [Thway].* Trans. Than Than Win. Honolulu: Center for Southeast Asian Studies, University of Hawai'i at Mānoa.

———. 2008. *A Man Like Him: Portrait of the Burmese Journalist, Journal Kyaw U Chit Maung.* Trans. Ma Thanegi. Ithaca, NY: Southeast Asia Program Publications, Cornell University.

Malalasekera, G. P. 1960. *Dictionary of Pali Proper Names.* London: Luzac.

Malalgoda, Kitsiri. 1976. *Buddhism in Sinhalese Society, 1750–1900: A Study of Religious Revival and Change.* Berkeley: University of California Press.

Mandalay Division, Commissioner of. 1931. "Letter to the Chief Secretary of Burma, Home and Political Department." In file 1/15 (D) 2916, NAD.

Manderson, Lenore. 1996. *Sickness and the State: Health and Illness in Colonial Malaya, 1870–1940.* Cambridge: Cambridge University Press.

———. 1998. "Shaping Reproduction: Maternity in Early Twentieth-Century Malaya." In Ram and Jolly 1998, 26–49.

Mani, Lata. 1998. *Contentious Traditions: The Debate on Sati in Colonial India.* Berkeley: University of California Press.

Marr, David G. 1981. *Vietnamese Tradition on Trial, 1920–1945.* Los Angeles and London: University of California Press.

Maung Maung. 1962. *Aung San of Burma.* With an introduction by Harry J. Benda. The Hague: published for Yale University Southeast Asia Studies by M. Nijhoff.

———. 1963. *Law and Custom in Burma and the Burmese Family.* The Hague: M. Nijhoff.

———. 1980. *From Sangha to Laity: Nationalist Movements of Burma, 1920–1940.* New Delhi: Manohar.

———. 1989. *Burmese Nationalist Movements, 1940–1948.* Hong Kong: Kiscadale Publications.

Maung Maung Aye. 1947. "Sū ka ta myui:" [Certain kinds of people]. *Thway thauk,* no. 15 (February): 29.

Maxim, Sarah Heminway. 1992. "The Resemblance in External Appearance: The Colonial Project in Kuala Lumpur and Rangoon." PhD diss., Cornell University.

McClintock, Anne. 1995. *Imperial Leather: Race, Gender, and Sexuality in the Colonial Conquest.* New York: Routledge.

McCoy, Alfred W., ed. 1985. *Southeast Asia under Japanese Occupation.* New Haven, CT: Southeast Asia Studies, Yale University.

———. 2000. "Philippine Commonwealth and Cult of Masculinity." *Philippine Studies* 48, no. 3: 315–346.

McDaniel, Justin Thomas. 2003. "Invoking the Source: Nissaya Manuscripts, Pedagogy and Sermon-Making in Northern Thai and Lao Buddhism." PhD diss., Harvard University.

———. 2008. *Gathering Leaves and Lifting Words: Histories of Buddhist Monastic Education in Laos and Thailand.* Seattle: University of Washington Press.

McPhedran, Collin. 2002. *White Butterflies.* Canberra: Pandanus Books.

Mendelson, E. Michael. 1975. *Sangha and State in Burma: A Study of Monastic Sectarianism and Leadership.* Ithaca, NY: Cornell University Press.

Mi Mi Khaing. 1984. *The World of Burmese Women.* London: Zed Books.

Minamida, Midori. 1980. "Thein Pe Myint no shōsetsu ni okeru jyoseizō no yukue" [The characterization of women by Thein Pe Myint]. *Journal of Osaka University of Foreign Studies* 47:17–27.

Ming, Hanneke. 1983. "Barracks-Concubinage in the Indies, 1887–1920." *Indonesia* 35 (April): 65–93.

Mitchell, Timothy. 2000. Introduction to *Questions of Modernity,* ed. Timothy Mitchell, xi–xxvii. Minneapolis: University of Minnesota Press.

Monin, P. 1940. "Kyvanup. min: ma kui pro pe pā" [Please tell my wife]. *Thuriya* 23, no. 2: 55–60.

Moscotti, Albert Dennis. 1974. *British Policy and the Nationalist Movement in Burma, 1917–1937.* Honolulu: University Press of Hawai'i.

Mran mā–aṅgalip abhidhān [Myanmar-English dictionary]. 1998. Yangon: Department of Myanmar Language Commission, Ministry of Education.

Mya Galay. 1934a. "Amyui: smī: myā: cit e* yañ kye: mhu lui lā: ap kroṅ:" [About the need to improve women's cultivation]. *Toe tet yay* 4 (January): 20–21, 59–60.

———. 1934b. "Mīn: ma myā: nhaṅ. pru praṅ re: [Women and reforms]. *Toe tet yay* 5 (February): 30–31, 70–72.

Mya Sein. 1958. "The Women of Burma: A Tradition of Hard Work and Independence." *Atlantic Monthly* (February): 122–125.

———. 1972. "Towards Independence in Burma: The Role of Women." *Asian Affairs* 59, no. 3 (October): 288–299.

———.1973. *The Administration of Burma.* Repr., Kuala Lumpur and Singapore: Oxford University Press. Originally published in 1938.

———. 1998. "Mran mā amyui: sa mī:" [Burmese women]. In *Mran mā amyui: sa mī: kre: mum* [A looking-glass of Burmese women], 181–196. Yangon: Myanmar nainggan sape hnik sanezin ahpwe. Originally published in 1958.

Mya Than. 1997. "The Ethnic Chinese in Myanmar and Their Identity." In *Ethnic Chinese as Southeast Asians,* ed. Leo Suryadinata, 115–146. Singapore: Institute of Southeast Asian Studies.

Naim, C. M. 2004. *The Selected Essays of C. M. Naim.* Delhi: Permanent Black.

Naing Naing Maw. 1999. "The Role of Myanmar Women in the Nationalist Movement, 1906–1942." MA thesis, Yangon University.

Nan Hninn Yu Yu. 1995. "Mran mā amyui: sa mī: cā re charā myā: (1044–1939)" [Burmese women writers (1044–1939)]. MA thesis, Yangon University.

National Council of Women in Burma. 1927. In file "Papers of Sybil Mary Dorothy Bulkeley," MSS EUR D1230/5, IOR.

National Council of Women in Burma. 1929. *Report by the National Council of Women in Burma on Conditions Affecting Labour in and near Rangoon.* MSS EUR D1230/6, IOR.

Nemoto, Kei. 2000. "The Concepts of Dobama ('Our Burma') and Thudo-Bama ('Their Burma') in Burmese Nationalism, 1930–1948." *Journal of Burma Studies* 5:1–16.

Ngwe U Daung. 1947. "Mok sā mok" [Let there be crest hair]. *Shumawa* (July): 11.

———. 1978. "Gyānay maggajaṅ: mhat tuiṅ myā:" [Landmarks in the history of journals and magazines]. In *Cā nay jaṅ samuiṅ: cā tam: myā:* [Essays on the history of journalism], 77–98. Yangon: Sape beikman.

Nijhawan, Shobna. 2010. "At the Margins of Empire: Feminist-Nationalist Configurations of Burmese Society in the Hindi Public (1917–1920)." Working paper, Department of Languages, Literatures, and Linguistics, York University, Toronto.

Nisbet, John. 1901. *Burma under British Rule—and Before.* Vol. 1. Westminster, UK: A. Constable and Co.

Nishino, Rumiko. 1993. *Jūgun ianfu to jūgonen sensō: Biruma ianjo keieisha no shōgen.* [Comfort women and fifteen years of war: Testimony of the Japanese manager of a comfort station in Burma]. Tokyo: Akashi shōten.

Nordholt, Henk Schulte. 1997a. Introduction to Nordholt 1997b, 1–37.

————. 1997b. *Outward Appearances: Dressing State and Society in Indonesia.* Leiden: KITLV Press.

Nu, U. 1954. *Burma under the Japanese: Pictures and Portraits.* New York: St. Martin's Press.

Nwe Nwe Myint. 1992. "Gantha loka cā cu cā raṅ: (1938–1941)" [*Ngan hta lawka* index (1938–1941)]. MA thesis, Yangon University.

Nyi Nyi. 1938. "Correspondence." *Ngan hta lawka* 24, no. 158 (March): 56.

O'Connor, Richard A. 1983. *A Theory of Indigenous Southeast Asian Urbanism.* Singapore: Institute of Southeast Asian Studies.

Okell, John. 1967. "Nissaya Burmese." *Journal of Burma Research Society* 50, no. 1: 95–123.

Ong, Aihwa. 1995. "State Versus Islam: Malay Families, Women's Bodies, and the Body Politic in Malaysia." In Ong and Peletz 1995, 159–194.

————. 1998. "Flexible Citizenship among Chinese Cosmopolitans." In *Cosmopolitics: Thinking and Feeling beyond the Nation,* ed. Peng Cheah and Bruce Robbins, 134–162. Minneapolis and London: University of Minnesota Press.

Ong, Aihwa, and Michael G. Peletz, eds. 1995. *Bewitching Women, Pious Men: Gender and Body Politics in Southeast Asia.* Berkeley: University of California Press.

Paragu. 1981. "Samuin: nok khaṃ mran mā vatthu rhaññ" [Burmese historical novels]. In *Vatthu rhaññ cā tam: myā:* [Essays on the novel], 1:76–128. Yangon: Sape beikman.

————. 1995. *Lay tī paṇḍita charā ū: moṅ krī* [Ledi pandita U Maung Gyi]. Yangon: Lawka sape.

Pe Maung Tin. 1956. *Mran mā cā pe samuiṅ:* [A history of Burmese literature]. Yangon: Thudhamawadi.

Pearson, Gail. 2004. "Tradition, Law and the Female Suffrage Movement in India." In L. Edwards and Roces 2004, 195–219.

Peleggi, Maurizio. 2002. *Lords of Things: The Fashioning of the Siamese Monarchy's Modern Image.* Honolulu: University of Hawai'i Press.

Petievich, Carla. 2004. "Rekhti: Impersonating the Feminine in Urdu Poetry." In *Sexual Sites, Seminal Attitudes: Sexualities, Masculinities and Culture in South Asia,* ed. Sanjay Srivastava, 123–146. New Delhi: Sage Publications.

Pham, Julie. 2005. "J. S. Furnivall and Fabianism: Reinterpreting the 'Plural Society' in Burma." *Modern Asian Studies* 39, no. 2: 321–348.

Phayre, Arthur P. 1969. *History of Burma: Including Burma Proper, Pegu, Taungu, Tenasserim, and Arakan, from the Earliest Time to the First War with British India.* Reprints of Economic Classics. New York: A. M. Kelly.

Po Ka. 1914. *The Citizen of Burma.* Rangoon: British Burma Press.

Po Yaygyan. 1997. "Adrift and Washed Ashore." *New Light of Myanmar* (9 May).

Pollock, Sheldon. 2002. "Cosmopolitan and Vernacular in History." In *Cosmopolitanism,* ed. Carol A. Breckenridge, Sheldon Pollock, Homi K. Bhabha, and Dipesh Chakrabarty, 15–53. Durham, NC: Duke University Press.

Pruitt, William. 1994. *Étude linguistique d nissaya birmans: Traduction commentée de textes bouddhiques* [Linguistic study of Burmese nissaya: Annotated translation of Buddhist texts]. Paris: Presses de l'École française d'Extrême-Orient.

Pu Galay, U. 1939. *Ka brā: prassanā* [The problem of mixed people]. Yangon: Kyi pwa yay.

Ram, Kalpana, and Margaret Jolly, eds. 1998. *Maternities and Modernities: Colonial and Postcolonial Experiences in Asia and the Pacific.* Cambridge: Cambridge University Press.

Rangoon Gazette. 1920. "New University Boycotted: University and Judson College Students on Strike." 7 December.

Ray, Bharati. 1995. "The Freedom Movement and Feminist Consciousness in Bengal, 1905–1929." In *From the Seams of History: Essays on Indian Women,* ed. Bharati Ray, 175–218. Delhi: Oxford University Press.

Reid, Anthony. 1988. *Southeast Asia in the Age of Commerce, 1450–1680: The Lands below the Winds.* New Haven, CT: Yale University Press.

Reyes, Raquel A. G. 2008. *Love, Passion and Patriotism: Sexuality and the Philippine Propaganda Movement, 1882–1892.* Singapore: NUS Press in association with University of Washington Press.

Reynolds, Craig J. 1995. "A New Look at Old Southeast Asia." *Journal of Asian Studies* 54, no. 2: 419–446.

Rice, W. F. 1915. "A Confidential Letter from the Chief Secretary to the Government of Burma to the Secretary to the Government of India, Home Department (Rangoon). In file 2987/16, "Rangoon Brothels/Prostitution in Rangoon," L/PJ/6/1448, IOR.

Richardson, David, trans. 1896. *The Dhamathat; or, The Laws of Menoo.* Rangoon: Hanthawaddy Press.

Riot Inquiry Committee. 1939a. *Final Report of the Riot Inquiry Committee.* Rangoon: Office of the Superintendent, Government Printing and Stationery.

———. 1939b. *Interim Report of the Riot Inquiry Committee.* Rangoon: Office of the Superintendent, Government Printing and Stationery.

Robertson, Maureen. 1992. "Voicing the Feminine: Constructions of the Gendered Subject in Lyric Poetry by Women of Medieval and Late Imperial China." *Late Imperial China* 13, no. 1 (June): 63–110.

Roces, Mina. 2004. "Is the Suffragist an American Colonial Construct? Defining 'the Filipino Woman' in Colonial Philippines." In L. Edwards and Roces 2004, 24–58.

———. 2005. "Gender, Nation and the Politics of Dress in Twentieth-Century Philippines." *Gender and History* 17, no. 2: 354–377.

Rodd, Laurel Rasplica. 1991. "Yosano Akiko and the Taisho Debate over the 'New Woman.'" In Bernstein 1991, 175–198.

Roff, William R. 1972. *Bibliography of Malay and Arabic Periodicals Published in the Straits Settlements and Peninsular Malay States, 1876–1941.* London: Oxford University Press.

Rupp, Leila J. 1997. *Worlds of Women: The Making of an International Women's Movement.* Princeton, NJ: Princeton University Press.

Sadan, Mandy. 2007. "Constructing and Contesting the Category 'Kachin' in the Colonial and Post-Colonial Burmese State." In *Exploring Ethnic Diversity in Burma,* ed. Mikael Gravers, 34–76. Copenhagen: NIAS Press.

Said, Edward W. 1978. *Orientalism.* New York: Pantheon Books.

Sangermano, Father Vicenzo. 1995. *The Burmese Empire a Hundred Years Ago.* With an introduction and notes by John Jardine. Bangkok, Thailand: White Orchid Press. Originally published in 1833.

Sape Beikman. 1964. "*Moṅ krī | ū: | lay tī paṇḍita*" [Ledi Pandita U Maung Gyi]. In *Mran mā. cvay cuṃ kyam:* [Myanmar encyclopedia], 9:251–254. Yangon: Sape beikman.

———. 1966. "Mran mā kumārī asaṅ: myā:" [Burmese Women's Associations]. In *Mran mā. cvay cuṃ kyam:* [Myanmar encyclopedia] 10:57–59. Yangon: Sape beikman.

Sarkar, Tanika. 2001. *Hindu Wife, Hindu Nation: Community, Religion and Cultural Nationalism.* New Delhi: Permanent Black.

Sarkisyanz, Manuel. 1965. *Buddhist Backgrounds of the Burmese Revolution.* The Hague: M. Nijhoff.

Sato, Barbara Hamill. 2003. *The New Japanese Woman: Modernity, Media, and Women in Interwar Japan, Asia-Pacific.* Durham, NC: Duke University Press.

Saunder, K. J., and W. C. B. Purser, eds. 1914. *Modern Buddhism in Burma: Being an Epitome of Information Received from Missionaries, Officials, and Others.* Christian Literature Society, Burma Branch.

Saw Moun Nyin. 1976. *Bamā amyui: sa mī:* [Burmese women]. Yangon: Thiha poun hneik htaik.

Schmidt, J. D. 2008. "Yuan Mei (1716–98) on Women." *Late Imperial China* 29, no. 2 (December): 129–185.

Scott, James C. 1976. *The Moral Economy of the Peasant: Rebellion and Subsistence in Southeast Asia.* New Haven, CT: Yale University Press.

Scott, James George. 1911. *Burma: A Handbook of Practical Information.* Rev. ed. London: A. Morning.

Scott, Joan W. 1986. "Gender: A Useful Category of Historical Analysis." *American Historical Review* 91, no. 5 (December): 1053–1075.

Shuttleworth, E. 1916. "Extent, Distribution and Regulation of the 'Social Evil' in the Cities of Calcutta, Madras and Bombay and in Rangoon Town." In file 2987/16, "Rangoon Brothels/Prostitution in Rangoon," L/PJ/6/1448, IOR.

Shway Yoe. 1989. *The Burman: His Life and Notions.* Rev. and repr. ed. Scotland: Kiscadale Publications. Originally published in 1910.

Shwe Khaing Thar. 1951. *Chaṅ yaṅ thuṃ: phvai. mhu* [Burmese clothes and hairdos]. Mandalay: Kyi pwa yay.

Silverberg, Miriam. 1991. "The Modern Girl as Militant." In Bernstein 1991, 239–266.

Singh, Surendra Prasad. 1980. *Growth of Nationalism in Burma, 1900–1942.* 1st ed. Calcutta: Firma KLM.

Sinha, Mrinalini. 1995. *Colonial Masculinity: The 'Manly Englishman' and the 'Effeminate Bengali' in the Late Nineteenth Century.* Manchester, UK, and New York: Manchester University Press.

———. 2000. "Refashioning Mother India: Feminism and Nationalism in Late-Colonial India." *Feminist Studies* 26, no. 3 (Autumn): 623–644.

Sinha, Mrinalini, Donna Guy, and Angela Woollacott, eds. 1999. *Feminisms and Internationalism.* Oxford: Blackwell.

Skidmore, Monique. 2004. *Karaoke Fascism: Burma and the Politics of Fear.* Philadelphia: University of Pennsylvania Press.

———, ed. 2005. *Burma at the Turn of the 21st Century.* Honolulu: University of Hawai'i Press.

Smart, Millicent B. 1913. *Burman Woman's House Doctor.* Rangoon: British Burma Press.

Smith, Donald Eugene. 1965. *Religion and Politics in Burma.* Princeton, NJ: Princeton University Press.

Smith, Martin. 1999. *Burma: Insurgency and the Politics of Ethnicity.* Rev. ed. London: Zed Books.

Socarras, Cayetano. 1966. "The Portuguese in Lower Burma: Filipe de Brito de Nicote." *Luso-Brazilian Review* 3, no. 2 (Winter): 3–24.

Spiro, Melford E. 1997. *Gender Ideology and Psychological Reality: An Essay on Cultural Reproduction.* New Haven, CT: Yale University Press.

Stephenson, H. 1936. "Letter to Commander Cochrane," 1 March. In file P&J(B)1508, "Rangoon University Strike, 21 March–22 July 1936," M/1/147, IOR.

Stevens, Sarah E. 2003. "Figuring Modernity: The New Woman and the Modern Girl in Republican China." *NWSA Journal* 15, no. 3: 82–103.

Stewart, J. A., and C. W. Dunn, comp. 1969. *A Burmese-English Dictionary.* Rev. and ed. Hla Pe, A. J. Allot, and J. W. A. Okell. London: School of Oriental and African Studies, University of London.

Stivens, Maila. 1998. "Modernizing the Malay Mother." In Ram and Jolly 1998, 50–80.

Stoler, Ann Laura. 1989a. "Making Empire Respectable: The Politics of Race and Sexual Morality in 20th-Century Colonial Cultures." *American Ethnologist* 16, no. 4 (November): 634–660.

———. 1989b. "Rethinking Colonial Categories: European Communities and the Boundaries of Rule." *Comparative Studies in Society and History* 31, no. 1 (January): 134–161.

———. 1992. "Sexual Affronts and Racial Frontiers: European Identities and the Cultural Politics of Exclusion in Colonial Southeast Asia." *Comparative Studies in Society and History* 34, no. 3 (July): 514–551.

———. 2002. *Carnal Knowledge and Imperial Power: Race and the Intimate in Colonial Rule.* Berkeley and Los Angeles: University of California Press.

Strassler, Karen. 2008. "Cosmopolitan Visions: Ethnic Chinese and the Photographic Imagining of Indonesia in the Late Colonial and Early Postcolonial Periods." *Journal of Asian Studies* 67, no. 2 (May): 395–432.

Subrahmanyam, Sanjay. 2002. "And a River Runs Through It: The Mrauk U Kingdom and Its Bay of Bengal Context." In Gommans and Leider 2002, 107–126.

Swe Swe Aung. 2000. "Women's Role in the National Development of Myanmar." MA thesis, Yangon University.

Symes, Michael. 1800. *An Account of an Embassy to the Kingdom of Ava: Sent by the Governor-General of India in the Year 1795*. London: W. Bulmer.

Tarlo, Emma. 1996. *Clothing Matters: Dress and Identity in India*. Chicago: University of Chicago Press.

"Tarup praññ n* khet kāla amyui: sa mī: myā: khoṅ: choṅ ne prī" [Modern women in China take the lead]. 1937. *Thuriya* (7 January): 51.

Taw Sein Ko. 1913. *Burmese Sketches*. Rangoon: British Burma Press.

Taylor, Jean Gelman. 1983. *The Social World of Batavia: European and Eurasian in Dutch Asia*. Madison: University of Wisconsin Press.

———. 1997. "Costume and Gender in Colonial Java, 1800–1940." In Nordholt 1997b, 85–116.

Taylor, Robert H. 1984. "Introduction: Marxism and Resistance in Wartime Burma." In *Marxism and Resistance in Burma, 1942–1945: Thein Pe Myint's Wartime Traveler*, ed. and trans. Robert H. Taylor, 51–69. Athens: Ohio University Press.

———. 2008. *The State in Myanmar*. Rev. and expanded. London: Hurst and Co. Originally published in 1987.

Tekkatho Htin Gyi. 1992. *Mran mā nuiṅ ṅaṃ ca taṅ: cā myā: aññhvan:* [An index to Burmese newspapers]. Vols. 1 and 2. Yangon: Sape beikman.

Tekkatho Win Mun. 1981. "Mran mā vatthu rhaññ samuiṅ:" [A history of Burmese novels]. In *Vatthu rhaññ cā tam: myā:* [Essays on the novel], 2:239–300. Yangon: Sape beikman.

Than Daing, Bo. 1967. 1950. *Lvat lap ye: are: tau puṃ mhat tam:* [Memoir of the independence revolution]. Yangon: Sape beikman.

Than Htut and Thaw Kaung. 2005. "Some Myanmar Historical Fiction and Their Historical Context." In *Selected Writings of U Than Htut (Taik Soe)*, 72–90. Yangon: Myanmar Historical Commission.

Than Than Win. 2004. "Translator's Introduction." In *Blood Bond*, by Ma Ma Lay, trans. Than Than Win, 11–14. Honolulu: University of Hawai'i Press.

Thant Myint-U. 2001. *The Making of Modern Burma*. New York: Cambridge University Press.

Thant Tut. 1980. *Mran mā nuiṅ ṅaṃ bhun: tau krī: kyoṅ: paññā re: samuiṅ:* [A history of Burmese monastic schools and education]. 4th ed. Yangon: Oung bin poun hneik taik.

Thein Pe Myint. 1943. *What Happened in Burma: The Frank Revelations of a Young Burmese Revolutionary Leader Who Has Recently Escaped from Burma to India*. Allahabad, India: Kitabistan.

———. 1970. *Sapit mhok kyoṅ: sā:* [The student boycotter]. Yangon: Bagan sa ouk.

———. 1974. *Kyvan tau e* akhyac ū | cā pe bhava jāt lam: cuṃ* [My first love: Various stories from my literary life]. Yangon: Yee lay sape.

———. 1998. *Thein Pe Myint vatthu tui poṅ: khyup sac* [A new collection of short stories by Thein Pe Myint]. Yangon: Ya pyi sa ouk taik.

Thein Pe Myint, Thakin. 1950. *Kuiy tve. mhat tam:* [Memoirs]. Yangon: Taing chit.

Timm, Annette F. 2002. "Sex with a Purpose: Prostitution, Venereal Disease, and Militarized Masculinity in the Third Reich." *Journal of the History of Sexuality* 11, nos. 1–2 (January–April): 223–255.

Tin Htway. 1972. "The Role of Literature in Nation Building: With Special Reference to Burma." *Journal of Burma Research Society* 55, nos. 1–2: 19–46.

Tin Kha. 1990. *Mran mā nuiṅ ṅaṃ cā nay jaṅ: mhat cu myā:* [Notes on Burmese periodicals]. Yangon: Sape beikman.

Tin Tin. 1940. "Tū ma myā: thaṃ re: pā" [Please write to the nieces]. *Journal gyaw* (January): 5.

Tin Tut. 1942. "Causes of the Attitude of the Burmese People in the Recent [War] Campaign in Burma," 2 October. Simla, India: Department of Reconstruction. Available in NAD.

Tone, Andrea. 1996. "Contraceptive Consumers: Gender and the Political Economy of Birth Control in the 1930s." *Journal of Social History* 29, no. 3 (Spring): 485–506.

Trager, Frank N. 1971. *Burma: Japanese Military Administration, Selected Documents, 1941–1945.* Philadelphia: University of Philadelphia Press.

Trager, Frank N., and William J. Koenig. 1979. *Burmese Sit-tàns, 1764–1826: Records of Rural Life and Administration.* Association of Asian Studies Monograph 36. Tucson: University of Arizona Press.

Tran, Nhung Tuyet. 2008. "Gender, Property, and the 'Autonomy Thesis' in Southeast Asia: The Endowment of Local Succession in Early Modern Viet Nam." *Journal of Asian Studies* 67, no. 1: 43–72.

Trivedi, Lisa N. 2003. "Visually Mapping the 'Nation': Swadeshi Politics in Nationalist India, 1920–1930." *Journal of Asian Studies* 62, no. 1: 11–41.

Tun Shein. 1919. "Enfranchisement of Burmese Women." *Thuriya* (8 November). Clipping in file 8115, "Sex Disqualification (Removal) Act," L/PJ/6/1642, IOR.

Turner, Alicia Marie. 2009. "Buddhism, Colonialism and the Boundaries of Religion: Theravada Buddhism in Burma, 1885–1920." PhD diss., University of Chicago.

Tusan, Michelle E. 2003. "Writing *Stri Dharma:* International Feminism, Nationalist Politics, and Women's Press Advocacy in Late Colonial India." *Women's History Review* 12, no. 4: 623–650.

Twomey, D. H. R. 1903. "Letter to the Secretary to the Government of India," 24 January. In file 517, "Marriages between European Officers in Burma and Burmese Women," L/PJ/6/629, IOR.

University Boycotters' Union. 1922. *The Voice of Young Burma: The Reproduction of the Articles Published by the Publicity Bureau of the University Boycotters.* Rangoon: New Burma Press.

Van Esterik, Penny, ed. 1996. *Women of Southeast Asia.* Monograph Series on Southeast Asia, Occasional Paper 17. De Kalb: Center for Southeast Asian Studies, Northern Illinois University.

Vanita, Ruth. 2004. "'Married among Their Companions': Female Homoerotic Relations in Nineteenth-Century Urdu Rekhti Poetry in India." *Journal of Women's History* 16, no. 1: 12–53.

Vicinus, Martha, ed. 1973. *Suffer and Be Still.* Bloomington: Indiana University Press.

Vickers, Adrian. 2004. "The Classics in Indonesian Studies: J. S. Furnivall's *Netherlands India.*" Paper presented at the 15th biennial conference of the Asian Studies Association of Australia, Canberra, 29 June–2 July.

Waite, Robert G. 1998. "Teenage Sexuality in Nazi Germany." *Journal of the History of Sexuality* 8, no. 3 (January): 434–476.

Weber, Charlotte. 2008. "Between Nationalism and Feminism: The Eastern Women's Congresses of 1930 and 1932." *Journal of Middle East Women's Studies* 4, no. 1 (Winter): 83–106.

Who's Who in Burma, 1961. 1962. Rangoon: People's Literature Committee and House.

Wilson, Liz. 1996. *Charming Cadavers: Horrific Figurations of the Feminine in Indian Buddhist Hagiographic Literature.* Chicago: University of Chicago Press.

Win Myint. 1972. *Manlay Sayadaw's Verses: Pyo, Kabya, Linka and Yadu.* Yangon: Paw pyu la sape.

Womack, William. 2003. "Politics and Press Censorship in British Burma: The Case of the Moulmein Chronicle." *SOAS Bulletin of Burma Research* 1, no. 1 (Spring): 58–60.

———. 2008. "Contesting Indigenous and Female Authority in the Burma Baptist Mission: The Case of Ellen Mason." In *Women's History Review* 17, no. 4 (September): 543–559.

Woycke, James. 1988. *Birth Control in Germany, 1871–1933.* London and New York: Routledge.

Wright, W. J. Paylight. 1914. *Regulated Vice and the Traffic in Women.* London: British Branch of the International Abolitionist Federation.

Ye Hlaing. 1935. "Myui: khyac may" [A female patriot]. *Tet thit* 1, no. 2 (August): 9–12.

Yegar, Moshe. 1972. *The Muslims of Burma.* Wiesbaden, Germany: O. Harrassowitz.

Yeni. 2007. "A Leader of Men." *Irrawaddy News Magazine* 15, no. 9 (September).

Yoshimi, Yoshiaki. 2000. *Comfort Women: Sexual Slavery in the Japanese Military during World War II.* New York: Columbia University Press.

Zoellner, Hans-Bernd, ed. 2006. "The Nagani Book Club—An Introduction." Working Paper no. 10:1. Southeast Asian Studies, Universität Passau.

NEWSPAPERS AND PERIODICALS

10,000,000
Asian Affairs
Atlantic Monthly
Burma Debate

Dagon
Deedok gyanay
Guardian
Irrawaddy News Magazine
Journal gyaw
Journal of Burma Research Society
Kyi pwa yay magazine
Myanmar alin
Nainggan thit you soun
Ngan hta lawka
Rangoon Times
Shumawa you soun magazine
Tet khit
Thuriya
Thway thauk
Toe tet yay
Youq shin lan hnyun
Zawana

Index

Page numbers in boldface refer to figures.

ABM (American Baptist Mission), 7, 33, 125; schools, 31, 58, 81, 149

Adas, Michael, 7, 28

advertisements, x, 118–119; for beauty and hygiene products, 106–116; and commodification of housewifery, 110–113, 116–117; for medicine, 96, 111, 114; the modern woman in, 2, 96, 149; the press and, 38–40, 42–44; promotion of consumption by, 97, 105–106; for sex-related products, 112–113, 116, 189n47

AFPFL (Anti-Fascist People's Freedom League), 41, 135–136, 185n46

All Asian Women's Conference (1931), 91

Allott, Anna, 196

Amar, Ludu Daw, 58, 146–148, 169, 180n78

AMSH (Association for Moral and Social Hygiene), 125–126, 192n37

amyo, 25, 118, 147, 152, 167; changing meaning of, 25, 76–78; women as protectors of the Burmese, 76–79, 86, 94, 97, 99, 116, 118

Andaya, Barbara, 4, 46, 133

Anderson, Benedict, 41–42

Anglo-Burmese Wars: First, 14–16; Second, 16, 158; Third, 16–17; and Treaty of Yadanabo, 14

anglophiles, 60, 148, 159

anticolonial resistance, x, 28, 185n48; and boycott of foreign goods, 42, 145–146; by monks, 82, 144; nationalist narratives of, 4; noncooperative, 82, 85; nonviolent, 50, 82–83, 87; participation of women in, 81, 83–88, 94, 129, 149, 186n65; Saya San rebellion, 82–83, 86; student, 80–84, 87; and workers' strikes, 84, 87

archives, ix–xi

Arnold, G. F., 54–55

Association for Moral and Social Hygiene, 125–126, 192n37

Aung San, 83, 135, 167, 185n46, 196n45

Aung San Suu Kyi, 2, 167–168

authorship: female, 40, 60–70; pseudonymous, 60–62, **61**, 67–69, 183n5

Ba Maw, 145, 165, 195n9, 198n4

Bayly, Christopher, 6

beauty products, 96–97, 100–101, **106–107**, 106–110, 114, 118–119

Bengali babu, 158, 197n80

Besant, Annie, 91–93
BIA (Burma Independence Army), 4, 160
Bingham, Adrian, 76
birth control, 111–113, 116, 170, 189n47
Blundell, Edmund Augustus, 38, 176n126
BNA (Burma National Army), 160
bo gadaw, 121, 136–138, 166–167, 194n91
Braun, Eric, 64, 181n107
British Commonwealth League, 48, 91
British Malaya, 17, 40
Brito, Filipe de, 128, 159
Brown, R. Grant, 47–48
Buddhism: gender ideologies of, 47, 51–52, 149, 179n48, 195n28; and *nat* (spirit) worship, 20; and nationalism, 12, 82–83, 86–88, 129–130, 132, 136, 185n48; Orientalist scholarship on, 49; state of, under colonialism, 4, 32, 64; study of, among laity, 35–37. *See also* Buddhist (Burmese); Buddhist women; *dhammasat;* sangha
Buddhist: Chinese, 22, 26; Indian, 191n13; Sinhala, 110
Buddhist (Burmese): culture, 12, 117–118, 121, 128–129, 133, 158, 179n48; customary law, 10, 23, 27, 47–48, 86, 93, 130, 186n62; and *dhammasat,* 25, 128–130, 133; education, 29–37, 52, 80, 181n107, 184n40; monks, 7, 23, 36, 39, 81–82, 143–144, 148; nuns, 52–53; organizations, 9, 37, 80, 85; texts, 9, 29, 36, 53, 60, 65–66, 68; women as custodians of, 12, 86–87, 121, 145–147. *See also* Buddhism; Buddhist women; sangha

Buddhist women: Christian depictions of, 32, 54; customary rights of, 47–48, 50, 86, 89–90, 93, 129–130, 193n63; literacy of, 52, 55; marriage of, to Chinese Buddhists, 22–23; marriage of, to Europeans, 121, 123–125, 132–136, 140; marriage of, to Indians, 28, 41, 122, 131, 133–140, 191nn12–13
Burma: British reoccupation of, 153, 160, 173n31; historiography of colonial, ix–x, 3–7, 169; Lower, 16–17, 19–20, 31, 52, 128; map of colonial, 15; Ministerial, 18, 173n20; pacification of, 18–19, 159; "scheduled" (frontier) areas of, 173n20; separation of, from India, 131, 178n31, 193n69; Upper, 16–19, 152, 181n116; usage of "Myanmar" versus, 12–13, 172n38
"Burma Proper," 18, 173n20
Burma Round Table Conference (1931), 51, 57
Burma Socialist Programme Party, x, 186n58
Burmanization, 125, 128, 131, 164
Butler, Sir Harcourt, 49–50
BWA (Burmese Women's Association), 85–87, 89–90, 93–94, 186n60

Callahan, Mary, 159–160
Carlson, Richard, 178n38, 186n58
cartoons, x, 40, 75–76, 151; of foreigners, 24, 132–133, 136, 138; of modern fashionable women, 110–111, 143–144, 146; political, 24, 168, 199n21
census, 25–27
Chakrabarty, Dipesh, 10
Chakravarti, Nalini, 130–131

Charney, Michael, 53
chettiar moneylenders, 21
Chinese, 20–22, 173n33; Burmese, 9,
    20, 22–23
Chins, 26, 173n20; in armed forces,
    159; colonial representations of,
    as a martial race, 157
cinema, 44, 96, 104–105, 119,
    189nn30–31, 198n1
clothing: changing styles of, 99–104;
    hybrid, 103–104, 106, 188n27;
    lace bodice (*zar bawli*), 99, 103,
    109; sheer blouse (*eingyi pa*), 99,
    103, 154, 188n16; textile industry
    and, 104–106, 189n34. *See*
    also fashion
Coedès, George, 46
cohabitation, 121, 123–124, 126–128,
    132–134, 169
college: female students in, 55–56, 81,
    83, 88, 161; Government, 55, 80,
    124, 135; Judson (Baptist), 31,
    55, 80, 125, 185n47; national,
    184n41. *See also* universities
colonial economy. *See* economy, colonial
colonial officials. *See* officials, colonial
colonial state. *See* state, colonial
colonialism: the civilizing mission
    and, 49–50, 169; demographic
    changes under, 20–22; and plural
    society, 5–6, 28, 169; and racism,
    121, 140–141; scholarship on,
    in Burma, ix–x, 2–7; scholarship
    on modernity and, 8, 10; state
    of Buddhism under, 4, 30, 32,
    64, 162. *See also* anticolonial
    resistance; economy, colonial;
    officials, colonial; state, colonial
concubinage. *See* cohabitation
consumerism: advertising and, 97,
    105–106; and commodification
    of domesticity, 96, 110–118;

conspicuous, 28–29, 96, 109;
    dutiful, 96–99, 116–119;
    frivolous, 8, 12, 97, 99, 149;
    intellectuals on, 109–110,
    143–147, 149; and modernity,
    2, 8, 11; the press and, 42–44;
    rise in, 44, 97, 118–119, 166;
    scholarship on, 97–99; and
    self-improvement, 97, 109,
    114–118. *See also* advertisements;
    beauty products; fashion;
    fashionable women
contraception. *See* birth control
cosmetics. *See* beauty products
cosmopolitanism: and discourse of
    scientific progress, 114; and
    discourse of social equality, 73–74,
    95; modern women as agents and
    symbols of, 8–9; scholarship on,
    9–10
Cousins, Margaret, 91–93
Cowen, John, 125–127, 192n37
Crosthwaite, Charles, 17–19, 123, 127,
    157
culture. *See* Buddhist (Burmese):
    culture; culture, European
    bourgeois
culture, European bourgeois, 26, 110,
    140–141, 124

Dagon (Dagon magazine), 180n85,
    180n90; women's column in, 11,
    59–69, 61, 67, 72–74
Dalhousie, Lord, 15–16
Deedok (Deedok journal), 75, 182n128;
    women's column in, 68
dhammakathika, 82
dhammasat, 25, 128–130, 133
dobama (our Burma), 131, 161, 168
Dobama Asiayone, 83–84, 95, 146, 160;
    manifesto of, 87; rhetoric of "us
    versus them," 131–132

domesticity: changes in, 63, 76, 117, 156; and childbirth and child rearing, 113–116, 119, 124; Christian conceptions of, 32, 62; commodification of, 96, 110–118; gender roles in, 63, 76–79, 94, 154; and science, 9, 32, 113–114; violence in, 117. *See also* housewives

dress. *See* clothing; fashion

East India Company, 14, 20

economy, colonial: capitalist, 5–6, 21, 156; ethnic division of, 5–7, 21–25; and growth of plural society, 5–6, 28, 44–45, 169; and large scale (im)migration, 21–24, 28–29, 41, 141, 174n41, 187n91; of sex, 121, 123–127, 132–137, 146; single-product (rice) export, 14, 20–21, 104, 174n40, 177n132

education: Anglo-vernacular, 31–38, 56, 113, 176n115; boys' schools, 35; coeducational, 34, 54–55, 169; employment and, 2, 55–59, 69, 156, 158, 169, 180n76; English, 9, 30–31, 34, 58; female, 30–38, 50–59, 64–66, 70–74, 90, 156–157; girls' schools, 31, 34, 53, 57, 81, 150; government grants for, 32–34; and lay schools, 30, 33–35, 53; literacy and, 38, 52–55, 59, 70–71; and mission schools, 30–36, 58, 81; monastic, 29–35, 52; and moral instruction, 35–37; and "national" schools, 37, 57–59, 81–82, 88, 135–136, 150, 184n37, 184nn40–41; public, expansion of, 30, 32–35, 55. *See also* college; universities

Edwards, Louise, 8, 70, 149

Edwards, Penny, 9, 116

employment of women, 2, 55–58, 69, 156, 169, 180n76; and Sex Disqualification (Removal) Act, 57, 90–91, 179n71

ethnicity: and British practice of "divide and rule," 26, 175n66; census and increased consciousness of, 25–27; changes in awareness of, 25–28, 44–45, 77–78; composition of army by, 159–160; economic specialization by, 5–7, 21–25; ethnic minorities, 25, 157–159; ethnic strife, 23–25, 28, 44–45, 120–122, 134, 169; plural legal system and increased consciousness of, 25–28; in precolonial Burma, 19–20, 25, 27

Eurasians, 6, 121, 123, 128, 140–141, 191n14; economic specialization of, 24; orphans, 31, 127; rise in the population of, 21–22, 120

Europeans (*bo*), 16–17, 104, 120–121, 191n14; dispute over, wearing of shoes at pagodas by, 42, 80, 98, 188n7; economic specialization of, 24, 28; manliness of, men, 157–158; merchants and firms, 20–21, 38–39; schools, 9, 30–31, 34, 58; unions between Burmese women and, 121, 123–125, 132–137, 140; wives and mistresses of (*bo gadaw*), 121, 136–138, 166–167, 194n91; women, 22, 47, 55, 85, 192n15

fashion: and advertising, 97, 105–108; *amauk* (crest hair), 100–101, 152–154; and beauty, 101, 106–109; *bo ke* (English haircut), 99, **101**, 153; changes in men's, 99, **100–101**; changes in women's, 99–104; criticisms of *khit hsan* (modern), 109–110, 143–144, 146;

defense of *khit hsan,* in the press, 149–154; film and, 104–105; hybrid, 103–104, 106, 188n27; *khit hsan,* 99–106, **102**; *sadohn* (chignon), 99–100, **102**–103, 105, 153; textile and apparel industry and, 104–106, 189n34; as trope for modernity, 8, 97–98, 145–147. *See also* fashionable women

fashionable women, 8, 96–105, **102**, **144**; criticisms of, in the press, 12, 109–110, 118–119, 143–149, 155, 160–162; defense of, in the press, 149–154; as icon of consumerism, 11, 96–97, 118, 161; as icon of self-fulfillment and self-realization, 11, 109, 118, 147, 157, 161–162, 166

feminism, 48, 51, 85, 130, 166, 170; international, 9, 91–93, 95; patriotic, 8–9, 11; relationship between nationalism and, 50, 70, 89–90, 92–95; scholarship on third-world, 95; and the "woman question," 64–65, 73

film. *See* cinema

foot-binding, 46, 49, 51

foreign, mistrust of, 2, 4–5, 165–166

Foucault, Michel, 188

Furnivall, John, 5, 18, 36, 99, 123, 171n14; and historiography of colonial Burma, 5–7, 10

Gandhi, 9, 81, 83, 87, 184n37

GCBA (General Council of Burmese Associations), 80–81, 85–87, 129

GCSS (General Council of Sangha Sammeggi), 82, 85

Göle, Nilüfer, 73

Great Depression, 5, 118, 122, 134, 141–142, 158, 162; and 1938 Burma riots, 41

Habermas, Jürgen, 42

Hall, Harold Field, 47–48, 158

Hart, Alice, 23, 139

Hicks, George, 199n11

Hla Pe, 165

Hmi, Daw, 56

housewives (*ein shin ma*): articles and featured columns about, 75–76; commodification of, 110–113, 116–117; and hygiene, 96–97, 106, 108, 110–118; as icon of dutiful consumption, 96–99, 116–119. *See also* domesticity; motherhood

Hpo Lat, 174n33

hygiene: as dominant marker of modernity, 113–116; products and household management, 96–97, 106, 108, 110–118; as school subject, 35, 54, 113–114; and self-improvement, 11, 96–97, 108–109

INC (Indian National Congress), 81, 85

Independent sa tañ: cā (Independent weekly), 59, 69, 75

Indian Civil Service, 5, 124, 132, 179n68

Indians (*kala*), 5–6, 31, 104, 174n44; accounts of Burmese women by, 50–51, 92; Buddhist, 191n13; *chettiar,* 21; economic specialization of, 24, 41, 159, 189n34; exodus of, during World War II, 153, 196n44; immigration and migration of, 21–22, 41, 131; Indo-Burmese population, 22, 122, 191nn12–13; marriage of, to Burmese women, 28, 41, 121–122, 131, 133–140, 191nn12–13; in Rangoon, 6, 22; representations of, as lower-class, 138–140; riots against, 23–24, 28, 41, 120–122, 134

Indo-Burmese: marriage, 28, 41, 121–122, 131, 133–140; population, 22, 122, 191nn12–13

intermarriage: Anglo-Burmese, 121, 123–125, 132–136, 140; changing attitude towards, 12, 120–122, 128–134, 140–142, 145; Indo-Burmese, 28, 41, 122, 131, 133–140; Japanese-Burmese, 121; Sino-Burmese, 9, 20, 22–23

International Alliance of Women for Suffrage, 48, 91

International Council of Women, 91

Islam: marriage between Muslim men and Buddhist Burmese women, 41, 121–122, 134, 137–138; Muslim Burmese, 122, 135–136, 191nn12–13; Muslim women, 49, 51, 71, 138–139, 191n8

Japanese occupation, 2, 152–153, 164, 173n31, 196n45, 198n4; Burmese accounts of, 165–166; and "comfort women," 165, 198n11; emergence of AFPFL during, 185n46, 196n45; emergence of Burmese national armies during, 160; marriage between Burmese women and Japanese men during, 121; Thailand-Burma Railway (Death Railway), 165, 198n8, 198n10

Jinarajadasa, Dorothy, 91–93

Journal gyaw (Weekly thunderer), 69, 105, 150

kabya ("mixed-race"), 120–123, 135–136, 139–141, 190n1

Kachins, 25–26, 173n20; colonial representations of, as a martial race, 157–158

Karens, 25–26, 31, 173n20; in armed forces, 159; colonial representations of, as a martial race, 157–158

Kartini, 72

Kaung, U, 30

Kawanami, Hiroko, 53

Khin Khin Lay, Dagon, 58–59, 62, 70, 159, 169

Khin Khin Nu, 105

Khin Myo Chit (Khin Mya), 37, 72, 76, 94, 183n5, 191n6

khit hmi thu, 2, 12, 168, 170; as consumer, 96–99, 109–111, 118; educated, 64–67, 73–74

khit hsan thu. See fashionable women

Konbaung dynasty, 14, 16, 53, 128, 181n116

Koop, John, 6

Kyi pwa yay (Improvement magazine), 58, 69

Laurie, Colonel W. F. B., 158

law, 17–19, 25, 29, 49; Buddhist customary, 10, 23, 27, 47–48, 86, 93, 130, 186n62; degree, 56; *dhammasat,* 25, 128–130, 133; English, 7, 27; martial, 17; plural legal system, 10, 27; Village Regulation Act, 17–18, 173n18

Ledi Sayadaw, 36, 60, 64, 72, 180n90, 181n107

Legislative Council, 17, 62, 65, 70, 90–91, 130–131, 160

Lieberman, Victor, 19–20, 27

Luce, Gordon H., 124–125

Lun, Saya (Thakin Kodaw Hmaing), 42, 59–60, 68, 72, 177n152, 180n87, 183n5

Ma Lay, Journal Gyaw Ma (Tin Hlaing), 69, 149–152, 161, 196n30, 196n32, 197n61; *Mon Ywe Mahu* (Not out of hate), 1, 12, 163–164; on sexism in Burma, 154–155; *Thway* (Blood), 12, 163–164, 166 magazines: women editors and writers for, 58–59, 69, 72; women's, 59, 64, 70; women's columns in, 40, 44, 66–69, 75–78. *See also titles of individual magazines*

makeup. *See* beauty products

marriage: advice columns on, 76; in *dhammasat,* 25–26; norms and customs, 48, 127–130, 133. *See also* intermarriage

masculinity: in Burmese fiction, 158–159; in crisis, 134, 146, 155–162; cult of, 157; Orientalist discourse on, 157–158

Maung Gyi, Ledi Pandita U, 60–68, 72–74, 159, 169, 180n9

Maxim, Sarah, 6

May Oung, U, 148, 179n68, 195n20

McClintock, Anne, 3

McCoy, Alfred, 157

McDaniel, Justin, 66, 68

Me Me Khin, Daw, 56

medicine: advertisements for, 96, 111, 114; in monastic education, 29, 52; Western, 9, 111; women employed in the field of, 56. *See also* motherhood: medicalization of

Mi Mi Khaing, 52

Mindon, King, 29, 130, 172n7

miscegenation, 120–122, 140–141. *See also* Eurasians; Indo-Burmese; *kabya; zerbadee*

missionaries (Christian), 7, 30–33, 38; depictions of Burmese women by, 32, 47–48, 54, 114; and establishment of modern education, 7, 30–38, 58, 81, 169; the press and, 38, 177n141

modern girl, 2, 8, 12, 96, 98, 155, 168; criticisms of, 143–144, 147–149

modern woman, 2, 12; consumerist, 96–99, 109–111, 118; educated, 59, 64–67, 70–74; *khit hmi thu,* 2, 12, 168, 170; scholarship on, 8, 70; women of the *khit kala* (present era), 2–4, 8–12, 75, 94, 108, 161, 167, 170. *See also* modern girl; "new woman"; *tet khit thami*

modernity: capitalist, critiques of, 147–148; colonial, 5, 167–168; "conditions of women" and debates about, 11, 49–51, 64, 71–73, 79, 89; and consumption, 113–119; exclusion of Burmese from, 5–7, 169; fashion as trope for, 8, 97–98, 145–147; hygiene as dominant marker of, 113–116; recent scholarship on, 8–9, 171n24; Western, 1, 145

Mon Ywe Mahu (Not out of hate), 1, 12, 163–164

monks: and blouse burnings, 143–144, 162; and education, 7, 30, 32–34, 52–53; Ottama, U, 81–82, 86, 129, 131, 144; and politics, 62, 82–83, 86, 144; scholar, 36, 64, 65, 72, 180n90; *tet hpongyi* (modern monk), 148–149, 186n68; and textual production, 36, 39; Wisara, U, 82. *See also* sangha

Mons, 19, 20, 26–27, 30, 128

motherhood: commodification of, 111–118; medicalization of, 111–116; nationalist discourse on, 76–79. *See also* domesticity; housewives

movie theaters. *See* cinema

Mya Sein, Daw, 51, 56–57, 74, 92, 94, 169; and protest for women's right to stand for parliamentary elections, 65, 90–91, 187n80

Mya Shwe, Daw, 56

Mya Yin, Daw, 56

Myanmar, 1, 24, 72, 167; usage of "Burma" versus, 12–13, 172n38

Myanmar alin (New light of Burma), 41, 60, 69, 150, 153, 167–168, 199n19

Naidu, Sarojini, 91, 93
naming convention (Burmese), 13, 47, 60, 180n77
National Council of Women: in Burma, 91, 187n80, 187n91; in India, 91
nationalism, 9, 161, 169; and Buddhism, 12, 82–83, 86–88, 129–130, 132, 136, 185n48; and *Dobama Asiayone,* 83–85, 95, 131–132, 146, 160; historiography of Burmese, 44; relationship between feminism and, 50, 70, 85–95; and remasculinization of Burmese men, 146, 155–162; role of press in, 41–44; role of women in, 76–80, 86–89, 93–95, 99; and *tat* (army) movement, 159–160. *See also* anticolonial resistance; nationalist; patriotism; *thakin*
nationalist: discourse of motherhood, 76–79; discourse of race, 121, 135–142; education, 37, 57–59, 81–82, 88, 135–136, 150, 184n37, 184nn40–41; organizations, 37, 41, 80–87, 129, 135–136; women's movements, 85–88
Nehru, Rameshwari, 91–93; *Stri Darpan* (Women's mirror), 50, 92
"new woman," 2, 49, 98, 149, 155, 157; and bobbed hair, 98–99; and education, 65; scholarship on, 8, 70
newspapers: anticolonial, 40–42; disruption of, during Japanese occupation, 153; history of, in Burma, 38–40; women editors and writers for, 58–59, 69;

women-owned, 58–59; women's columns in, 75. *See also titles of individual newspapers*
Ngan hta lawka (World of books), 58, 76–77, 147
Nijhawan, Shobna, 50–51, 92
Nisbet, John, 19
nissaya, 65–66, 68
Nu, U (Thakin), 83, 165, 185n46, 185n52

officials, colonial: in Indian Civil Service, 5, 124, 132, 179n68; views of Burmese men, 157–158; views of Burmese press, 41–42; views of Burmese women, 46–51, 54, 114; views on cohabitation and intermarriage, 123–127. *See also names of individual officials*

patriotism: gender roles in, 86–89; *kabya* (mixed people) and, 135–136; *myo chit may* (female patriot), 79, 88, 97, 149, 154; patriotic organizations, 82, 85–88; and wearing of *pinni* blouse and *yaw longyi,* 86, 88, 98, 110, 146; *wunthanu,* 78, 94–95, 149, 160, 184n24. *See also* anticolonial resistance; nationalism; nationalist
Pe Maung Tin, U, 124
Pearson, Gail, 93
Peleggi, Maurizio, 188n27
Phayre, Sir Arthur, 33
pinni (homespun cotton), 86, 88, 98, 110, 146
plural society, 5–6, 28, 169
politics, 85, 89. *See also* anticolonial resistance; feminism; monks: and politics; nationalism; nationalist; patriotism; *and names of individual political organizations*

press: as advertising medium, 39, 42–44, 106; Burmese language, 39–40; and Christian missionaries, 38, 177n141; commercial incentives for, 39, 42–44, 69, 73; disruption of, during Japanese occupation, 153; early history of, 38–40; English language, 38–40; on fashionable women, 12, 109–110, 118–119, 143–155, 160–162; freedom of, 41; and the public sphere, 41–44; role of, in Burmese nationalism, 41–44. *See also* magazines; newspapers
prostitution, 123–127, 134
Pu Galay, U, 120–122, 135
purdah, 47, 49, 139
Pwa Hmi, Daw, 56
Pwa Shin, Daw, 58

race: categories of, 25–26; census and increased consciousness of, 25–27; class and, 26, 138–142, 167; and ethnic and national identity, 25–27, 121, 132, 140–142, 167; mixed, 120–123, 135–136, 139–141, 190n1; nationalist discourse of, 121, 135–142. *See also* Chinese; Eurasians; Europeans; Indians; Indo-Burmese
racism: biological, 139–140; cultural, 121, 140–142
Razak, U, 135–136
Reid, Anthony, 46, 52
religion: categories of, 26; Orientalist scholarship on, 49; plural legal system and, 101; source for ethnic and national identity, 25–27, 140–142; women's authority in the realm of, 51–53. *See also* missionaries; monks; sangha; *and individual religions*

Rice, W. F., 125
riots: first anti-Indian (1930), 23, 28; second anti-Indian (1938 Burma riots), 23–24, 28, 41, 120–122, 134
Roces, Mina, 145, 161

San, Independent Daw, 59, 65, 74, 90–92
sangha (monastic community): dissension within, 62, 181n97; effects of colonialism on, 4, 30, 64, 162; exclusion of women from, 52–53, 179n48; politicization of, 81–82; reaction of, to Thein Pe Myint's *Tet hpongyi* (Modern monk), 149; relationship of, to knowledge production, 52–53. *See also* education, monastic; monks
Sato, Barbara, 98
Saw Moun Nyin, 105
Saw Sa, Daw, 56
Scott, Sir George, 49
Second World War, 153, 163, 180n85, 185n46
sexuality: and advertisements for sex-related products, 112–113, 116, 189n47; of imperial personnel, 124–127; and sexual emancipation of modern women, 2, 8, 98, 157
Shans, 25–26, 173n20
sheer blouse (*eingyi pa*), 99, 103, 154, 188n16; criticisms of, 109–110, 143–144, 146
Shin Saw Pu, Queen, 52, 178n40, 181n90
Shuttleworth Report, 127
Shwe Khaing Thar, 110
Sinha, Mrinalini, 90, 197n72
social class: class endogamy, 25, 140; divisions in, 25–26, 121–122,

140, 142; educated middle-class, 28, 38, 75, 80, 85, 104, 161; and European bourgeois culture, 26, 110, 124, 140–141; middle-class women, 87, 91, 161; in precolonial Burma, 25–26, 142; representations of Indians as lower-class, 138–140; upper-class Burmese, 58–59, 92, 99; working class, 30, 92, 104; working class women, 8, 79, 87, 92, 187n91

Spiro, Melford, 128

state, colonial: and administrative reforms, 17–19; and census, 25–27; concern with health and reproduction, 113–114; and educational reforms, 7, 32–35, 70–71; and employment of women, 57–58, 179n71, 180n76; laissez-faire policies and practice of, 18–19; and Legislative Council, 17, 62, 65, 70, 90–91, 130–131, 160; and military recruitment, 159–160; policy on prostitution, 125–126; and political prisoners, 82, 86–87; the press and, 38–42; and territorial organization, 15, 18, 173n20. See also anticolonial resistance; economy, colonial; officials, colonial

Stevens, Sarah, 149

Stoler, Ann, 26, 140

Stri Darpan (Women's mirror), 50, 92

Stri Dharma (Woman's duty), 91

Supayalat, Queen, 65, 181n90, 181n116

Symes, Michael, 20

Tarlo, Emma, 97, 103

tat (army) movement, 159–160, 198n89

Taw Sein Ko, 9, 30, 35, 71–72, 175n77

Taylor, Jean Gelman, 145

Taylor, Robert, 82, 85, 187n68

"temporary unions." See cohabitation

tet hpongyi (modern monk), 148–149, 186n68;

tet khit thami, 2, 12, 96, 98, 168; criticisms of, 143–144, 147–149

thakin, 83–85, 87, 92, 95, 180n87; collaboration with Japanese, 196n45, 198n4; and Nagani (Red Dragon) Book Club, 185n52; and rhetoric of "us versus them," 131–132, 136, 144, 161, 168, 194n72; thakinma, 87, 95. See also Dobama Asiayone

Thant Myint-U, 128

Thein Pe Myint, 88, 186n68; Heroine, 88; "Khin Myo Chit," 88–89; "Lady Khin," 109; Tet hpongyi (Modern monk), 148–149; The Student Boycotter, 88–89

theosophists, 91–93, 187n82

1300 Revolution, 84–87

Thirty Comrades, 196n45, 198n4. See also thakin

thu gyi (hereditary headman), 17–18, 173n13

thumya bama (their Burmese), 131–132, 136, 144, 168, 194n72

Thuriya (The sun), 40, 42, 58, 60, 146, 153

Thway (Blood), 12, 163–164, 166

tika (commentary), 60, 194n75

Toe tet yay (Efficiency magazine), 69, 72, 105, 183n5; women's column in, 75–78

Tone, Andrea, 190n47

tradition. See Buddhist (Burmese): culture; culture, European bourgeois

universities: Calcutta, 31, 33, 36;
    Rangoon, 36, 124, 149, 156,
    158; students' union, 83–84, 160,
    185n47; women in, 55–58, 66,
    102
University Boycott: of 1920, 36,
    80–82, 135; of 1936, 83–**84**,
    87–88, 185n47

Village Regulation Act, 17–18, 173n18

Westernization: association of female
    gender with, 145; of elite, 7; of
    fashion, 97, 99, **101**, 145, 153;
    of home, 117; rejection of, 1–2;
    of youth, 147–148, 159. See also
    tet khit thami
women (Southeast Asian), autonomy
    and economic independence of, 46,
    48–52, 149
women of the *khit kala* (present era),
    2–4, 8–12, 75, 94, 108, 161, 167,
    170; educated, 59, 65–66, 70–73
women's authority: in administration,
    52, 89, 178n38; in economic
    sphere, 48–51; in family, 48–49,
    117; in knowledge production,
    52–53, 62, 66; in spiritual realm,
    51–52

women's movements: feminist-
    nationalist, 89–95; international,
    9, 91–93, 95; nationalist, 85–88;
    for suffrage, 64, 70, 85, 95. *See
    also titles of individual women's
    organizations*
women's status: discourse on the
    "conditions of women," 11,
    49–51, 64, 71–73, 89–95, 169;
    "traditional," in Burma, 46–51;
    "traditional," in Southeast Asia,
    46, 48–52, 149
World War II. *See* Second World War
wunthanu athin, 82, 85–88
Wunthanu Konmaryi Athin (Patriotic
    Women's Associations), 85–87,
    129

xenophobia, 2, 4–5, 165–166

YMBA (Young Men's Buddhist
    Association), 37, 80, 85–87
Youq shin lan hnyun (Screen show
    weekly), 75, **101**, 105, 117
YWBA (Young Women's Buddhist
    Association), 85–87, 186n60

zerbadee (Muslim Burmese), 122,
    191nn12–13

About the Author

Chie Ikeya holds a PhD in history from Cornell University and is presently an associate professor of history at Rutgers University, New Brunswick, where she teaches women's and gender, Asian, and global and comparative histories.

OTHER VOLUMES IN THE SERIES

HARD BARGAINING IN SUMATRA: Western Travelers and Toba Bataks in the
Marketplace of Souvenirs
Andrew Causey

PRINT AND POWER: Confucianism, Communism, and Buddhism in the
Making of Modern Vietnam
Shawn Frederick McHale

INVESTING IN MIRACLES: El Shaddai and the Transformation of Popular
Catholicism in the Philippines
Katherine L. Wiegele

TOMS AND DEES: Transgender Identity and Female Same-Sex Relationships
in Thailand
Megan J. Sinnott

IN THE NAME OF CIVIL SOCIETY: From Free Election Movements to People Power
in the Philippines
Eva-Lotta E. Hedman

THE TÂY SƠN UPRISING: Society and Rebellion in Eighteenth-Century Vietnam
George Dutton

SPREADING THE DHAMMA: Writing, Orality, and Textual Transmission in
Buddhist Northern Thailand
Daniel M. Veidlinger

ART AS POLITICS: Re-Crafting Identities, Tourism, and Power in Tana Toraja, Indonesia
Kathleen M. Adams

CAMBODGE: The Cultivation of a Nation, 1860–1945
Penny Edwards

HOW TO BEHAVE: Buddhism and Modernity in Colonial Cambodia, 1860–1931
Anne Ruth Hansen

CULT, CULTURE, AND AUTHORITY: Princess Liễu Hạnh in Vietnamese History
Olga Dror

KHMER WOMEN ON THE MOVE: Exploring Work and Life in Urban Cambodia
Annuska Derks

THE ANXIETIES OF MOBILITY: Migration and Tourism in the Indonesian Borderlands
Johan A. Lindquist

THE BINDING TIE: Chinese Intergenerational Relations in Modern Singapore
Kristina Göransson

IN BUDDHA'S COMPANY: Thai Soldiers in the Vietnam War
Richard A. Ruth